The Right to Be Parents

The Right to Be Parents

LGBT Families and the
Transformation of Parenthood

Carlos A. Ball

NEW YORK UNIVERSITY PRESS
New York and London

NEW YORK UNIVERSITY PRESS
New York and London
www.nyupress.org

References to Internet websites (URLs) were accurate at the time of writing.
Neither the author nor New York University Press is responsible for URLs
that may have expired or changed since the manuscript was prepared.

Library of Congress Cataloging-in-Publication Data
Ball, Carlos A.
The right to be parents : LGBT families and the transformation of parenthood / Carlos Ball.
p. cm.
Includes bibliographical references and index.
ISBN 978-0-8147-3930-3 (hardback)
ISBN 978-0-8147-3931-0 (ebook
ISBN 978-0-8147-3932-7 (ebook)
1. Parent and child — United States. 2. Gay parents — Legal status, laws, etc. — United
States. 3. Custody of children — United States. I. Title.
KF540.B35   2012
346.7301'73 — dc23   2011045382

New York University Press books are printed on acid-free paper,
and their binding materials are chosen for strength and durability.
We strive to use environmentally responsible suppliers and materials
to the greatest extent possible in publishing our books.

Manufactured in the United States of America

To Richard, Emmanuel, and Sebastian,
the LGBT family of my own.
And to Nancy Polikoff,
for her advocacy on behalf of all LGBT families.

Contents

Introduction

In 1996, three years after a Virginia judge took her five-year-old son Tyler away from her so that he could be raised by her mother, Sharon Bottoms made the most difficult decision of her life: believing that Tyler had suffered enough and wanting to spare him further emotional turmoil, she told her lawyers to drop the custody fight.

It had all started three years earlier, when Sharon told her mother Kay that she did not want the boy to spend time in his grandmother's house because Kay's live-in boyfriend had repeatedly molested Sharon when she was a girl. Kay, who had been helping her daughter by looking after Tyler in her home for several hours a week, became so infuriated by Sharon's decision that she contacted a lawyer. A few weeks later, the attorney filed a court petition contending that Sharon was not a fit mother entitled to keep custody of Tyler because she was a lesbian living with her female partner.

Sharon was twenty-two years old when she met April Wade at a Memorial Day picnic in 1992. The two women started dating and, later that summer, the twenty-six-year-old April moved in with Sharon and Tyler. After a series of difficult relationships—including one with her former husband and father of Tyler, who had never shown any interest in the boy—Sharon felt like she had finally met the person with whom she wanted to spend the rest of her life.

Almost a year later, a hearing was held in circuit court in Virginia to determine whether Sharon should retain custody of her son. At the hearing, Kay testified that Tyler "shouldn't be raised by lesbians" and charged that he "is going to be mentally and physically harmed because of [Sharon and April's] relationship."[1] Also during the proceeding, Richard Ryder, a prominent Richmond attorney who represented Kay, made much of the fact that Wade and April sometimes hugged and kissed in front of the child, that the two women shared a bedroom, and that they had sex about once or twice a week (though never in the child's presence).

Upon the conclusion of the six-hour hearing, the judge stripped Sharon of custody of her son because she had "openly admitted in this court that she is living in an active homosexual relationship."[2] That relationship, the judge opined, was illegal (sodomy was a crime in Virginia) and immoral. In addition to granting Kay custody of Tyler, he also prohibited Sharon from visiting with her son in April's presence.

The local newspaper reported that Sharon, after the judge issued his ruling, stood outside the courtroom and "sobbed uncontrollably."[3] A few feet away from her, a clearly pleased Ryder told the gathered media that the judge had been appropriately troubled by Sharon's open lesbianism. Shortly after his court victory, the lawyer appeared on a national television interview and urged Americans to remember that "the Roman Empire fell because of lesbianism, homosexuals, and things of this nature."[4]

Eighteen months later, the Virginia Supreme Court rejected Sharon's effort to overturn the trial judge's ruling. Eventually, Sharon decided it would be best for her son if she ended the custody fight with her mother. But she continued to challenge the restriction prohibiting her from visiting with Tyler in April's presence. In 1999, the Virginia Court of Appeals, more than six years after the litigation began, upheld the visitation restriction imposed by the trial judge.[5]

▲

The Virginia Supreme Court's ruling in Sharon Bottoms's case was remarkable for several reasons. First, although the state's highest court, like the trial court, emphasized that sodomy was a felony offense in Virginia, it did not explain that the sodomy law applied to *everyone* who had consensual oral or anal sex, regardless of whether they were gay or straight. The court also conveniently failed to reveal that no Virginia court had ever taken custody away from a heterosexual parent and granted it to a nonparent because he or she engaged in consensual sex while in the privacy of the home. That punishment seemed reserved only for parents, like Sharon, who were in same-sex relationships.

Second, the court dismissed the rights of parents to have custody of their children as mere "technical rights."[6] This trite characterization was wholly inconsistent with the long-standing principle in American family law that the best interests of children are almost always served when children remain in their parents' custody. Indeed, a parent may not be deprived of custody by a nonparent, even a grandparent, unless there is a finding—usually by clear and convincing evidence—that the parent is unfit or has abandoned the child, or that there exist other extraordinary circumstances that would justify taking the child away from the parent.

The strength of the presumption in favor of parental custody was readily evident from prior Virginia cases. In one lawsuit, decided only six years before Sharon Bottoms's case, a child's paternal grandmother filed for custody after the boy's mother's boyfriend shot and killed his father in his presence. The court concluded that the fact that the child *would have to grow up in the same household as his father's killer*—who was acquitted of murder after the jury concluded he acted in self-defense—did not meet the "extraordinary circumstances" standard justifying the taking of custody away from a parent in favor of a nonparent.[7]

Two years later, the same court heard a case in which maternal grandparents sought custody of their grandchildren because their father had a history of alcohol abuse, neglected his family, and killed the children's mother. Despite the fact that the lower court had concluded that the father was an unfit parent, the appellate court held that it would not be in the children's best interests to deprive him of custody while he appealed his murder conviction.[8]

The only possible conclusion that can be reached when we place these two rulings alongside Sharon Bottoms's case is that, according to the Virginia Supreme Court, living with a parent who is in an open lesbian relationship is more harmful to a child than living with someone who has killed one of his parents.

When she first started battling her mother over custody of Tyler, Sharon moved out of the apartment she shared with her partner April, hoping that doing so would increase the chances of regaining custody of her son. Several weeks later, however, she changed her mind and moved back in with April, telling the media that "I want to fight as a family."[9] Unfortunately for Sharon, and her son, the Virginia Supreme Court eventually ruled that her living with April in an open lesbian relationship meant that she was an unfit mother. Although the court also noted that Sharon had had several unsuccessful relationships, had gone through periods of unemployment, and had twice spanked the boy hard, it was her lesbian relationship that troubled the judges the most. If Sharon had been a straight mother rather than an openly lesbian one, it is highly unlikely that the court would have taken custody away from her.

At the hearing held before the trial judge, Kay Bottoms had failed to present any evidence establishing a link between Sharon's relationship with April and actual or even potential harm to Tyler. It is not surprising that such evidence was unavailable, given that a court-ordered psychological study of mother and son found that Sharon was "warm" and "responsive" toward the child, that the boy "behave[d] as if entirely secure and at ease with his mother," and that he felt "familiar and comfortable" in her presence.

The report also concluded that Tyler was a "bright, self-confident, socially responsive little boy who [was] experiencing no undue emotional discomfort, cognitive deficits or developmental delays."[10]

But the Virginia Supreme Court overlooked all this evidence and instead *presumed* that if the boy sometimes used bad language or had temper tantrums, it must have been because of Sharon's relationship with April. In the end, the court made it resoundingly clear that it was not possible, in its view, to be both a good mother and an open lesbian.

▲

This book traces the history of legal reforms that, in seeking to gain legal recognition of lesbian, gay, bisexual, and transsexual (LGBT) families, have fundamentally changed how American law defines and regulates parenthood. It is not possible to fully comprehend why these legal changes have occurred without understanding the backgrounds, hopes, fears, and aspirations of the LGBT parents who have been behind key lawsuits. For that reason, this book chronicles the human stories of courageous and determined LGBT parents who, for several decades now, have battled in the courts to gain legal recognition of and protection for their relationships with their children. So while this is a book about reforms in the law of parenthood in general, and that of LGBT parenting in particular, it is also about many of the LGBT parents who have made those reforms possible.

One of the principal questions this book explores is how courts have gone about determining the role that parents' sexual orientation and gender identity should play in litigation involving the well-being of children. Many in our society hold damaging stereotypes about LGBT individuals. One of the most invidious of these stereotypes is the notion that children are harmed when they are "exposed" to LGBT people. At its worse, this belief is based on the view that LGBT individuals are hypersexual beings who constitute sexual threats to children. Only slightly less problematic is the presumption that LGBT individuals are likely to influence their children's sexual orientation and gender identity in harmful ways.

These misconceptions have all too often found their way into court rulings in family law cases. This book argues that neither the sexual orientation nor the gender identity of parents should be relevant in making judicial determinations regarding parental rights. For too long, questions related to sexual orientation and gender identity have served as proxies for parental competence. Rather than relying on generalizations and assumptions of harm to children, courts should deem the sexual orientation and gender identity of

Sharon Bottoms (*left*) and her partner, April Wade, a few days after a Virginia trial court took away custody of her son in 1993. Used with permission of the *Richmond Times-Dispatch.*

individuals to be irrelevant in determining whether they are capable of being good parents.

▲

Twenty years before Sharon Bottoms's case, a California appellate court also stripped a lesbian mother of custody and granted it to the children's grandparents. When Lynda Chaffin moved from Washington State to California in 1968, she left her six- and eight-year-old daughters with her parents because she was unable, for financial and health reasons, to take them with her. (Lynda had divorced her husband several years earlier and the court had awarded her custody.) When Lynda was able to, she moved her daughters to California, after which her parents sued for custody. A trial judge in late 1973 granted custody to the grandparents largely because Lynda was a lesbian; she then fled with her daughters and remained in hiding for almost a year.

In November 1974, she turned herself in and the Los Angeles County Sheriff's Department sent the children to their grandparents' house in Washington. Lynda appealed the custody order, but the appellate court sided with the grandparents. In doing so, it noted that the mother "does not merely say she is homosexual. She also lives with the woman with whom she has engaged in homosexual conduct, and she intends to bring up her daughters in that environment. The trial court was not required . . . to disregard the potential psychological influence that appellant's homosexual relationship might have upon her daughters. . . . In exercising a choice between homosexual and heterosexual households for purposes of child custody a trial court could conclude that permanent residence in a homosexual household would be detrimental to the children and contrary to their best interests."[11]

When Lynda Chaffin in 1975 was denied custody of her children, the case received no media coverage, except that provided by the gay press.[12] In contrast, Sharon Bottoms's case was covered by dozens of media outlets across the country, from local newspapers to national television networks. In 1993, *Time* magazine used the case as the main focus of a cover story titled "Gay Parents: Under Fire and on the Rise."[13] And when the Virginia Supreme Court in 1995 affirmed the trial court's ruling taking custody away from the lesbian mother, several major newspapers wrote editorials critical of its decision.[14]

Although the courts' reasoning in the Chaffin and Bottoms rulings was essentially the same, LGBT parenting in the United States changed dramatically during the intervening twenty years. In 1975, only a small number of lesbian and gay parents were willing to be open about their sexual orientation. In addition, few of the lesbians and gay men who were out of the closet considered the possibility of having children. Becoming a parent, much like marrying someone of the same sex, was simply not within the realm of the possible for most openly gay people in the 1970s.

But there were changes in the air. As a result of the work of gay rights advocates, Washington, D.C., in 1976 became the first jurisdiction in the country to enact a law prohibiting judges from making custody decisions based solely on parents' sexual orientation.[15] And in 1977, as the Carter White House was preparing to sponsor a conference on families, advocates gained visibility for lesbian and gay parents by attempting—ultimately unsuccessfully—to get organizers to add gay parenting to the agenda. In 1979, the first reports of adoptions by openly gay individuals appeared in the mainstream press.[16]

In 1982, the Feminist Women's Health Center in Oakland opened the first sperm bank in the country whose explicit mission was to assist all women, regardless of marital status or sexual orientation, to become parents. Three years later, the first manual explicitly aimed at helping lesbians decide whether and how to have children became available in print.[17] In 1989, the book *Heather Has Two Mommies* was published, making it the first children's book with a main character raised by a lesbian couple.[18] (The book's first printing of four thousand copies sold out before they even reached bookstores.) Also in 1989, major newspapers and magazines, including the *New York Times* and *Newsweek*, ran feature stories profiling lesbians raising children.[19] And a year later, the first children's book featuring a gay father was published.[20]

In 1991, the Oakland sperm bank reported that more than two hundred lesbians had used its services since its doors opened almost a decade earlier. That same year, a West Hollywood medical practice announced that it had helped more than one hundred lesbians conceive through alternative insemination. (Alternative insemination is the process by which a woman attempts to become pregnant through the introduction of sperm into her uterus via a means other than sexual intercourse.) In 1993, a pediatric clinic specializing in offering services to the children of lesbians and gay men opened in San Francisco. Also that year, a second "how-to" parenting guide was published; unlike the first one, this one was aimed not just at lesbians, but also at gay men.[21] The new guide discussed not only the different ways that lesbians and gay men could become parents, but also the specific challenges they faced in raising children. A few months after the guide's publication, the *New York Times* ran a front-page story titled "Gay Parents Become Increasingly Visible."[22] That same year, an anthropologist published a book providing a rich account of lesbian parenting, including the different motivations that led some lesbians to choose to become mothers.[23]

All of this meant that by the time the Virginia Supreme Court in 1995 held that Sharon Bottoms should be stripped of custody of her son because she was living with another woman, many Americans had become aware that having and raising children were not exclusively heterosexual pursuits. The issue of parenting by lesbians and gay men was now a subject of discussion around office watercoolers, in the opinion pages of newspapers, and even on the floors of state legislatures. Although many people, including the majority of judges on the Virginia Supreme Court, were clearly troubled by lesbian and gay parents, the fact that such parents existed, and that their numbers were growing, was now impossible to deny.

▲

Lynda's Chaffin case from 1975 was one of the first legal claims involving a lesbian or gay parent to reach an appellate court in the United States. Lynda's children, like Sharon Bottom's son, were born from a heterosexual marriage. Until relatively recently, the great majority of children raised by lesbians and gay men were conceived in earlier, almost always dissolved, different-sex marriages. As a result, practically all the early legal cases involving LGBT parents entailed a custody or visitation dispute between a lesbian or gay parent and a former heterosexual spouse. (There were also cases like Lynda Chaffin's, which involved a custody dispute between a lesbian or gay parent and a family member, but they were less common.)

Few lesbian and gay parents dared to come out of the closet before the 1970s. Following the Stonewall riots and the emergence of the modern gay rights movement, a small—and, as the decade progressed, growing—number of lesbian and gay parents chose to be open about their sexual orientation while seeking custody of or visitation with their children after separating from their different-sex spouses. In turn, the latter often attempted to use their ex-spouses' newly revealed homosexuality to persuade judges to deny or limit their custodial and visitation rights. The main legal issue in these cases, which continue to be litigated today, is what role same-sex sexuality and relationships should play in the determination of parental rights.

At first, courts were almost uniformly hostile to the idea that openly lesbian and gay parents should be awarded custody over straight parents, as well as to the notion that they should have unrestricted rights to visit with their children. Chapters 1 (lesbian moms) and 2 (gay dads) tell the stories of some of these early cases, stories that are as much about the courage and determination of lesbian and gay parents fighting to retain contact with their children as they are about the narrow-minded judges who rejected the idea that individuals could be both good parents and open about their same-sex sexual orientation. Indeed, it is in these early cases that we most clearly see courts improperly making family law rulings based on the same-sex sexual orientation and relationships of parents rather than on their ability to provide their children with caring and nurturing homes.

Both chapters also profile more recent cases involving disputes between gay and straight parents. As we will see, some heterosexual parents continue to try to use their former spouses' same-sex sexual orientation and relationships to gain advantages in custody and visitation disputes. But it is today more difficult (though certainly not impossible) for them to succeed in these efforts than it was just a few years ago. Almost all jurisdictions have adopted what is known as the "nexus test" in parenting cases in which the same-sex sexual orientation and relationships of one of the parties becomes an issue. That test, when properly applied, requires that specific evidence of actual or potential harm to the child be introduced before a court can take into account a parent's sexual orientation and relationships in making custody and visitation decisions.

A crucial issue in all the cases explored in the book's first two chapters is the legal relevance of the decision by lesbian and gay parents to be open about their sexual orientation. The very nature of parenting law, and of the "best interests of the child" standard that forms the normative foundation of that law in the United States, gives judges—in particular those at the trial level—considerable discretion to determine what promotes and what undermines the well-being of children. It is therefore possible for judges, even while ostensibly applying the nexus test, to conclude that whatever difficulties the children are experiencing, they are the result of the lesbian and gay parents' sexual orientation and relationships. The key issue, as we will see, is one of causation. When a court applies the nexus test correctly by requiring that the heterosexual parent demonstrate a link between the other parent's homosexuality and harm to the children, the lesbian or gay parent is almost always able to persuade the court that sexual orientation should not be a factor in making custody and visitation decisions.

▲

While the first two chapters explore how courts have determined whether parents who are open about their sexual orientation can be good parents, the three chapters that follow grapple with the question of how courts decide whether any given person is a parent to begin with. Most individuals, including some who later identify as lesbian or gay, become parents through heterosexual intercourse. Indeed, almost all the lesbian and gay parents profiled in chapters 1 and 2 became parents in this way.[24] Given their biological links to the children, the issue in their cases was not whether they were the legal parents of their children (they clearly were), but was instead whether they were capable of promoting and protecting their children's well-being.

In contrast, chapters 3, 4, and 5 explore cases involving children of so-called planned lesbian and gay families. These are families headed by lesbians or gay men who intend from the beginning to have and raise children, either by themselves or with partners, while being open about their sexual orientation. Most planned lesbian and gay families are created with the assistance of reproductive technology or through adoption. Although litigation involving children in planned lesbian and gay families has also given rise to the question of what role sexual orientation should play in determining whether someone is capable of being a good parent, the primary legal question in these cases has been an even more fundamental one—namely, who is eligible or qualified to be *a parent* to begin with.

Another difference between the cases profiled in chapters 1 and 2 and those chronicled in chapters 3, 4, and 5 is that the former all involve disputes between lesbian or gay parents and heterosexual parents. In contrast, legal disputes concerning planned lesbian and gay families usually involve either lesbian and gay litigants on both sides (chapters 3 and 4), or lesbian and gay litigants battling the government (chapter 5).

The first members of the LGBT community who had children outside heterosexual marriages were lesbians who, starting in the late 1970s, used alternative insemination as a way of conceiving children. At first, the number of lesbians who became parents in this way was quite small, limited mostly to a handful of women living in the San Francisco area. But by the end of the 1980s, there were hundreds of lesbians across the country pursuing parenthood through alternative insemination (and, starting in the 1990s, through other forms of reproductive assistance such as in vitro—or outside the womb—fertilization). Interestingly, many of these women tried to become pregnant by using sperm donated by gay friends or acquaintances.

It did not take much time for courts to start seeing custody and visitation cases involving planned lesbian families. The main legal issue in these cases was who was legally eligible to qualify as a parent. A lesbian mother who gave birth to a child conceived through alternative insemination, for example, was obviously the child's parent. But what about a lesbian partner who had helped care for the child with the biological mother's consent and encouragement but who lacked a biological link to the child? In answering that question, judges had to grapple with the issue of whether it was possible for a child to have two mothers. As we will see in chapter 3, while courts at first generally rejected the idea that same-sex partners of legal parents could be awarded the necessary parentage status required to seek custody or visitation after the end of their relationships with the biological parents, some appellate courts, starting in the mid-1990s, began ruling that it was often in children's best interests to continue having relationships with both adults who helped care for them, even in the absence of a biological connection with one of them.

The cases profiled in chapter 3 pitted lesbian mothers against one another. On one side of the legal and emotional conflicts were biological mothers who strongly believed it was in their children's interests not to have judicially mandated contact with their former same-sex partners. On the other side were lesbians who insisted that the law should recognize them as parents because they functioned as such and the children considered them to be their parents. As we will see, these clashing positions have forced courts to grapple with the question of what distinguishes a parent from someone who, while having enjoyed ongoing contact with a child, remains a legal stranger to that child. In short, disputes between lesbian mothers and their former partners require courts to determine what makes a parent.

Courts have also, in the context of planned lesbian and gay families, grappled with the issue of whether known sperm donors (often gay men) have parental rights over children conceived and raised by lesbian mothers, frequently with the assistance of their female partners. As explained in chapter 4, these cases not only raise the disputed question of what role biology should play in determining parenthood, but also test the law's willingness to recognize that the well-being of children is not necessarily dependent on their having a father. In addition, the cases raise the controversial question of whether it is sometimes in a child's best interests to have more than two parents.

Planned lesbian and gay families are formed not only through the donation of sperm, but also through the sharing of ova. As a result, chapter 4 also explores the parental rights of lesbian women who provide ova to their partners in order for the latter to carry children to term.

All the cases profiled in chapters 3 and 4 show the extent to which lesbian and gay parenting cases have forced courts to grapple with the question of what makes a parent. There are those—including some lesbian and gay litigants—who have contended that biology should continue to be the crucial, often dispositive, factor in determining parentage status.[25] Others have argued that additional factors, such as the intent of the parties and the extent to which individuals function as parents, should also be taken into account.

As we will see, when courts adopt the former view, they often do so at the expense of the actual relationships of love and care children have developed with the most important adults in their lives. In contrast, when courts embrace the latter perspective, they are better able to account both for the actual relationships that children have with parental caretakers and the wide diversity of familial structures in the United States today. For these reasons, this book defends an expansive legal understanding of parenthood, one that is not limited to formal links (such as biological ones) but also looks to questions of intent and function. The judicial inquiry under this approach centers on whether a couple jointly decided to raise a child together after agreeing that one of them would be biologically related to that child. The approach also seeks to assess whether the individual who lacks the biological link with the child successfully established a parental relationship with that child.

Planned lesbian and gay families are formed not only through alternative insemination and other types of reproductive assistance, but also through state-created mechanisms such as foster care and adoption. As chronicled in chapter 5, child welfare agencies in some large cities, starting in the early 1970s, began placing gay teenagers with gay foster parents. This was followed, in some parts of the country, by judicial approval of adoption petitions brought by lesbian and gay applicants who were open about their sexual orientation.

As with every other important issue involving LGBT parents, courts have played a crucial role in determining the extent to which foster care and adoption are available to lesbians and gay men. This issue has become highly politicized as some social conservatives have successfully pushed to legally restrict the ability of lesbians and gay men to serve as foster care and adoptive parents. As a result, chapter 5 also tells the stories of LGBT individuals who have challenged those restrictions with varying degrees of success over the last thirty years. In addition, the chapter profiles some of the lesbian and gay litigants who have persuaded courts to recognize joint adoptions and second-parent adoptions. (The former permit same-sex couples to adopt children together after courts terminate the rights of their biological parents, while the latter allow same-sex partners of legal parents to adopt their children.)

As with cases involving the use of reproductive technology, the principal issue in the foster care and adoption cases has been whether the law should recognize the lesbian or gay individuals in question as parents. And, as is true of cases involving disputes between lesbian and gay parents and former heterosexual spouses, the foster care and adoption cases have required courts to confront the question of whether it is possible for individuals to promote and protect the well-being of children while being open about their same-sex sexual orientation and relationships.

It has not just been lesbians and gay men who have found themselves litigating parenting issues in court over the last few decades; transsexual individuals have as well. Transsexual parenting cases, like lawsuits involving lesbians and gay men, fall under two broad categories. The first comprises legal disputes in which the main issue is whether the gender identity of transsexual parents affects their ability to be good parents. As a result, chapter 6 profiles cases in which transsexual parents have battled in the courts to maintain relationships with their children in the face of claims by former spouses that their identification with a gender other than their biological one renders them unfit parents. As we will see, transsexual parents in some ways face even greater challenges than lesbian and gay ones because they are at greater risk of having their parental rights *terminated altogether.*

In addition, transsexual individuals, like lesbians and gay men, sometimes find themselves needing to persuade courts that they be deemed parents of children whom they helped raise but with whom they lack biological connections. For this reason, chapter 6 also profiles parenting cases in which transsexual individuals have sought to have their relationships with their children legally recognized despite the absence of biological links. As with many lawsuits involving lesbians and gay men, the family law disputes involving transsexuals that fall under this second category have grappled with the fundamental question of what makes a parent.

▲

It is helpful, in thinking about the law of LGBT parenting, to compare it to the issue of same-sex marriage. Although the latter has clearly been the gay rights issue that has received the most attention nationally over the last twenty years, there has been, as this book makes clear, a quieter revolution going on related to parenting by LGBT people. As a legal matter, the issue of same-sex marriage is primarily a constitutional one involving weighty policy questions about the nature and purpose of marriage and the social impact of expanding the institution to include same-sex couples.

Even though the law of LGBT parenting also frequently addresses big questions (such as what role biology should play in determining parentage status), they arise mostly in highly individualized litigation, as parties go before courts to determine whether the best interests of particular children will be promoted by creating or maintaining a relationship with a particular LGBT person or couple. This type of individualized assessment does not usually make for lofty constitutional or policy pronouncements. Nonetheless, LGBT parenting cases have worked in the aggregate to transform the legal definition of family and parenthood in fundamental ways.

Many LGBT parenting cases differ from more traditional gay rights litigation (e.g., cases challenging same-sex marriage bans and other discriminatory policies, such as the military's former exclusion of openly gay service members) in that the objective is not necessarily to achieve wide policy reforms, but is instead to gain legal recognition and protection for one familial arrangement or for one parent-child relationship. It is for this reason that—with some important exceptions (e.g., lawsuits challenging foster care and adoption restrictions, as well as efforts to persuade courts to recognize the parentage status of the former same-sex partners of legal parents)—most of the cases discussed in this book were handled by private attorneys rather than by movement lawyers working for organizations such as the ACLU and Lambda Legal. In this way, LGBT parenting cases are generally more diffuse and less centralized than are some of the other types of gay rights litigation.[26]

Another distinguishing characteristic between LGBT parenting cases and most other types of gay rights litigation is that what is ultimately at issue in the former is not the rights of LGBT individuals as such, but is instead the interests of the children involved. It is those interests that must guide policy makers and judges as they grapple with the multiplicity of issues raised by the existence of LGBT parents.

Even though LGBT parenting lawsuits are usually about obtaining justice for one family, or for one parent and his or her children, that does not mean that LGBT parenting litigation has not led to significant legal reforms. Indeed, as I explain in this book, LGBT litigants have been at the forefront of cases establishing how the law determines when individuals who have no biological (or adoptive) links to children should nonetheless be deemed their parents, at least for certain purposes (e.g., establishing custody and visitation rights). They have also been instrumental in helping to ascertain the government's authority to determine who is eligible to become foster care and adoptive parents. Finally, LGBT litigants have played crucial roles in determining how the law should respond to changes in reproductive assistance technologies.

It bears noting that LGBT parent litigants have not been alone in encouraging courts to reconsider some of the foundational principles of how legal parenthood is determined and understood. It is also the case that a growing number of heterosexual families fall outside the traditional model of a married couple raising children to whom they are both biologically related. Like LGBT individuals, some heterosexuals adopt children while others conceive them with the assistance of reproductive technology and donated sperm and eggs. But it is in some ways easier for the law to grapple with diversity among heterosexual families because straight people have the option of marrying in all fifty states. And marriage, in parenting law, makes a big difference. Married individuals in all states, for example, can adopt their spouse's children, while unmarried partners (regardless of sexual orientation) in some states cannot. In addition, the laws of all states allow a husband who consents to his wife's insemination with another man's sperm to be deemed the child's parent. But in most states, the same kind of explicit protection is not available to unmarried couples (regardless of sexual orientation) who conceive through alternative insemination.

Marriage, of course, does not always help to settle the parenting status of heterosexuals raising children because some of them choose not to marry. These heterosexuals have much in common with unmarried same-sex couples. Indeed, much of what I have to say in this book about how parenting law should treat lesbian and gay couples who are raising children together applies as well to unmarried straight couples doing the same. But there is, obviously, one important difference between unmarried same-sex and unmarried different-sex couples: their sexual orientation. Overcoming the prejudices and stereotypes that attach to having a same-sex sexual orientation constitutes a unique challenge for lesbian and gay parents, and thus the subject of such parents, and of how the law should grapple with their existence, merits its own exploration and analysis.

▲

Many of the issues raised by LGBT parenting lawsuits are sometimes addressed by legislatures. For LGBT parents, however, courts have generally been a more hospitable venue, largely because of the already-noted individualized assessment that is involved in family law adjudication. It is often easier to persuade a judge that a particular LGBT person, serving as a parent, can advance the well-being of a particular child than it is to convince legislators that sexual orientation or gender identity should be deemed irrelevant in matters related to parenting. Indeed, as illustrated by laws restricting the ability of LGBT individuals to adopt, when legislatures have gotten involved in these matters, it has frequently been to limit rather than to expand the opportunities of LGBT individuals to become parents.

This is not to suggest that legislatures do not sometimes enact laws that benefit LGBT parents. For example, as we will see in chapter 3, Delaware and the District of Columbia have enacted statutes recognizing functional or de facto parents, which can benefit nonbiological LGBT parents. In addition, as explained in chapter 4, many states no longer require that a woman who has been alternatively inseminated be married in order to terminate the parental rights of known sperm donors, a change that benefits all unmarried women, including lesbians, who want to raise children without the assistance of fathers. Nonetheless, as this book makes clear, it has been courts, and not legislatures, that have been primarily responsible for most of the changes in LGBT parenting law over the last four decades.

▲

As we will also see in this book, the progress that LGBT parents have made through the courts has varied greatly among jurisdictions. The best interests of the child standard, as already noted, grants judges significant discretion to determine what promotes and what undermines the well-being of children. Whether that discretion is helpful to an LGBT parent litigant often depends on the particular judge who is hearing the legal claim. Sometimes trial judges in the same county, for example, reach vastly different conclusions in similar cases; some are quick to infer harm to children from a parent's same-sex relationship, while others reject sexual orientation–based assumptions and demand specific evidence of harm.

Although appellate courts can provide some uniformity by determining which rules of law apply, the best interests of the child standard nonetheless leaves much discretion to trial judges. It is also important to remember that the precedential weight of state appellate court rulings ends at the borders of the state in which they are issued. (The vast majority of family law issues in the United States are litigated in state, rather than in federal, courts.) As a result, LGBT parents in one state can have markedly different legal rights than those in a neighboring one.

All of this means that there is frequently some uncertainty regarding many of the specific legal issues related to LGBT parenting. But that uncertainty is not necessarily a bad thing, at least when compared with the state of the law thirty years ago. As this book shows, there was *considerable* legal certainty then, but it was based on the belief, shared by most judges, that LGBT people had no business being parents. As this book also makes clear, that uniformity of view has broken down, permitting LGBT individuals, at least in some states on some issues, to prevail in having their relationships with their children recognized and protected by the law.

▲

When Barbara Holmes became pregnant in the fall of 2001 through a relationship with a man—to whom she was not married and who expressed little interest in the child—she moved back in with her parents outside Indianapolis.[27] After her son, Clark, was born, Barbara's parents helped take care of the boy for several years. This was of great help to Barbara, a certified public accountant whose job required her to travel out of town every week.

After Clark turned six, Barbara got her own place and moved out of her parents' home with her son. A few months later, she met Karen Walterson and the two women started dating. But when Barbara told her mother about her relationship with Karen, she replied that homosexuality was a sin and that the relationship would harm Clark.

In the summer of 2007, Karen quit her job, moved in with Barbara, and assumed a large share of the child-care responsibilities. Also that summer, Barbara's mother had a stroke and was hospitalized, after which her father told her that it was her homosexuality that had caused her mother's serious physical ailment. He also told her that Karen was not welcome in her mother's hospital room. After Barbara's mother was released from the hospital, she continued to berate her daughter about her homosexuality, warning her that if she insisted in being open about it, she would lose her job and Clark would be harassed at school.

In the months that followed, Barbara's parents at first refused to invite Karen to family gatherings, only to grudgingly relent when their daughter insisted that Karen was part of her family. But much tension remained in the relationship between Barbara and her parents, a strain that culminated in a three-way shouting match on Christmas eve. During that altercation, Barbara's father told her that he never wanted her to visit their home again. He also stated that if anything bad were to happen to Clark, she would have to answer to him, a remark that Barbara understood as a threat.

After the blowup, Barbara and her parents stopped talking to each other. A few months later, in April 2008, her parents filed a court petition seeking the right to visit with Clark several times a month. In September of that year, Barbara and Karen traveled to California to get married. (Several weeks later, California voters approved a state constitutional amendment banning same-sex marriages.)

The trial court appointed a guardian ad litem (GAL)—that is, someone whose role in the lawsuit was to represent Clark's interests. The GAL interviewed Barbara, her parents, Karen, and Clark. He learned that Clark called Barbara "Mommy" and Karen "Mom." He also determined that Barbara's parents strongly objected to their daughter's same-sex relationship and to the role that Karen was playing in Clark's life. Even though the GAL concluded that her parents' homophobia justified Barbara's refusal to allow them to visit with Clark, the trial judge ordered that the grandparents be allowed to visit with the boy for ten hours a month and on certain holidays and birthdays. Barbara appealed that ruling to the Indiana Court of Appeals, which in 2009 reversed the trial's judge order after concluding that Barbara's parents were not entitled to forced visitation over her objections.[28]

The difference between the Indiana court's ruling and that of the Virginia Supreme Court in Sharon Bottoms's case fourteen years earlier is striking. The latter court was unable to see beyond Sharon's lesbianism, leading it to conclude, without any basis in fact, that her same-sex relationship with her partner was harming her son. In contrast, the Indiana court recognized that the source of the conflict between Barbara and her parents was not the former's same-sex relationship but the latter's refusal to accept it. That court was also willing to apply, in a case involving a lesbian mother, the long-recognized principle that a legal parent should be permitted to make decisions about what she believes is in her child's best interests over the objections of nonparents unless there is clear evidence that the parent is unfit.

The Virginia court had ruled that once Sharon Bottoms decided to have an open relationship with her lesbian partner, she could no longer retain custody of her son. But the Indiana court did not make Barbara choose between leading an open life as a lesbian—which included sharing her home with her partner—and her son. Instead, the judges ruled that it was for Barbara, and not for the courts or the child's grandparents, to decide whether she was to be in an open relationship with another woman.

The difference between the Virginia and Indiana rulings is an example of the progress that LGBT parents have made in some of the nation's courts over the last two decades. Most chapters in this book contain similar stories of progress. This does not mean that courts today are always able to look beyond sexual orientation and gender identity in order to apply legal principles fairly in cases involving LGBT parents and their children. Far from it. As all the chapters in this book show, LGBT parents continue to lose legal cases because of the refusal of some judges to move beyond antiquated and unrealistic understandings of what every family should look like. But, as a general matter, LGBT parents are making progress in the courts. This book explores why and how that has come to be.

PART I

What Makes a Good Parent?

1

Mothers on Trial

In the spring of 1970, Sandy Schuster, a thirty-two-year-old mother of four children, was attending a service at a fundamentalist church in Seattle when she was transfixed by the sight of a beautiful woman walking down the church's aisle holding the hands of her two young sons. That twenty-eight-year-old woman, Madeleine Isaacson, taught Sunday school at the church, and after a few weeks, the two struck up a conversation that led to a blossoming friendship. It turned out that they had much in common—both were deeply religious, completely devoted to their children, and in unhappy marriages of eight years.

When Madeleine, two months after they first met, told her new friend that she was in love with her, Sandy reacted with alarm. While studying nursing at Stanford before she married, Sandy had read the work of Sigmund Freud, leading her to now explain to Madeleine that she was likely going through a phase that could be traced back to childhood experiences. Madeleine insisted, however, that she was in love, and after a while Sandy admitted that the feeling was mutual. Although the women's realization that they were lesbians might have led them to question their commitment to Christianity, they instead came to see their coming into each others' lives as a gift from God.

Less than a year after they met, the two women put their kids and a handful of belongings in a van and fled to California. Sandy left a note for her husband Jim, and Madeleine called her husband Jerry from the road, explaining what they were doing. The two men immediately joined forces, tracked them down in Oceanside, and, while their wives were looking the other way, grabbed one of Sandy's children and both of Madeleine's sons and rushed them back to Washington State.

The two women had no choice but to return to Seattle and try to settle the whole mess in court. Throughout the divorce and custody proceedings that followed, Jim and Jerry's main legal argument would be that the mothers' lesbian relationship rendered them unfit to have custody of their children.

If Sandy and Madeleine insisted on not hiding their lesbian relationship, the fathers argued, they should not be permitted to continue living with their children.

▲

Before there was an organized political and legal movement seeking to decriminalize sodomy, end the military's decades-long policy of excluding gay service members, and pursue same-sex marriage as a civil rights goal, there were lesbian mothers fighting for the custody of their children in the courts. There had always been mothers who were lesbians—in the same way that there had always been fathers who were gay—but before the sexual and political convulsions of the 1960s and early 1970s, few dared to acknowledge their homosexuality to themselves, much less to others. Some lesbian mothers had become aware of their attraction to other females during their adolescence but decided later to marry men in the hope that it would help them deny (or at least hide) their sexual orientation. But the experiences of many lesbian mothers tracked those of Sandy and Madeleine—that is, they married men first, had children second, and realized they were lesbians third.

Beginning around 1970, in the wake of the Stonewall riots and the growing influence of the women's movement, lesbian mothers for the first time started considering the possibility of being open about their sexual orientation while not losing custody of their children. For some, this was too big of a risk to take. Indeed, many lesbians in the 1970s who separated from or divorced their husbands continued to hide their sexual orientation in order not to jeopardize custody of their children. But a growing number of others began to chafe against having to choose between leading open lives as lesbians and raising their children.

Most lawyers and activists in the 1970s advised lesbian mothers to avoid contested litigation with their husbands if possible. Once the decision to get a divorce was made, it was better to try to reach an agreement with the husband that would grant him generous visitation rights in return for the mother retaining custody. Pursuing this strategy minimized the risk that a court would use a mother's lesbianism to deny her custody outright, or to condition it on her not having intimate relationships with other women. When an agreement was not possible, however, there was no choice but to have a judge decide the custody issue. And once custody was in play, many fathers did not hesitate in trying to use their ex-spouses' lesbianism against them. This, in turn, forced judges to grapple with the question of what role the mothers' sexual orientation played in their ability to be good parents to their children.

The question of child custody (and in some instances visitation) was the first legal issue involving LGBT people in the United States that began appearing repeatedly in court dockets. Indeed, family law judges were the first group of jurists in the country to routinely grapple with the legal relevance of homosexuality.

Custody cases between disputing parents are decided under a standard known as the "best interests of the child," one that purposefully grants trial judges broad discretion to take many different factors into account in determining the custody and visitation rights of former spouses. These factors include the economic and emotional stability of the parents; the parents' track record of caring for the child in the past and their willingness to care for him or her in the future; and, if the child is mature and old enough, the child's preference.

The wide discretion enjoyed by trial judges under the best interests of the child standard made it possible for them to bring their views on homosexuality to bear on lesbian custody proceedings. Many judges who were troubled by a mother's homosexuality specifically relied on that fact to deny or limit her custodial rights. In fact, it seemed that early custody trials involving lesbians frequently devolved into lengthy proceedings largely focused on the causes, manifestations, and effects of their homosexuality. During a 1967 California custody trial, for example, a lesbian mother was asked the names and addresses of everyone with whom she had been sexually intimate during the previous two years, how often she had sex, and whether she had ever been a prostitute. As if this were not enough, the judge asked her to explain "what occurs [in] a homosexual act. Just what does this entail? *What do you do?*" When the mother refused to answer the question on the ground that it might incriminate her—sodomy was illegal in California at the time—the judge insisted that he needed "in a contested custody matter in which this issue of homosexuality is the main thread . . . to have some detailed knowledge of what these activities are."[1] The result of this type of obsessive focus on homosexuality by judges meant that the children and their well-being were almost always lost in the process.

▲

Sandy and Madeleine's divorce and custody cases landed before Washington State judge James Noe in December 1972. Noe asked a social worker and a psychiatrist to visit the home the couple shared with their children and write reports on what they found. As was usually the case in early custody disputes involving lesbian mothers, the court wanted to know how the mothers' openness about their sexual orientation affected the children.

In her report to the court, the social worker wrote that the danger of homosexuality was that it might lead to "feelings of guilt and self-rejection and a tendency to withdraw from society." Yet, she found that Sandy and Madeleine answered their children's questions about their relationship clearly and honestly, which made the children feel comfortable with their familial arrangement. The social worker concluded that "this is a most happy, well organized, [and] creative family." The court-appointed psychiatrist agreed, writing in his report that "the children certainly are getting good physical and emotional care, are being loved and are able to show love in return."[2]

Judge Noe was a deeply religious man. As a result, it may have helped Sandy and Madeleine that their husbands raised concerns not only about their open lesbianism but also about their Christian fundamentalism. Although the judge was not at all troubled by the women's strong faith, he did ask them during the proceedings to reflect on a biblical passage from Romans 1 in which Paul condemns those who lusted after the flesh more than after God. What effect, the judge wanted to know from the women, did the "Word of God [have] . . . on [your] lifestyle"?[3]

Although Sandy and Madeleine knew the passage well, they reread it at home and, as was their usual practice with the Bible, spent time discussing it. Their conclusion, which they later shared with the judge, was that God disapproved of lust, whether gay or straight, but He did not disapprove of love. And what they felt for each other, above all else, was love. Judge Noe, who appeared partially reassured by the women's answer, ruled in the end that the two women could have custody of their children because the latter seemed happy and well-adjusted under their mothers' care. But the judge was sufficiently troubled by the fact that the women lived together in an open lesbian relationship that he conditioned the mothers' custody on their finding separate residences.

▲

Sandy and Madeleine, knowing that their children were thriving in their joint household, did not agree with the judge's order that they live apart. This meant, as we will see below, that the legal battle between the two women and their former husbands continued for years to come. At the very least, however, the court had awarded them custody of their children. Some lesbian mothers in the 1970s were not so lucky. One of them was Mary Jo Risher.

Mary Jo was born in 1937 and grew up in Little Rock, Arkansas. The daughter of a railroad worker and a waitress, she attended the Arkansas Baptist School of Nursing in the mid-1950s. A few months before she graduated, she met and married Doug Risher as he was about to join the air force. Marrying Doug in 1957 came as a relief for Mary Jo because she thought it would bring to an end the attraction she had felt for other women since high school.

The couple's first child, Jimmy, was born in 1958. After Mary Jo suffered several miscarriages, the couple adopted a second son, Richard, born in 1967. Shortly after the adoption, the family moved to Dallas, where Doug took a job as an airplane mechanic and Mary Jo became chaplain of the local chapter of a fraternal organization (the Order of the Eastern Star) and president of the Dallas County Council of PTAs. The marriage, however, was not a happy one. The couple separated in July 1970 and divorced less than a year later.

After the divorce, Mary Jo for the first time began acting on her attraction to women, visiting lesbian bars, making lesbian friends, and eventually dating women. The second woman she dated was Ann Foreman, a divorced mother with a young daughter who worked as a bank auditor. The two women fell in love and decided, after six months of dating, to move in together with their children.

Ever since they separated, Doug had heard rumors that his ex-wife was a lesbian, rumors that were confirmed when Mary Jo, Ann, and the three children began sharing a home. Although Doug had initially agreed that Mary Jo should have custody of their two sons, he had by now remarried and wanted more contact with the children. The fact that his former wife was living openly with another woman gave him the opportunity he was seeking to take custody away from her.

Unlike most legal rulings, custody determinations are never final. A parent who has lost (or waived) custody can always petition the court alleging that there has been a "material change in circumstances" justifying a modification of the initial custody award. The presumption in these cases is that a change in custody should be avoided in order not to disrupt the child's life. But if the petitioning party can show that, due to changed circumstances, a custody modification would be in the child's best interests, a court must grant it.

These points of legal doctrine meant that even when lesbian mothers kept their lesbianism out of initial custody proceedings, there was always the possibility that, if they were living openly as lesbians, their ex-husbands would try to use it against them in future proceedings. In addition, given the social prejudices prevalent at the time, it was likely that many judges would deem a mother's lesbianism, especially if she was an in open relationship with another woman, as a sufficiently material and detrimental change of circumstance to justify stripping custody away from her and granting it to the father.

In October 1975, a sheriff's deputy knocked on Mary Jo's door and served her with legal papers declaring that Doug was seeking custody of the boys because Mary Jo and Ann were "living in a homosexual relationship as man and wife." The document also alleged that Mary Jo and Ann held "wild parties, on numerous occasions in the presence of the children, inviting other homosexuals to these gatherings, for the purpose of openly engaging in homosexual activities." The children, the document concluded, "should be removed from [this] immoral and undesirable environment."[4]

Although the accusations contained in this legal document were patently false, they were representative of the challenges faced by lesbian mothers who wanted to retain contact with their children over their former husband's objections. It was true, of course, that Mary Jo lived with her partner and that the two sometimes had lesbian friends over. But their home was not, as Doug alleged, a hypersexualized one where children were exposed to the intimate conduct of adults.

Mary Jo hired two lawyers to help her fight Doug's effort to take away custody. The lawyers tried to persuade the presiding family court judge in Dallas that Doug, during the custody proceedings, should not be permitted to raise issues related to their client's lesbianism before the jury. (Texas law is unusual in that it calls on juries to hear custody cases; most states call on judges, rather than on juries, to make custody decisions.) The lawyers insisted that their client's sexual orientation was wholly irrelevant to the question of whether she was a good mother. But the judge refused to exclude evidence of Mary Jo's lesbianism, ruling that Doug was entitled to raise questions about her ability to be a good parent and role model to the children, given the fact that she was a lesbian who lived openly with another woman in a romantic relationship. Despite his ruling, the judge refused to allow several potential jurors from hearing the case after they opined, during the jury selection process, that a lesbian mother should *never* be granted custody of her children.

From the moment the trial began on December 16, 1975, Doug's lawyer, a young and ambitious attorney by the name of Mike McCurley, made it clear that he was going to put Mary Jo's lesbianism on trial by aggressively probing how it affected her ability to properly care for eight-year-old Richard. (The custody of Mary Jo's seventeen-year-old son Jimmy was not at issue because she had agreed shortly before the trial began that he could live with his father.) While Mary Jo was on the witness stand, McCurley asked many questions about her relationship with Ann, including whether she loved her as a spouse (the answer was yes), whether she had sex with women other than Ann (the answer was no), and whether she was physically affectionate with Ann in the home (the answer was yes, but never in front of the children).

McCurley then asked a series of questions aimed at establishing that Mary Jo was more committed to her lesbianism (and to Ann) than to her son. But when McCurley explicitly asked whether she loved Ann more than she loved her son, Mary Jo objected to the question, complaining that it was "like asking one of these jury members to make a choice between their wife or husband [and] their child."[5] She added that she could love Ann as her partner and Richard as her child without any conflict or tension between the two.

One of the key witnesses at the custody trial was Jimmy, Mary Jo's oldest son. While on the witness stand, Jimmy shared his view, while answering McCurley's direct questions on the matter, that his mother "played the masculine role and Ann played the woman's role" at home.[6] Jimmy also told the jury that his mother's relationship with Ann was a constant source of embarrassment to him, that he preferred to live with his father, and that it would be best for his brother to be removed from his mother's home because it is better to be raised by a man and a woman than by two women.

▲

Ever since lesbian and gay parents started coming out of the closet, critics have claimed that their sexual orientation will interfere with the "normal" sexual and gender development of their children. The concern is that the children of these parents will either turn out to be lesbian or gay themselves or, at the very least, be insufficiently masculine (if they are boys) or feminine (if they are girls). In the mid-1970s, studies showing that lesbian and gay parents did not affect the sexual orientation or gender identity of their children were still several years away. But this did not prevent lesbian mothers and their lawyers from calling on psychiatrists, psychologists, and pediatricians with expertise in sexual orientation matters to testify in custody trials.

Lawyers who specialized in lesbian custody cases in the 1970s recommended that great care be paid to the choice of experts. As Nan Hunter and Nancy Polikoff put it in the first comprehensive law review article published on lesbian custody cases, "the expert witnesses for the lesbian mother may well form the most important part of her case."[7] It was crucial, Hunter and Polikoff explained, that the expert "address the fears that a court might have about placing a child in a lesbian home environment. The expert [should] explain to the court that, although the causes of homosexuality are not certain, there is no evidence to suggest that being raised by homosexual parents is a cause."[8] And this, of course, made a great deal of sense since the vast majority of gay people were raised in heterosexual households.

One of the first gay rights organizations that reached out to parenting experts was the National Gay Task Force (later known as the National Gay and Lesbian Task Force). The organization was cofounded in 1973 by Bruce Voeller, a former Rockefeller University biology professor who, as we will see in the next chapter, battled with his former wife in court over his right to visit with his children after he started living openly as a gay man. One of the first steps that Voeller took as executive director of the new organization was to put together a packet of statements written by leading scientists—including Evelyn Hooker, a professor of psychiatry at UCLA, Judd Marmor, a professor of psychiatry at USC, and Benjamin Spock, the famous pediatrician and author—stating their professional opinion that sexual orientation was not a factor in the ability of individuals to be good parents, and that, as Dr. Spock put it, there was "no evidence that homosexual parents are more apt to raise homosexual children."[9]

These experts' views were bolstered in December 1973 when the American Psychiatric Association removed homosexuality from its official manual of mental and emotional disorders. (Two years later, the American Psychological Association passed a resolution supporting this action. And, a year after that, it approved another resolution opposing the use of sexual orientation as the primary factor in making custody determinations.) This change affected lesbian custody cases because, from then on, when an expert hired by a straight father raised the specter of mental illness or deviancy while discussing the mother's lesbianism, the American Psychiatric Association's decision could be used to question the witnesses' scientific credibility.

▲

The use of expert testimony in Mary Jo Risher's case was typical of cases involving lesbian mothers in the 1970s. Doug's lawyer called a family counselor to the stand, who testified at length about the importance of parents "modeling sexual identification." He also claimed that a child in a heterosexual family was more likely to learn "the important roles and functions that he is to play as an adult."[10] (Doug sought to bolster the counselor's reasoning by opining during his testimony that it was "important for children to have the mother and father image in their lives, and certainly two women showing affection to each other is not my idea of a good environment for a child.")[11]

The issue of gender role modeling also came up during the testimony of Dr. Robert Gordon, a court-appointed psychologist who was tasked with the responsibility of assessing Mary Jo's track record as a mother. Gordon was a crucial witness because the jury was likely to give considerable weight to the testimony of this ostensibly neutral expert. It undoubtedly hurt Mary Jo's chances of retaining custody of her son, therefore, when Gordon took the stand and questioned her judgment as a mother. The doctor was particularly troubled by the fact that when he interviewed Richard, the boy had volunteered that he was wearing jeans that belonged to Ann's daughter. Although Gordon admitted during cross-examination that the jeans were unisex and that children at the time often wore unisex clothing, it was his opinion that Mary Jo showed poor judgment in allowing her son to wear the jeans. As a lesbian mother, the doctor explained, Mary Jo had to be particularly mindful of promoting her son's proper gender development.

The second example provided by Gordon of Mary Jo's poor judgment as a mother was also sartorial in nature. At the same interview, Richard wore a shirt with the letters "YWCA" on it. In Gordon's opinion, it was inappropriate for Richard to wear such a shirt. It did not matter to him that the boy was taking gymnastic lessons at the YWCA or that there were other boys in the class. Instead, it was his expert opinion that while it was generally not inappropriate for boys to attend classes at the YWCA and girls to do the same at the YMCA, Richard's situation was different because his mother was a lesbian. According to this expert, it was imperative that such a mother "encourage . . . masculine identifications" in her son.[12]

Doctor Gordon's testimony was indicative of how the sexual orientation of lesbian mothers in custody cases placed unique burdens on them to show that they were good parents to their children. Indeed, the doctor could not have been more explicit in his view that Mary Jo's lesbianism threatened the ability of her son to properly identify as a masculine boy, a position that Mary Jo had to refute if she wanted the expert's psychological seal of approval.

Knowing that the jurors would likely be troubled by the suggestion that Mary Jo's lesbianism might make her son either gay or feminine (or both), her lawyers called on Dr. Dolores Dyer, a state-certified clinical psychologist who had extensive experience working with children. Dr. Dyer explained on the witness stand that Richard, in response to questions she had posed to him about his interests and what he wanted to be when he grew up, gave "very typical male stereotype [answers]. . . . He wants to be a policeman; he plays with bicycles. . . . He wants to be a lion."[13] She added that, "as a psychologist, I go along with the position of the American Psychological Association which no longer endorses homosexuality as a mental illness in that we no longer consider a homosexual . . . deficient in stability of judgment or impair[ed in] their ability to function."[14]

A crucial part of Mary Jo's legal case, then, was aimed at neutralizing the accusation that her being open about her sexual orientation was harmful to her child. Although technically it was Doug, as the party seeking the custody modification, who had the burden of showing that the modification would be consistent with Richard's best interests, it was Mary Jo who, as a practical matter, had to establish she could be a good mother to her son even though she lived in an open relationship with another woman. It seemed clear during the trial that whether she would be able to retain custody of Richard depended on her ability to persuade the jury of this.

▲

During closing arguments, Doug's attorney asked the jury not to make the young boy "a guinea pig in someone else's experiment."[15] The lawyer also chastised Mary Jo for "refusing to give up her lifestyle" for her child while contending that the boy would be better off in the "fine Christian family atmosphere" that Doug had created in his new home with his new wife.[16] For his part, Mary Jo's lawyer implored the jury not to punish her because she was a lesbian and even more important, not to "punish [her son] because his mother is a homosexual."[17]

After a trial that had lasted more than a week, and in which almost twenty witnesses testified, it was time for the jury, three days before Christmas, to begin deliberating. The judge instructed the jurors that it was their job to decide whether there had been "a material and substantial change of conditions" since Mary Jo had first been awarded custody of Richard more than three years earlier that justified transferring custody to his father.[18] The judge asked the jury to come back with a simple yes or no answer.

The jury of ten men and two women deliberated for a day and a half before returning with a verdict: their answer was yes. Upon hearing that one word, Mary Jo rested her head on her lawyer's shoulder and began crying, first in soft whimpers and then in loud howls. As Doug was surrounded and congratulated by his lawyers and friends, the judge officially closed the proceedings. This permitted TV camera operators and newspaper photographers to swarm the courtroom to chronicle the despair of a mother who had just lost her child. An Associated Press photograph of a crying and distraught Mary Jo appeared the following day in newspapers across the country.

Tony Liscio, the jury's foreman and a former football player with the Dallas Cowboys, told the congregated media that he had been one of two jurors who had voted to allow Mary Jo to keep her son. But Liscio was unable to persuade the others, explaining that "it was a lifestyle of a lesbian that most jurors felt affected the trial."[19] He added that "not having a man [in the home] had an effect on the [jury's] decision."[20]

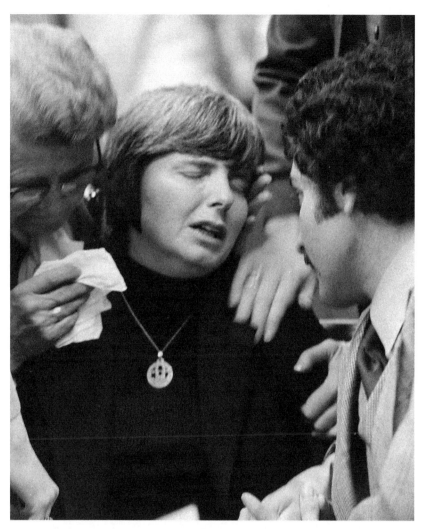

Mary Jo Risher being consoled after a Dallas jury took away custody of her son in 1975. Used with permission of the Associated Press.

A few days later, Mary Jo drove Richard to her mother's house. At an arranged time, Doug drove up and took the boy with him. Mary Jo would later be awarded visitation rights, allowing her to see Richard every other weekend. (She was, however, required to pay child support.) Although Mary Jo wanted to appeal the jury's ruling, her lawyers failed to post an appeal bond within the prescribed time limits.[21] As a result, the Court of Civil Appeals refused to hear her case and Mary Jo never regained custody of her son.[22]

In the end, Mary Jo lost her case because she was unable to persuade the jury that she could be both a good mother and live as an open lesbian while sharing her home with the woman she loved. The question of Mary Jo's attributes and capabilities as a parent were both determined and overshadowed by her sexual orientation. To put it simply, Mary Jo lost custody of her son because the jury concluded that her open lesbianism made her a bad mother. The absence of evidence presented during the trial that Richard had been harmed in any way by his mother's relationship with Ann made the outcome a travesty of justice. The jury's verdict had much to do with prejudice and little to do with the proper application of the law.

▲

Even when lesbian mothers in the 1970s were able to keep custody of their children, it sometimes came with the condition that they not live with their partners. That was what Judge Noe in Seattle had required when he ordered that Sandy Schuster and Madeleine Isaacson cease living together as a condition of their keeping custody of their children. Around the time of Judge Noe's ruling, Sandy and Madeleine were becoming politically active around the issue of lesbian mothers and their children. In 1973, the couple was featured in the first documentary film made in the United States about a family headed by two lesbians (titled *Sandy and Madeleine's Family*). The following year, Sandy published a pamphlet about lesbian mothers titled *Love Is for All*, an outgrowth of her thesis for a master's degree in psychiatric nursing she received from the University of Washington.

Upon hearing of Judge Noe's ruling, the two women despaired that they might no longer be able to live together with their six children in the sprawling country house they had shared for the previous two years. They were a family and the thought of being required by a court of law to break up their home was devastating. But as they considered their dilemma, they came up with a seemingly ingenious solution: they would move out of their house and rent adjoining units in an apartment building, an arrangement that would allow them to continue living as a family unit while still abiding by the letter (though not exactly the spirit) of the judge's order.

Soon after Jim Schuster and Jerry Isaacson learned of their former wives' new living arrangement, they went back to court. In their legal papers, the fathers claimed that a modification of Judge Noe's custody ruling was now required because (1) both men had recently remarried; (2) the mothers had violated the court's order by living together; and (3) the mothers had brazenly publicized their lesbian relationship through the documentary and frequent public appearances and media interviews. For their part, Sandy and Madeleine filed a counterpetition asking that the earlier court order requiring them to live apart be rescinded.

A custody modification trial was held before superior court judge Norman Ackley in September 1974. The proceedings lasted five and a half days. The fathers called twenty-one witnesses to the stand, three of whom were psychiatrists or psychologists. The mothers called twelve witnesses, seven of whom were doctors. The court also appointed its own psychiatrist, the same doctor who had testified during the first custody hearing.

The fathers' lawyer was Clay Nixon, a prominent and flamboyant attorney who had practiced law in Seattle for almost fifty years. Nixon, who "invariably wore a white vest, a fresh rose in his buttonhole, and, frequently, a broad-brimmed white hat," was a lifelong Republican who had vigorously supported Senator Joseph McCarthy's anticommunist crusades of the 1950s.[23] At the new custody trial, Nixon charged that homosexuality "is a disease similar to leprosy." He claimed that Sandy and Madeleine were requiring their children to believe that homosexuality is "the preferred way of life." The attorney also charged that the relationship between the two women was not one of love but a "union of lust."[24] Not surprisingly, the expert witnesses called by Nixon suggested that children were more likely to become gay if they were raised by lesbian mothers. The mothers' expert witnesses discredited this theory, as did the court-appointed expert.

After the last witness testified, Judge Ackley orally announced his decision from the bench. The judge explained that he was persuaded by the court-appointed psychiatrist's testimony "that although the children will grow up knowing more about homosexuality and human sexuality in general, this knowledge need not predispose them to become homosexuals."[25] The judge added that even though he was troubled by "the publicity which [the mothers] have elicited about their unorthodox life style[,] . . . it has apparently not hurt the children yet."[26] Ackley concluded that the children were "healthy, happy, normal and loving," and that their current living arrangement was in their best interests. He also found that the fact that the mothers "moved into adjoining apartments, where they . . . lived together as one household . . . did not prove to be against the best interests of the children."[27] He therefore denied the fathers' custody modification petition and lifted the requirement that Sandy and Madeleine live apart.

▲

Although Judge Ackley did not state so explicitly, he applied a legal standard to the question of the mothers' sexual orientation and relationship that has become known as the "nexus test." Nixon had argued throughout the proceedings that the mothers' homosexuality was reason alone to strip them of custody. Ackley implicitly disagreed with that position by focusing instead on the *impact* of the mothers' lesbianism on the children.

From the earliest lesbian custody cases, lawyers for the mothers argued that courts should not rely on presumptions of harm based on their clients' same-sex sexual orientation and relationships, but should instead provide them with a fair opportunity to show that they could be good parents to their children. The lawyers added that if courts insisted on accounting for a parent's sexual orientation and relationships, they should do so only if there was specific evidence that those factors negatively affected the children. The crucial issue under this proposed approach was whether a nexus or link existed between sexual orientation and actual or potential harm to the child. As Hunter and Polikoff explained in their article on lesbian custody cases published in 1976, "the only effective control against a decision based on prejudice . . . is a requirement that harm to the child be demonstrated before any factor, such as the mother's lesbianism, can be considered."[28]

Although a California appellate court, as early as 1967, had held that it was improper to automatically deny custody to a lesbian mother because of her sexual orientation, many courts in the 1970s failed to follow suit.[29] Another California appellate court in 1973, for example, upheld the decision of child welfare authorities to take two children away from a lesbian mother and place them in a foster home because "the continuous existence of a homosexual relationship in the home where the minor is exposed to it involves the *necessary likelihood* of serious adjustment problems."[30] And a year later, when the same mother sought to regain custody of two other children who had not been part of the earlier proceedings, the court ordered that they remain in foster care in another state because the preadolescents were "approaching a particularly sensitive period of their lives with respect to their emotional and physical development, and the mother's unconventional sexual relationship becomes of particular significance at this point in their lives."[31]

For his part, a trial judge in Ohio in 1975 concluded that a mother was unfit because she lived with another woman in a lesbian relationship, an arrangement the court viewed as presumptively harmful to the children. According to the judge, the issue was not so much the mother's sexual orientation as it was her decision to live openly with another woman. In awarding custody to the children's grandmother, the judge explained that "I don't say that a mother cannot be fit to rear her children even if she is a lesbian, but I wonder if she is fit when she boldly and brazenly sets up in the home where the children are to be reared."[32]

And there was more. In Washington State, a judge in 1976 denied custody to a lesbian mother, granting it instead to the heterosexual father, after noting that her living with another woman meant that her home life was "abnormal and not a stable one," and therefore "highly detrimental" to the children.[33] That same year, a New York trial court judge held that a lesbian mother's cohabitation with another woman was a sufficient ground to deny her custody. According to the judge, the women's living arrangement created an "improper environment for the child." He also concluded that the child was "emotionally disturbed by virtue of this environment." Although the judge in this last finding appeared to apply the nexus test by focusing on the supposed harm caused by the mother's same-sex relationship, he pointed to *no evidence* showing a link between that relationship and the child's purported emotional disturbance. In the end, the judge not only stripped the lesbian mother of custody and awarded it to the father, but he also imposed extensive restrictions on the mother's visitation rights—including no overnight stays, no visitation in the presence of gay people, no visits to places where gay people might congregate, and no involvement of the child in "homosexual activities or publicity."[34]

▲

Clay Nixon, in appealing Judge Ackley's ruling denying his clients' request that the court strip Sandy and Madeleine of custody of their children, continued to argue that living with their openly lesbian mothers was harming the children. In particular, Nixon claimed that the children's home environment negatively affected their sexual and psychological development. To support this allegation, Nixon pointed to Sandy's eight-year-old daughter. The attorney suggested that the girl "expressed some doubt about her heterosexual orientation" and "an ambivalence towards sexual roles."[35] Yet, the only evidence in the record that Nixon relied on to support his contention was the fact that the third grader had told one of the psychiatrists that she was not sure whether she wanted to get married and have a family.

Nixon also questioned the competency of several of the mothers' expert witnesses—one doctor was a "confessed homosexual," another (male) doctor cohabited with a woman outside of marriage, while a third espoused "liberal social theories." Finally, Nixon claimed that the mothers' political activities on behalf of lesbian rights proved that their "concern for their children is at least secondary and that the cause of homosexuality is primary and that they intend to devote their future energies to that cause." Time and again, Nixon returned to the mothers' openness about their sexual orientation as *the* reason to deny them custody. Nixon claimed that the mothers' insistence in leading open (and proud) lives as lesbians required the court to strip them of custody of their children.

In their response, Sandy and Madeleine's lawyers noted that Nixon was impermissibly trying to re-litigate the facts of the case before the appellate court. It was true that there had been conflicting testimony at the custody hearing on whether the mother's lesbianism was negatively affecting the children, but Judge Ackley had found the mothers' witnesses more credible on that crucial point. The bottom line, the lawyers argued, was that the trial judge had not abused his discretion in concluding that modifying the custody arrangement was inconsistent with the children's best interests.

The mothers' legal position on appeal was supported by an amicus (or "friend of the court") brief filed by an organization called the Lesbian Mothers' National Defense Fund (LMNDF), a Seattle-based group that was less than a year old.

▲

In the summer of 1974, four lesbians living in Seattle—three of them mothers—formed a new organization aimed at protecting the rights of lesbian mothers. Although there had been earlier lesbian mother groups in other parts of the country, they largely focused on the challenges and joys of child rearing. This new group was different because its goal was to help lesbian mothers retain legal custody of their children after separating from their husbands. Indeed, it was Sandy and Madeleine's case, as well as that of another lesbian mother from Washington State, that led the four women to form the new group.[36]

One of the ways that the LMNDF helped lesbian mothers was by raising money on their behalf. Lesbian custody cases were expensive to litigate, not only because of the usual attorney and court fees involved, but also because of the need to hire expert witnesses to counter the arguments frequently raised by ex-husbands that the mothers' sexual orientation and relationships threatened the children's well-being.

A few weeks after its inaugural meeting in 1974, LMNDF held its first fund-raiser. A local female band and a puppet group provided the entertainment. The children helped with publicity by making colorful posters that were put up around town. The group provided a keg of beer, asked for $2 donations, and netted $120. The LMNDF sent most of that money to a lesbian couple in Ohio that was embroiled in a protracted custody fight over the children of one of them. (The ex-husband's attorney, who was running for county prosecutor, vowed to rid the county of "the evil" of lesbians raising children. The trial judge ended up denying custody to the mother after concluding that to lesbians, "orgasm . . . means more . . . than children or anything else.")[37] By October 1975, a little more than a year after it was founded, the LMNDF had distributed almost $5,000 it had collected through fundraisers and membership fees to more than twenty-five lesbian mothers across the country who were fighting for the custody of their children in the courts.

The LMNDF, which adopted the motto "Raising Children Is a Right, Not a Heterosexual Privilege," grew steadily, attracting members not only from the Seattle area, but from other parts of the country as well. In addition to raising money, the organization kept a list of lawyers who were interested in helping with lesbian custody cases. It also collected and distributed materials (e.g., legal briefs, academic articles, and press clippings) that might prove helpful to mothers in custody fights. And it published a bimonthly newsletter, called *Mom's Apple Pie*, which it mailed to its members, informing them of ongoing cases, legal developments, fund-raising appeals, and helpful books and articles.[38]

Inspired, and often assisted, by the LMNDF, similar groups began forming in other parts of the country. These organizations included Dykes and Tykes in New York City, the Lesbian Mothers' Union in Oakland, the Lesbian Defense Fund in Vermont, and the Lesbian Mothers' Defense Fund in Ann Arbor, Michigan. All these groups were run by volunteers, many of whom were lesbian mothers.

In Philadelphia, a lesbian mother by the name of Rosalie Davies founded a legal advocacy group in 1974 called Custody Action for Lesbian Mothers (CALM) after she lost a protracted court battle with her ex-husband over custody of her two children. Davies told the media at the time that she had lost her case because she was a lesbian and that, during the proceedings, her sexuality had been "at trial like an ancient witchcraft trial."[39] Knowing from firsthand experience the importance of competent legal representation in custody fights, Davies founded CALM to make such representation available to lesbian mothers in the Philadelphia area. In 1979, Davies received her law degree from Temple University and then spent much of the next two decades fighting legal battles on behalf of lesbian mothers.

It was also not unusual in the 1970s for lesbians to come together in local communities to form groups aimed specifically at raising money to help pay expenses associated with a particular custody case. One of those groups was the Rachele Yaseen Defense Fund, which raised $12,500 on behalf of a lesbian mother who fought a long battle in Illinois with her former husband for custody of their six-year-old daughter. Despite the fact that the father's lawyer, during the custody hearing, asked the mother questions such as how big was the bed she shared with her lesbian partner, and that the father's expert witness, a psychologist, testified that the child had "sexual identity problems" that would only be solved if she lived in "a normal man-woman environment," the judge awarded custody to the mother.[40]

Much of the support provided to lesbian mothers who found themselves in custody battles with former husbands came from volunteer-run, nonlegal organizations. In contrast, some of the more established groups that aimed to promote the rights of women and sexual minorities, like the American Civil Liberties Union and the National Organization for Women, had not made lesbian custody issues a priority. It was in part for this reason that two California lesbian lawyers—Roberta Achtenberg and Donna Hitchens—founded the Lesbian Rights Project in San Francisco in 1977. The primary mission of this advocacy organization was to provide legal assistance to lesbian mothers. In the early 1980s, the group expanded its scope to other LGBT rights issues and, in 1989, changed its name to the National Center for Lesbian Rights. To this day, the organization continues to play an instrumental role in protecting the rights of LGBT parents in court.

▲

The amicus brief submitted by the LMNDF in Sandy and Madeleine's custody case focused on constitutional rights. Specifically, it argued that it would violate lesbian mothers' due process, privacy, and equal protection rights if courts applied a presumption of unfitness based on their sexual orientation.

When the Washington Supreme Court finally ruled on the case in 1978, however, it did not base its decision on the mothers' constitutional rights.[41] Instead, it focused on the fact that the fathers had never appealed Judge Noe's initial determination in 1972 that the mothers should be granted custody. Given the absence of an appeal on that issue, the court found no reason to disturb Noe's ruling. The court also held that the mothers' failure to live apart, as ordered by Noe, was an insufficient ground on which to modify the initial custody ruling. As a result, the court affirmed Judge Ackley's refusal to transfer custody to the fathers.

Somewhat ironically, three out of the four justices in the majority thought Judge Ackley had erred in rescinding the order requiring the mothers to live apart. The fourth justice believed that Ackley got it right both in denying the motion to modify custody and in lifting the prohibition against the women living together. But because the three dissenting judges concluded that the mothers should not be allowed to retain custody of the children, they did not bother to address the issue of whether Sandy and Madeleine should live apart. Given that only three justices voted to force Sandy and Madeleine to live in separate households, the two women were able both to retain custody of their children *and* to remain living together.

As the divisions among the justices showed, the case was a close one. (This was perhaps the best that could have been expected from a court that had recently upheld the firing of a teacher solely because he was gay.)[42] Nonetheless, the ruling in Sandy and Madeleine's case constituted the first time that a state's highest court held that lesbian mothers, who lived in open relationships with other women, could retain custody of their children. More than eight years after they first met, the lesbian couple finally had the peace of mind that came with knowing that no one could take their children away from them.

▲

At the time that Sandy and Madeleine's long battle for their children finally ended, Marianne MacQueen, a lesbian mother from Ohio, was living a nightmare: Her ex-husband, after abducting her son and taking him to another state, was petitioning a court to terminate her parental rights.

Marianne was twenty-two in 1967 when she met her husband Roy Talbert in Nashville. The couple's first years of marriage were relatively happy. Marianne worked as a schoolteacher and Roy finished graduate school at Vanderbilt University. After their son Matthew was born in 1971, however, the relationship began to deteriorate. In 1972, the family moved to Yellow Springs, Ohio, where Roy got a job at a social services agency. But the couple separated shortly after that, and Roy agreed that Matthew could stay living with his mother.

In 1974, Marianne met and fell in love with Moya Shea, a woman in town who was raising her three-year-old son Jason by herself. A few months later, the couple moved in together and Matthew and Jason became as close as brothers.

For his part, Roy moved to Virginia, where he got a teaching position at a small college. In 1975, Roy asked Marianne for a divorce. Shortly after that, he informed her that he was remarrying and that he wanted Matthew to spend more time with him. Although Marianne arranged for Matthew to travel to Virginia on a few occasions, she told Roy that she had concerns about the boy having two different lives in two different places. Tension between the two ex-spouses grew as Roy began complaining that he was unable to see Matthew as much as he wanted.

In February 1976, Roy and his new wife Linda traveled to Ohio to visit with Matthew. The couple came to Marianne and Moya's home, ostensibly to take the boy out to dinner. Matthew never came back. The couple abducted the boy, taking him to Virginia, where Roy immediately filed for temporary custody.

An angry and distraught Marianne contacted a lawyer in Virginia to see what she could do to get her child back. When the attorney found out that Marianne was a lesbian who lived openly with another woman, he advised her to waive custody in return for her receiving visitation rights. There was no way, the lawyer explained, that a Virginia court would ever grant custody to a lesbian who did not hide her sexual orientation.

After an agonizing few weeks in which she despaired over her apparent lack of options, Marianne accepted the lawyer's advice and entered into a settlement agreement with Roy that allowed her to visit with Matthew for eight weeks during summers and on alternating Christmas and Easter vacations. In a matter of just two months, Marianne had gone from being with her son every day to visiting with him for a few weeks a year while the boy spent most of the time with his father—and his new wife—in another state.

For the next two years, Marianne did her best to make her visitation periods with Matthew as enjoyable for him as possible. But deep down she was extremely depressed by the forced separation from her son. For his part, Roy resented the time that Matthew spent visiting with Marianne. As he saw it, his wife Linda had become the boy's day-to-day mother. Eventually Roy decided that it would be best if Linda and he raised the boy without the involvement of his lesbian ex-wife.

In August 1978, Linda, with Roy serving as co-petitioner, filed papers in a Virginia circuit court seeking to adopt Matthew. In order for the court to grant such a request, it would first have to terminate Marianne's parental rights.

The case was assigned to Judge B. A. Davis, III. Davis served in the U.S. Army during World War II, after which he earned a law degree from Washington and Lee University. He practiced law in the southwestern Virginia town of Rocky Mount for more than twenty years, before the state's General Assembly appointed him to serve on the bench starting in 1973.

A hearing regarding Matthew's future was held before Judge Davis in October 1978. As in many other court proceedings involving lesbian mothers, the main issue became whether it was possible for a woman who was in an intimate relationship with another woman to be a good mother to her child. Roy testified that he was concerned about Marianne's "bohemian lifestyle" and the fact that she and Moya, after participating in a commitment ceremony, considered themselves married. He added that he thought having Matthew split his time between liberal Yellow Springs, Ohio (the home of famously progressive Antioch College), and conservative rural Virginia would be confusing to the boy.[43]

When she took the stand, Marianne spoke openly and honestly about her relationship with Moya, explaining how the two women had formed a household built around love for each other and their children. She described the two of them as "married in the sense that we have a primary relationship and that we have committed ourselves to living our lives together and to supporting each other."[44] She also explained why she was so vigorously fighting her ex-husband's efforts to terminate her parental rights:

> I want to be able to see [Matthew] grow and participate in his growth. I guess not being with him all the time has probably made me appreciate him even more than if I were. And when I have him in the summer, . . . I feel like I am constantly marveling at this gift that I have. And in the summer there were a number of times when Matt would come running up to me and want me to hold him and I would hold him and sort of cradle him in my arms like a baby, and he would say, "My mommy, my mommy. You are my mommy." And I don't want to break that tie.[45]

Marianne added that if she ever felt like her relationship with Moya was harming her son in any way, she would end it immediately.

Judge Davis took an active role throughout the hearing, repeatedly asking the witnesses—who were Roy; his wife, Linda; Marianne; Matthew's teacher; and four residents of Yellow Springs (including a former psychology professor and a therapist/counselor) who had seen Marianne interact with her son many times—what impact Marianne's lesbianism had on Matthew. None of the witnesses—not even Roy or Linda—provided any specific examples of how Marianne's relationship with Moya might harm Matthew.

After the completion of the one-day hearing, the Office of the Virginia Commissioner of Welfare, which was apparently not aware of Marianne's lesbianism, submitted a report to the court recommending that Linda's adoption petition not be granted. Judge Davis then informed the commissioner's office that evidence had come to light during the hearing that the boy's mother was a lesbian. Two weeks later, the office filed a supplemental report retracting the earlier, more specific recommendation and replacing it with the vague suggestion that the court do what was in the child's best interests. In contrast, reports written by the county services agency where Roy lived and the one where Marianne resided concluded that allowing the boy's mother to continue visiting with him, which would require the court to deny the adoption petition, would be in his best interests.

In March 1979, Judge Davis issued a ruling terminating Marianne's parental rights, making her a legal stranger to her son. Without pointing to any specific evidence in the record, Davis wrote that the "open lesbian relationship now engaged in by [his mother], a . . . relationship she says will continue, would have a detrimental effect on Matthew if he is permitted to visit and live with his mother, especially during his formative years."[46] The judge added, again without pointing to any evidence introduced at the hearing, "that his being exposed to this relationship would result in serious emotional and mental harm to this child." On the same day, Davis issued a separate order granting Linda's request to adopt Matthew.

▲

All the other lesbian mother cases chronicled in this chapter raise the question of whether the mothers should gain or retain legal custody of their children. Marianne's case was different. She had already conceded custody to her husband as part of a settlement agreement. The issue in Marianne's case, therefore, was whether she would remain Matthew's legal parent at all.

Adoption decrees, unlike custody determinations, are final and cannot be reopened because of changed circumstances. Given the severe ramifications of the case—if Judge Davis's ruling was allowed to stand, Marianne might not see her son again until he turned eighteen and could decide for himself whether he wanted to see her—the American Civil Liberties Union agreed to represent Marianne in her appeal to the Virginia Supreme Court. Marianne had until then been represented by a local Virginia lawyer. But from now on her attorney would be Marcia Robinson Lowry, then director of the ACLU's Children's Rights Project. (Several years later, Lowry formed a group called Children's Rights, an influential national advocacy organization working to reform child welfare systems.)

In February 1980, a full year after Judge Davis's rulings, Virginia's highest court announced that it would not hear the case for at least another year. By this time, Marianne had not seen Matthew in two years, and it had been more than ten months since Roy had allowed her to speak to her son on the phone. The idea of having to wait at least another year before seeing Matthew again was unbearable for Marianne.

To try to get her client to at least be able to visit with her child during the pendency of the appeal, Lowry filed a habeas corpus petition in federal court on behalf of Marianne, contending that her son was being "detained" unlawfully based on a judicial ruling that unconstitutionally terminated her parental rights in the absence of a finding that she was an unfit mother. This use of the federal writ of habeas corpus was controversial at the time, with courts disagreeing on whether the writ—usually relied on by prisoners to challenge the constitutionality of their imprisonment—could be used in cases involving the termination of parental rights.[47]

Federal district court judge James Turk refused to entertain the writ petition until the Virginia Supreme Court ruled on the appeal.[48] Turk, however, urged Roy and Marianne to work out a visitation schedule. But all Roy did in response was allow Marianne to visit with Matthew for a few hours on a Saturday afternoon in June 1980. And even that small concession came with the condition that she not bring along her partner Moya (or any other lesbian). After that one short visit, Roy told Marianne that there would be no more.

In June 1981, the Virginia Supreme Court, without providing a reason, announced that it would not hear the case until October. Given the new delay, Lowry went back to Judge Turk imploring him to issue an order requiring Roy to permit Marianne to visit with her son. This time Turk did so, allowing her to spend a few precious days with Matthew that summer.

When Marianne went to pick up her son at her ex-husband's house, Linda met her at the door. In Matthew's presence, Linda warned her that there better not be any other lesbians present during the visitation period. "If anything happens to Matthew," Linda added, "you will have to answer to me." Marianne calmly responded by saying that she would not allow anything bad to happen to him; she was, after all, the child's mother. "No you are not," Linda replied through clenched teeth. "*I am* his mother."[49]

In October 1981, the parties finally gathered in Richmond for the oral argument before the Virginia Supreme Court. David Molesco, Roy and Linda's lawyer, told the court that day that Marianne had chosen a "lifestyle" that was not suitable for being a mother. Her relationship with the child, he charged, could be nothing but harmful and should be severed completely. One of the justices specifically asked Molesco whether he was contending that a parent's homosexuality was a sufficient ground on which to terminate a parent/child relationship. The lawyer, without hesitation, answered that that was precisely what he was arguing.

For her part, Lowry told the court that there were many relevant factors in determining whether a parent was fit to have contact with her child. The key, she emphasized, was the effect of a parent's conduct on the child. She added that sexual orientation by itself, like religious beliefs, was an improper basis

Marianne MacQueen (*back left*) was able to visit with her son Matthew (*front right*) on only a few occasions between 1976 and 1981. Also present in this photo from 1982 are Marianne's partner Moya Shea (*back right*) and her son Jason (*front left*). Used with permission of Marianne MacQueen.

on which to terminate a parent's rights. She also told the court that terminating Marianne's parental rights without the existence of a compelling state interest violated her constitutional rights as a parent.

Like the Washington Supreme Court in Sandy and Madeleine's case, the Virginia Supreme Court did not reach the constitutional issues raised in Marianne's appeal. Instead, in overturning Judge Davis's ruling in late 1981, the court concluded that the evidence showed that Marianne was a good and caring parent. The court added that, "aside from the lesbian relationship involved here, the petitioners were unable to give any valid reason why this woman should be permanently deprived of her child."[50]

The court held that there had to be some evidence that Marianne's lesbianism was harming Matthew before it would uphold the termination of her parental rights. The justices explained that "regardless of how offensive we may find [Marianne's] life-style, its effect on her son's welfare is not a matter of which we can take judicial notice." In the end, the court sided with Marianne because there was no proof in the record that her "living in a lesbian household" had harmed the boy in any way. In doing so, the court rejected Roy and Linda's efforts to have it hold that being in an open lesbian relationship was a sufficient ground on which to conclude that a mother was unfit to care for her child.

Roy and Linda's lawyer had implored the court to adopt a per se standard of unfitness, noting that the type of sex purportedly engaged in by Marianne and Moya was a felony offense in Virginia, even when consensual. The court refused to do so, explaining that, "if we follow this argument to its logical conclusion, we soon would be considering whether a convicted murderer, rapist, robber, burglar, habitual offender, or some other lawbreaker, whose conduct is unlawful and whose life-style is dangerous to himself, his family, and the public generally, should be declared unfit per se as a parent and his children made fair targets for adoption."

By analogizing homosexuality to murder and rape, and by making it clear that it did not approve of Marianne's lesbian "lifestyle," the court seemed eager to establish its socially conservative bona fides. At the same time, however, the court stuck by a long line of Virginia precedents holding that a parent's rights cannot be terminated without evidence that his or her conduct was harmful to the child. As a result of the appellate court's decision, Judge Davis's order granting the adoption petition was reversed, and Marianne, after waiting for almost three years following that ruling, became a legal mother again.

But her fight was not over. Roy and Linda asked the Virginia Supreme Court to reconsider its decision, which it refused to do. A few months later, Marianne for the first time took the legal offensive by suing Roy because he was not abiding by the visitation schedule they had agreed to six years earlier. Eventually, however, Marianne made the decision that another extended court battle with Roy would only further harm her son. She therefore accepted a compromise that allowed her to spend twenty-seven days each summer (as well as one week in December) with her son.

After several years in which she saw her son for a total of only a handful of days, Marianne was relieved to have at least regained the legal right to visit with her child. The legal victory, however, did not allow her to set the clock back. Matthew was four years old when his father abducted him in 1976; he was ten when the court reinstated Marianne's right to see him again. Marianne missed six years of her child's life for no reason other than the fact that she was a lesbian who refused to hide her sexual orientation.

At the end of the day, Marianne's case, like those of Sandy Schuster, Madeleine Isaacson, and Mary Jo Risher, boiled down to the question of whether it was possible for a woman to be a good mother while at the same time being open about her lesbianism. It is more than likely that all four women would have easily gained or retained custody of their children had their former husbands not attempted to use their being in same-sex relationships as the reason for stripping them of custody (and, in Marianne's case, of all parental rights). Although, of the four women, only Mary Jo Risher ultimately lost her case, all of them paid a heavy price when their motherhood was subjected to heightened judicial scrutiny because of their sexual orientation.

During the years of litigation that followed the mothers' coming out of the closet, the burden remained on them to show that they could be good parents despite their lesbianism. That burden should have never been placed on them. Instead, the courts should have made it clear from the beginning that presumptions of harm based on group membership have no place in what are supposed to be individualized assessments regarding which former spouse is best able to advance a particular child's well-being.

All that the four mothers asked of the courts was that their capabilities as parents be assessed without relying on the presumption that when lesbian mothers raise their children alongside their female partners, they must harm their children in some way. Although some of the courts hearing the cases eventually eschewed that presumption, it took years of hard-fought litigation for them to do so. It is both indisputable and ironic that the protracted litigation pursued by the ex-husbands inflicted much greater harm on the children than the mothers' sexual orientation ever did.

▲

Given the nature of child-centered legal disputes, in which judges have a great deal of discretion as they make decisions based on a multiplicity of factors, the precedential value of victories by lesbians in cases such as Marianne's was by necessity limited. To put it simply, just because a lesbian mother won a case did not translate into another lesbian mother, even in the same jurisdiction, winning hers. Nonetheless, LGBT parenting advocates welcomed the results of cases like Marianne's because they helped make two basic points: first, that neither having a same-sex sexual orientation nor being in a same-sex relationship rendered a parent unfit; and second, that before a parent's sexual orientation and relationships could be held against her in a custody or visitation case, there had to be a proved link or nexus between those factors and actual or potential harm to the child.

Starting around the mid-1980s, a growing number of appellate courts began rejecting the per se standard in favor of the nexus test in cases where the sexual orientation of a parent was at issue.[51] This trend continued so that by the turn of the century, a clear majority of the appellate courts that had ruled on the issue had adopted the nexus test.[52]

There were several factors that contributed to the near complete judicial acceptance of the proposition that the impact of a parent's sexual orientation on the well-being of children had to be assessed on a case-by-case basis rather than relying on presumptions of harm. One factor was the greater visibility of lesbians and gay men across society and the accompanying increased tolerance of homosexuality. Although discrimination based on sexual orientation had by no means ended, there was, by the turn of the century, considerably less social stigma attached to same-sex sexual conduct and relationships than there had been in the 1970s and 1980s. In addition, during those intervening years, the gay rights movement made same-sex marriage one of its political and legal priorities. As a result of the movement's push for marriage as a civil rights goal, many heterosexual Americans came to understand that committed same-sex relationships did not differ from their own in any meaningful ways.

Furthermore, as we will see later in this book, growing numbers of lesbians and gay men, beginning in the 1980s, started forming planned families, primarily through the use of reproductive assistance or adoption. In contrast to lesbians and gay men who had become parents as a result of heterosexual relationships, these individuals became parents *after* they came out of the closet. The visibility of this new group of parents played a crucial role in demonstrating to judges, and to the general public, that an individual's ability to be a good parent was not dependent on his or her sexual orientation.

Another factor that contributed to the increasing judicial acceptance of the nexus test was the growing consensus among experts in the fields of psychology and child welfare that what mattered in promoting the well-being of children was not the parents' sexual orientation, but was instead the amount of care, love, and support that parents provided their children. This growing consensus followed the findings of dozens of published studies that sought to address the very question asked by the nexus test—that is, whether the same-sex sexual orientation and relationships of lesbian and gay parents harm their children.

▲

Studies on parenting by lesbians and gay men fall into three broad categories. Those in the first group have reported on the children's psychological and social development, covering topics such as behavior, emotional well-being, self-esteem, school performance, and peer relations. The studies in the second category have investigated the quality of the relationship between lesbian and gay parents and their children. The third category of studies has looked at the children's gender identity/development and sexual orientation. The studies in all three categories have almost uniformly concluded that there are no significant differences between the children of lesbians and gay men and those of heterosexuals.

The findings regarding the children's psychological and social development have been remarkably consistent. In the 1980s, several researchers studied children raised by lesbian mothers following their divorce from the children's fathers. These studies concluded that the children did not experience greater psychological difficulties or more problems with self-esteem or peer relationships than did the children of heterosexuals.[53] Starting in the 1990s, as the number of lesbians who were having children using assisted reproductive technology grew, social scientists also began studying children who had been raised from birth by lesbians without the assistance of fathers. These studies, like the ones from the previous decade, failed to find significant differences between children raised by lesbian mothers and those raised by heterosexual parents in matters related to psychological and social development.[54]

Even more studies of planned lesbian families were published in the first decade of this century. Like the earlier ones, they found no significant differences in the physical and emotional well-being of children conceived by lesbians through alternative insemination.[55] Recently, social scientists working in this area have also begun to look at adoption, allowing them to study not only planned families headed by lesbians, but also those planned by gay men. The adoption studies have found that adopted children raised by lesbian and gay parents are as well-adjusted and happy as are adopted children raised by heterosexuals.[56]

Several studies have also shown no significant differences between the quality of mother-child relationships in lesbian-headed families and parent-child relationships in heterosexual households.[57] The one difference that has been found in some studies is that it appears that the quality of the relation-ship between the nonbiological mothers and the children in lesbian families is higher (i.e., there is more warmth and interaction) than the quality of the relationship between fathers and children in heterosexual families.[58]

Social scientists have also studied the children's gender identity/develop-ment and sexual orientation. Regarding the former (which looks at issues such as the children's degree of comfort with their gender and their interest in pursuits and activities that are traditionally associated with one gender or the other), several studies have found no differences between children raised by lesbian mothers and those raised by heterosexual parents.[59] Other studies have suggested that there may be some differences in the extent to which the children of lesbians abide by traditional gender role expectations—some studies have found, for example, that daughters of lesbian mothers express a greater interest in pursuing occupations and careers (e.g., in law, medicine, and engineering) that have traditionally been dominated by men than do the daughters of heterosexual mothers—but that hardly rises to the level of harm.[60]

The sexual orientation of the children of lesbians and gay men has also been studied. Several early investigations found that children of lesbians and gay men were not more likely to have a same-sex sexual orientation than were children of heterosexuals.[61] More recent studies have replicated those findings. For example, a 2010 study of eighteen young adult children raised from birth by lesbian mothers found that none of them identified as lesbian or gay, and only one identified as bisexual.[62]

One study from 1996 did find that a higher percentage of female young adults raised by lesbian mothers were willing to consider same-sex relation-ships in the future than were the children of heterosexuals.[63] A more recent study of adolescents raised by lesbian mothers found that a higher number of their daughters had engaged in same-sex sexual conduct than had the daughters of heterosexual parents.[64] (The same was not true of the sons of lesbian mothers who participated in both these studies.)

Rather than proving that the children of lesbian parents are more likely to engage in same-sex sexual conduct, these studies may simply reflect the fact that the children of lesbian mothers who engage in such conduct may be more willing to *acknowledge* it than the children of heterosexual parents. Nonetheless, some opponents of LGBT parenting have tried to use these findings to support their claim that lesbian and gay parents are more likely to raise children who end up being lesbian or gay themselves. This conclusion is undermined by the studies' clear findings that the vast majority of LGBT parents' children are heterosexual. That finding, when coupled with the fact that most lesbian and gay individuals were raised by straight parents, suggests that the sexual orientation of parents may play a minor or insignificant role in determining their children's sexual orientation.

In addition, even if it were proved that more children of lesbian and gay parents grow up to be lesbian or gay themselves, that outcome would only be troubling if there is something wrong with having a same-sex sexual orientation. This is a normative rather than an empirical question. If one believes there is nothing wrong with being lesbian or gay, then a causal link between the same-sex sexual orientation of parents and their children, even if proven, is not problematic.

There are those who question the validity of the studies on LGBT parenting by claiming that they are methodologically flawed because they rely on small and nonrandomly selected samples of lesbian and gay families, and because they do not follow the children over the course of several years. This criticism overlooks the fact that in certain fields, such as developmental psychology, researchers rarely use large and randomly selected survey samples. As one leading psychologist has explained, "such large-scale survey research methods are often too blunt to address adequately the complex and nuanced questions that generally are at issue when scholars attempt to assess and compare the course of development in different circumstances. It is more common for researchers to use what might be called 'convenience' samples, and to explore those samples intensively, rather than to study large samples more superficially."[65]

Critics have also overlooked that some recent studies of LGBT parenting do rely on bigger samples[66] and do use randomly selected families.[67] In addition, there are several large and ongoing longitudinal studies being conducted that follow children from preadolescence through puberty to adulthood.[68] These studies have also found no significant differences in the children raised by lesbian and gay parents and those raised by straight parents.

Professional associations have taken note of the clear consensus among social scientists that children are not harmed by their parents' same-sex sexual orientation. For example, the American Psychological Association in 1995 issued a report, after reviewing forty-three social science studies of families headed by lesbians and gay men, which concluded that "not a single study has found children of gay and lesbian parents to be disadvantaged in any significant respect relative to children of heterosexual parents."[69] A few years later, the American Academy of Pediatrics agreed, releasing a report stating that "parents' sexual orientation is not a variable that, in itself, predicts their ability to provide a home environment that supports children's development."[70]

▲

Valerie and Shawn Damron were married in 1991 and had two daughters. The couple lived in Minot, North Dakota, where Valerie was a special education teacher and Shawn a noncommissioned officer with the U.S. Air Force stationed in Minot's sprawling air base. In 1999, Shawn became friends with Ann Elliott, a member of his unit. Shawn introduced Ann to his wife and the two women became fast friends. They also eventually became lovers.

In late 2001, Valerie and Shawn divorced and the couple agreed that Valerie would have physical custody of their two daughters, one aged eight and the other two. Several months later, Valerie and Ann exchanged rings and made a lifetime commitment to each other. They also bought a three-bedroom house together and moved in with the two girls.

As time went on, Shawn became increasingly agitated by the fact that his daughters were living with his former wife's lesbian partner. Knowing that Ann's lesbianism placed her at risk of being dismissed from the air force, Shawn began telling some of his work colleagues that Ann was a lesbian and that she and his former wife were lovers. During the summer that followed the divorce, the air force launched an investigation of Ann's private life. A few weeks later, Ann identified herself as a lesbian to her commanders, leading to her eventual discharge from the military.

Shawn then went to court and filed a custody modification petition, the principal basis for which was that his ex-wife was living openly as a lesbian and that his two daughters resided in the house she shared with her lesbian partner. Valerie opposed the petition, arguing that it would not be in the children's best interests to be removed from their "current happy, loving, family environment."[71]

The case was assigned to district court judge Gary Hilum, who scheduled a hearing in late 2002. At that hearing, the oldest daughter's teacher testified that the girl was excelling in school and that she got along well with her mother and with Ann. The school's principal, who was also Valerie's work supervisor, testified that Valerie was a wonderful teacher and mother. And Valerie's former psychologist told the court that Ann was an important source of support for Valerie, and that most of the stress in her life was caused by her difficult relationship with her former husband rather than by her sexual orientation.

When Shawn took the witness stand, he told the court that Valerie was an immoral person, that being a lesbian was wrong, and that he did not want his children to have any contact with Ann. As he explained to Judge Hilum, Valerie's relationship with Ann "sets the wrong moral character for my children."[72] But when Valerie's lawyer asked Shawn to go beyond moral condemnation and state specifically how Valerie and Ann's relationship was harming his children, he acknowledged that he did not know. In addition, while Shawn expressed a fear that his daughters would be harassed and teased due to their mother's lesbianism, he admitted that he knew of no instance in which an adult or peer had made negative comments to his daughters because of their mother's sexual orientation.

Despite the lack of evidence that the children's living arrangement was harming them in any way, the judge in early 2003 granted Shawn's petition by taking physical custody away from Valerie and granting it to him. Judge Hilum explained his reasoning as follows:

> [Valerie] is engaged in an open homosexual relationship in the home in which she resides with the children. This open homosexual relationship may endanger the children's emotional health and impair the children's emotional development. We will not know the answer to either of these questions until the children are older[,] at which time it will be too late. . . . Although there is no question that Valerie is a fit parent, because of the mores of today's society, because Valerie is engaged in a homosexual relationship in the home in which she resides with the children, and because of the lack of legal recognition of the status of a homosexual relationship, the best interests of the children would be better served by placing custody of the children with [Shawn].[73]

It is striking that the judge stripped Valerie of custody without pointing to any specific evidence that her care was harming the children. The judge also did not account for the fact that Shawn's petition was to *modify* a previous custody order and that, therefore, the law called for a presumption against a change in custody in order to promote continuity and stability in the children's lives. In fact, to the extent that Judge Hilum applied a presumption, it was a presumption of harm based exclusively on the mother's lesbian relationship. Although the judge did not explicitly so hold, he essentially ruled that a lesbian mother who shares a home with her female partner is not entitled to retain custody of her children.

▲

Judge Hilum's order stripping Valerie Damron of the physical custody of her children relied heavily on the 1981 decision by the North Dakota Supreme

Court in *Jacobson v. Jacobson*. The *Jacobson* court held that a parent's homosexuality could properly become the "overriding factor" in a custody case once a trial judge determined that both divorcing parents were "fit, willing, and able" parents.[74] In deciding that the straight father and not the lesbian mother should have custody of the children, the court noted that the relationship between the mother and her lesbian partner was not a legal one, suggesting that it might therefore be unstable.

The court's analysis was puzzling for two reasons. First, it was curious for a court to rely on the purported lack of stability of a same-sex relationship to deny custody to a lesbian mother in the context of a legal dispute arising from a *failed different-sex* relationship. Indeed, heterosexual relationships, including most obviously those that end in divorce, fail with some frequency, and yet no court would ever use that fact against a heterosexual parent who was claiming custody of her children.

Second, it was troubling for a court to rely on the law's unwillingness to recognize same-sex relationships as a reason to limit the rights of lesbian and gay parents. Same-sex couples in North Dakota at the time of *Jacobson* (like today) did not have the option of having their relationships legally recognized. That recognition ban applied to *all* same-sex couples and did not result from an individualized assessment that would support the court's suggestion that the particular same-sex relationship before it might not be sufficiently stable to promote the children's welfare.

Since there was no specific evidence of harm caused by the mother's lesbianism introduced in *Jacobson*, the trial court had ordered that custody be granted to her. The state supreme court, however, overruled the lower court, holding categorically that whenever a lesbian mother "is engaged in a homosexual relationship in the home in which she resides with the children," the interests of those children are best served by granting custody to the straight father.

▲

Whether Valerie Damron would succeed in her appeal to the North Dakota Supreme Court depended on whether the appellate court concluded that her relationship with her partner Ann, and their sharing of the home where the children lived, inflicted actual or potential harm on the children. In his brief to the state supreme court, the father's lawyer charged that "Valerie made a very selfish decision when she decided to subject her children to her open lesbian relationship. In doing so, she subjected them, if not now in the near future, to a great deal of confusion regarding sexual relationships and human sexuality."[75] Although the lawyer conceded that Valerie might not have a choice regarding her sexual orientation, "she did have a choice as to how to conduct herself in relation to her children."

In sharp contrast, Valerie's lawyer argued in his brief that the children *benefited* from having Ann in their lives. Specifically, the brief pointed to evidence introduced during the hearing before the trial judge that Ann was a good and reliable caretaker of the children, that she was committed to their welfare, and that they loved her and considered her to be part of their family.

The brief also noted that it was not surprising that the father had been unable to introduce any evidence that Valerie's sexual orientation and her relationship with Ann harmed the children, "given the nearly universal conclusions in the medical and social science literature that children who grow up with gay or lesbian parents fare as well emotionally, cognitively and socially as do children whose parents are heterosexual."[76]

The North Dakota Supreme Court eventually ruled in favor of Valerie. Although it did not refer to the studies on LGBT parenting, it did note the complete absence of any evidence in the record that Valerie's relationship with Ann was harming the children. This was crucial to the court, because it proceeded to hold "that, in the absence of evidence of actual or potential harm to the children, a parent's homosexual relationship, by itself, is not determinative of custody."[77] In overruling its 1981 decision in *Jacobson v. Jacobson*, the court explained that North Dakota law would now follow that of most jurisdictions in the country by requiring that straight parents who wanted to use the same-sex orientation and relationships of their former spouses in custody and visitation cases introduce specific evidence of harm.[78]

The North Dakota court in Valerie Damron's case recognized that the key issue is one of causation. In other words, allegations, fears, and suppositions about the consequences for children of their parents living with same-sex partners are not enough. Instead, what is required is the drawing of specific connections between the adults' same-sex relationships and actual or potential harm to the children.

After noting that there was no evidence in the record that Valerie's "homosexual household" had endangered the children's well-being or affected their emotional development, the court proceeded to overrule the lower court's judgment, returning the children to Valerie's care. Valerie's case is illustrative of how a court's correct application of the nexus test almost always allows lesbian and gay parent litigants to show that their same-sex relationships should not be a factor in the adjudication of custody and visitation issues.

For Valerie, her legal victory was extremely important because it allowed her to keep her family unit intact; she was not, in the end, forced to choose between her children and her partner. For LGBT parents across the country, her victory was important because it resulted in yet another appellate judicial opinion rejecting the idea that parents' same-sex sexual orientation and relationships were, by themselves, relevant in the adjudication of custody and visitation issues.

▲

It is important to note that despite Valerie Damron's victory before the North Dakota Supreme Court, not every lesbian mother litigating custody and visitation issues against a former husband in the last few years has succeeded in persuading courts to demand evidence of actual or potential harm to children. It is not the case that every time a lesbian (or gay male) parent loses when litigating against a former heterosexual spouse, it is because courts make improper assumptions about the impact of the parent's same-sex sexual orientation and relationships. Sometimes, of course, granting custody to a parent who happens to be heterosexual over a parent who happens to be lesbian or gay is consistent with the best interests of the children involved. To argue that every lesbian or gay parent should prevail in every (or almost every) custody or visitation case involving a former heterosexual spouse is as misguided as it is to hold that they should lose in every (or almost every) case.

But there continue to be cases in which courts are allowing a parent's sexual orientation to improperly color the assessment of what is in the children's best interests. Indeed, although the nexus test adopted by the court in Valerie's case was clearly an improvement compared to the categorical approach it replaced, its application by no means guarantees that courts will not be improperly swayed by a divorced parent's same-sex relationship. Some courts, even after ostensibly applying the nexus test, have concluded that a parent's decision to be in an open same-sex relationship, especially one that entails the sharing of a home, always harms children. Although these courts might be willing to ignore a parent's same-sex relationship when it is *hidden* from the children, they view the parent's participation in such a relationship as evidence that the parent is being indiscreet about his or her personal life, to the detriment of the children. This means that parents can be denied custody simply for living with their same-sex partners.

This type of reasoning is reflected in a 1998 ruling by the Alabama Supreme Court. After the lesbian mother in that case separated from the heterosexual father, she and her child moved in with her female partner. The father was comfortable with this arrangement so long as the two women were "discreet" by not sharing a bedroom and by telling the child and others that they were roommates rather than partners.

When the mother refused to lie to her daughter about the nature of the women's relationship and to force her partner to sleep in a different room, the father petitioned to modify custody. In upholding the taking of custody away from the mother, the Alabama Supreme Court stated that it was not doing so because of her lesbian relationship, but because she went from having "a discreet affair to . . . creat[ing] . . . an openly homosexual home environment."[79] The fact that the mother was sharing a bedroom with her partner and that she was unwilling to tell her daughter that the two women were mere roommates meant, according to the court, that "she has chosen to expose the child continuously to a lifestyle that is neither legal in this state, nor moral in the eyes of most of its citizens." As a result, the court refused to permit the lesbian mother to continue living with her child.

Another appellate court, this one from Mississippi in a 2005 ruling, upheld the taking away of a lesbian mother's physical custody of her children and the granting of it to the heterosexual father, because the mother had supposedly "exposed" the children to the sexual nature of her relationship with her lesbian partner. Yet, the "exposure" consisted of nothing more than the fact that the children knew that their mother and her partner shared a bedroom.[80]

The fact that these types of decisions continue to be issued means that some lesbian (and gay male) parents must stay in the closet if they want to have continued contact with their children after they separate from their different-sex spouses. In fact, two mothers in two different cases decided in the last decade were able to retain custody of their children only because they persuaded the courts that they were not lesbians even though they shared their respective beds with another woman.[81]

The judicial rulings that continue to improperly take sexual orientation into account in making custody and visitation decisions have also led some parents to make the excruciatingly difficult decision to terminate their committed relationships with the adults whom they love in order to retain custody of their children. This happened to a woman from Indiana by the name of Vanessa Downey. After Vanessa divorced her husband in 1996, the two entered into a settlement agreement that called for joint legal and physical custody. Several years later, Vanessa's ex-husband filed a motion asking the court to grant him sole custody because his former wife was living with another woman. In the years following her divorce, Vanessa had a three and a half year relationship with a woman. When that relationship ended, she met a new partner, with whom she had been for a year at the time her ex-husband filed his motion.

At a preliminary hearing held in 2000, the presiding judge informed both parties that he would, at the final hearing, entertain arguments on the issue of whether Vanessa should be prohibited from continuing to live with her partner. A few days later, Vanessa ended her relationship with her partner in order not to jeopardize her ability to retain custody of her children.

The trial judge eventually ordered that Vanessa not live with a same-sex domestic partner if she wanted to keep shared custody of the children. Although that order was overturned by an appellate court in 2002, Vanessa's legal victory did not take away the pain and sadness that came with having to terminate a relationship with a woman whom she loved in order not to risk losing custody of her children.[82]

The fact that some lesbian mothers are still losing custody cases simply because they are open about their sexual orientation shows the limitations of the nexus test in eradicating the effects of judicial bias in this area of the law. Such an eradication will be achievable only by adopting a rule explicitly holding that having a same-sex sexual orientation and participating in a same-sex relationship are legally *irrelevant* in the adjudication of custody disputes. This rule would make it clear to judges that they cannot take the parties' sexual orientation into account, in the same way that judges are not supposed to consider a parent's gender in deciding whether he or she is entitled to custody.

At the same time, judges applying this rule would still be free to consider whether the specific ways in which parents carry out sexually intimate relationships with other adults might negatively affect the children. But such a determination would be sexual orientation–neutral because it would require judges to treat the relationships of lesbian (and gay male) parents as they treat those of straight ones.

It has not been only lesbian mothers who have fought in the courts to maintain contact with their children following the dissolution of opposite-sex marriages. As we will see in the next chapter, many gay fathers have needed to do the same. As in parenting cases involving lesbian mothers, the crucial issue in gay father ones has been the weight that courts have given to the refusal by parents to choose between being open about their same-sex sexual orientation and maintaining their relationships with their children.

2

Fathers Come out of the Closet

Like many gay men born during the first half of the twentieth century, Bruce Voeller married a woman in the hope that his feelings of attraction for other men would go away. Bruce, who had wanted to be a scientist since he was a young boy, graduated from Reed College in Oregon in 1956 and then moved to New York to pursue a Ph.D. in biology at Rockefeller University. After marrying Kytja Voeller in 1960, the couple bought a house in northern New Jersey and started a family.

A year later, Bruce completed his studies and joined the faculty at Rockefeller as an assistant professor of biology. As the decade progressed, he became a leader in his field, publishing many scientific articles and books. He also financially supported his wife while she attended medical school, and he was a constant presence in the life of his three young children.

In addition to his passion for science, Bruce was drawn to politics. The late 1960s was a time of growing political activism by LGBT people in places like New York City, where Bruce worked. As Bruce witnessed the activism around him, he realized, as he would later put it, that he "had been living a lie" by pretending to be straight.[1]

He eventually came out of the closet and joined a group called the Gay Activists Alliance (GAA). That organization, which was founded in 1969 in the wake of the Stonewall riots, became famous for its well-organized direct actions—known as "zaps"—such as confronting homophobic politicians in public and showing up unannounced at marriage bureaus demanding licenses for same-sex couples. Although Bruce was supportive of, and sometimes participated in, the zaps, his main interest was in lobbying politicians and other individuals in power to address discrimination against gay people. For most of 1972, he headed the GAA's federal and state affairs committee. Later that year, members elected him president of the organization, a full-time position that required him to give up his academic career.

As head of the GAA, Bruce repeatedly clashed with its more radical members, who grew suspicious of his efforts to seek allies from within the political establishment. In October 1973, Bruce resigned as president of the group and immediately started working on forming a new organization, eventually named the National Gay Task Force (NGTF), which had national ambitions and whose primary goal was to persuade straight Americans that gay people were not that different from them. In its early years, with Bruce serving as its executive director, the NGTF worked to have the American Psychiatric Association remove homosexuality from its list of mental disorders; led a national advertising campaign to protest the stereotypical portrayal of gay people on television; and coordinated the introduction of the first congressional bill aimed at prohibiting employment discrimination based on sexual orientation.

One of the ramifications of Bruce's coming out of the closet was that he and his wife Kytja decided to separate in 1971. Bruce moved out of their New Jersey home and into a Manhattan apartment. The couple filed for a divorce a few months later, and the court issued a temporary order granting Kytja custody of the three children and Bruce the right to visit with them every other weekend and during some holidays.

Kytja was troubled by Bruce becoming, seemingly overnight, a prominent gay rights activist. It seemed that Bruce was now spending almost all of his time in the company of other gay people. Indeed, when the children visited him in Manhattan, they sometimes met Bruce's gay friends in the movement. On a few occasions, Bruce took the children to the Firehouse, an old Victorian building in lower Manhattan that served as the GAA's headquarters. Kytja grew convinced that Bruce's openness about his sexual orientation and his association with other gay people were harmful to the children.

By the time the divorce decree became final in early 1973, the former spouses found themselves at loggerheads over how and when Bruce should exercise his visitation rights. Unable to resolve their differences, Kytja filed a motion with the New Jersey superior court asking that Bruce be denied the opportunity to have overnight visits with the children. The motion also requested that the children not be "exposed" to any activities or publicity concerning the gay rights movement.

▲

While most of the legal cases involving lesbian mothers from the 1970s were about custody, almost all the early gay father cases were about visitation rights. It was then still relatively unusual for fathers to be awarded custody following a divorce. Fathers who sought custody were confronted with the perception among most judges that a mother's care and nurture was more important to a child's well-being than that of a father. This perception was most clearly reflected in the "tender years doctrine," under which many courts presumed that young children of divorced parents would be better off cared for by their mothers.

If it was difficult for fathers in general to be awarded custody of their children, it was practically impossible for openly gay fathers. Since custody was not a realistic outcome for most divorcing gay fathers, they had to settle for the opportunity to try to visit with their children as frequently as possible.

Although there was then (as there is now) a presumption that noncustodial parents were entitled to visitation, it was also understood that that right was not absolute. If visitation with a parent might be physically or emotionally harmful to the child, a court could prohibit it altogether. As a result, there was no guarantee that a judge would recognize the visitation rights of a gay father who was in an ongoing relationship with another man and who wanted to be open with his children about his sexual orientation.

In addition, courts had the authority (as they do now) to impose restrictions on visitation rights in order to advance what they believed to be the children's best interests. This meant that trial judges exercised a great deal of discretion in making visitation rulings and were able, explicitly or implicitly, to take into account the sexual orientation of gay fathers in determining how and when the visitations should take place.

The possibility that a court might deny or significantly restrict visitations with their children was a deeply disconcerting prospect for most gay dads. For noncustodial parents, who are by definition no longer part of their children's principal household, visitation provides the only opportunity to continue to maintain a viable and nurturing relationship with their children. And for gay dads in particular, a prohibition or restriction on visitations sent a message to their children that there was something dangerous (at worse) or troubling (at best) about their fathers' sexual orientation.

▲

For Bruce Voeller, the decision to fight his former wife's efforts to restrict his visitation rights was an easy one. Bruce was deeply committed to his children. Although he had worked hard in pursuing a successful academic career, he had also made sure to leave enough time to spend with them. And as a gay rights activist, Bruce was acutely aware of the legal and political implications of the courts' use of sexual orientation to restrict parental rights. Indeed, for Bruce, such restrictions were one of many ways in which society discriminated against gay people. As a result, he was unwilling to sit idly by as his former wife tried to use his sexual orientation, and his gay rights activism, to limit his ability to see his children.

Bruce shared these legal difficulties with Marilyn Haft, who at the time was heading the ACLU's Sexual Privacy Project. Haft was looking for gay rights cases to litigate, and Kytja Voeller's effort to restrict Bruce's visitation rights was a good one for the civil liberties group to take on because it might set a precedent that would help other lesbian and gay parents.

Since the visitation issue was going to be litigated in New Jersey, Haft suggested that they seek the help of a Newark lawyer by the name of Seymour Wishman. Although Wishman had been out of law school for only seven years, he had already built a reputation as an exceedingly able trial attorney who supported progressive causes. Wishman, however, was primarily a criminal defense lawyer and he had a particular dislike for divorce and family law disputes. He also knew little about gay issues and had never worked on gay rights matters before. As a result, his initial inclination when Haft first phoned him was to turn down the case.

But it so happened that between that phone call and the time that he met with Bruce and Haft several weeks later, Wishman learned that a trial judge in northern New Jersey had allowed a divorcing gay father to visit with his children for only four hours a month, and then only if a court-approved third party was present. Hearing about the other case made Wishman realize that Bruce's case was not an isolated one. In addition, when Wishman met with Bruce for the first time, he was quickly taken by his charismatic personality and his passionate explanation of why his former wife's effort to try to limit his opportunities to visit with his children was wrong and unjust. All of this led Wishman to agree to take on the case pro bono.

The visitation trial was held in late 1973 before superior court judge Benedict Lucchi, a forty-nine-year-old jurist who had been appointed to the bench only two years before. The proceeding was the first of its kind anywhere in the country—never before had a trial been held in which the main issue was the impact of a father's homosexuality on his children. The trial lasted for six days, and witnesses included Bruce, Kytja, and three character witnesses who testified on Bruce's behalf. One of those witnesses was Harold Brown, a former high official in New York City Mayor John Lindsay's administration who had recently told the *New York Times* that he himself was gay.[2]

The trial also included the testimony of three doctors. Bruce and his lawyers called two of these experts. One of them was Dr. John Money, a psychologist at Johns Hopkins University who was a pioneer in the fields of sexual and gender identities. In 1969, he coedited a book called *Transsexualism and Sex Reassignment*, which was highly influential in the medical community's eventual acceptance of surgery as a treatment for individuals who experience a disconnect between their biological sex and their gender identity.[3] Another expert witness who testified on Bruce's behalf was Dr. Richard Green, a psychiatrist and colleague of Money's at Johns Hopkins. Not only was Green the other coeditor of the transsexualism book, he was the founding editor of the journal *Archives of Sexual Behavior* and the founding president of the International Academy of Sex Research. Green was also a strong proponent within the American Psychiatric Association of declassifying homosexuality as a mental illness, which the organization agreed to do in 1973, shortly after the Voeller child visitation trial ended. A few years later, Green conducted some of the earliest research on LGBT parents and their children.[4]

Both Money and Green testified that a parent's sexual orientation was irrelevant to the question of whether he could be a good parent to his children. The two doctors also opined that Bruce had a close and healthy relationship with his children and that his living as an openly gay man, and his activism on behalf of gay rights causes, was not harming them.

Presenting a different view was Richard Gardner, a psychiatrist called to testify by Kytja Voeller's attorney. Gardner had become nationally known a few years earlier when, in response to the growing rates of divorce, he wrote a book advising children on how to cope with their parents' separation.[5] (A decade after the Voeller trial, Gardner once again received national attention when he coined the term "Parental Alienation Syndrome" to claim, controversially, that children of divorce who accused a parent [usually the father] of sexual abuse were often lying and that they were encouraged to do so by the other parent [usually the mother]. His proposed treatment for this supposed condition was to take custody away from the latter and give it to the former.)[6]

While on the stand at the Voeller visitation trial, Gardner acknowledged that Bruce had done a good job as a father and that the children were healthy and well-adjusted. He therefore recommended that Bruce be permitted to visit with his three children. He also opined, however, that Bruce's insistence on being open about his sexual orientation with his children, when coupled with his highly visible work as a gay rights activist, was detrimental to the children's well-being. Gardner was also troubled by the fact that, when visiting with their father, the children spent time with his "homosexual lover" and with other friends and acquaintances who were gay. Gardner warned that "the total environment to which the father exposed the children could impede healthy sexual development in the future," and that "the father's milieu could engender homosexual fantasies causing confusion and anxiety which would in turn affect the children's sexual development." Even more ominously, Gardner told the court that "it is possible that these children upon reaching puberty would be subject to either overt or covert homosexual seduction which would detrimentally influence their development."[7]

Wishman and Haft argued in their legal papers filed with Judge Lucchi that their client had a constitutional right to visitation with his children, a right that should not be limited because he was gay. When Judge Lucchi issued his opinion in the summer of 1974, he agreed with Bruce's lawyers on that point. The fact that a father is gay, the judge held, is by itself an insufficient reason to deny or restrict his visitation rights, given that the relationship between parents and their children is subject to constitutional protection. No court had ever before recognized the constitutional rights of gay fathers; on that point, Bruce and his lawyers gained an important victory.

But Judge Lucchi proceeded to distinguish the issue of whether the visitation rights of gay parents could be denied or restricted solely on the basis of their sexual orientation from the issue of whether, as he put it, "exposure to a specific homosexual parent may have a detrimental effect on a child."[8] On this second question, the judge held that the court had the authority to impose restrictions on Bruce's visitation with the children if his ex-wife was correct that his "involvement with and dedication to furthering homosexuality has created an environment exposure to which in anything more than a minimal amount would be harmful to the children."

Lucchi concluded that the children were being harmed by Bruce's life as an openly gay man and by his work as a gay rights activist. The judge noted that Bruce's salary as executive director of the NGTF was considerably lower than it had been as a biology professor, suggesting that his family was suffering economically from his gay rights activism. In addition, Lucchi pointed out that Bruce had had several lovers since separating from his wife, that he was currently living "with a male lover in a building occupied almost entirely by homosexuals," and that "a business undertaking in which he is currently involved is owned primarily by homosexuals."

The judge was also troubled by the fact that Bruce had taken his children to gay rights marches and rallies, as well as to the Firehouse, the GAA headquarters. In addition, he concluded that drawings made by the children, some of which had figures holding signs that stated "Gay Is Proud" and "We Want Equal Rights!!," were the result of Bruce's "prodding and indoctrination."

Bruce's lawyers had argued before Judge Lucchi that drug addicts and those convicted of serious crimes did not lose their rights to visit with their children unless there was specific evidence that they would physically harm the children. Gay fathers, the lawyers insisted, should be treated no differently. Judge Lucchi responded in his opinion that when "a bank robber is allowed full visitation rights," it is done with the expectation that the parent not expose "the child to any aspects of this most unacceptable line of endeavor." He concluded that "a homosexual who openly advocates violations of the New Jersey statutes forbidding sodomy . . . may also be restricted."

In the end, Judge Lucchi granted the mother's request that Bruce's visitation rights be significantly restricted. Bruce was permitted to see his children for a few hours every other Sunday and on Christmas, Easter, and Thanksgiving. He was also allowed to spend three weeks with his children in the summer as long as the visitation did not take place in his home. In addition, the judge ordered that, during the periods of visitation, Bruce "(1) not cohabit or sleep with any individual other than a lawful spouse, (2) not take the children or allow them to be taken to 'The Firehouse,' (3) not involve the children in any homosexual related activities or publicity; and (4) not be in the presence of his lover." Although Bruce and his lawyers appealed the judge's ruling, an appellate court two years later summarily affirmed the trial court's visitation restrictions in a one-page opinion.[9]

As in the lesbian mother cases profiled in the previous chapter, the issue in Bruce's case boiled down to whether he could be a good parent to his children while at the same time living openly as a gay man. Like the lesbian mothers, Bruce found himself needing to prove to the court that his homosexuality did not affect his ability to be a good father to his children. Ultimately, Bruce lost his case because the court assumed, without pointing to any specific evidence based on the children's conduct or happiness, that his openness about his sexual orientation was harmful to them.

One of the interesting questions arising from Bruce's case is the extent to which the outcome would have been different had he not been so actively involved in the gay rights movement. Although it appears that Bruce's gay activism was an important reason for his legal defeat, there were several other courts, in the years that followed, which similarly restricted the ability of non-activist gay fathers to visit with their children. Indeed, what seems to have mattered most to early courts in restricting the visitation rights of gay fathers was not the extent of their political activism, but was instead the degree to which they were open about their sexual orientation. As the following case from Missouri shows, simply living as an openly gay man, which could entail such seemingly innocuous activities as spending time with gay friends and attending a gay church, was often deemed by judges to constitute a sufficient ground on which to limit a gay father's ability to see his children.

▲

In 1968, a year before the Stonewall riots, a former Pentecostal minister who had been defrocked by his church because of his homosexuality founded a Christian church in Los Angeles with the objective of offering religious services to the LGBT community. The minister, Troy Perry, called his new church the Metropolitan Community Church (MCC). At the time, almost all religious denominations held a negative view of homosexuality and of gay people. The MCC offered sexual minorities a rare opportunity to worship God as part of a tolerant and welcoming religious community. Soon, new MCC congregations started springing up throughout the country and, eventually, throughout the world. Today, the church has more than forty thousand members in almost three hundred congregations in over twenty countries.

One of the MCC congregations that came together in the 1970s was in Kansas City, Missouri. For Daniel Pearson, a gay man living outside Kansas City who had divorced his wife of almost a decade in 1978, the ability to attend services at the local MCC was of great comfort because it allowed him to reconcile his sexual orientation with his Christianity. On a few occasions, he took his ten-year-old son Henry—with whom he visited on some weekends—to his place of worship.

When Jane Pearson learned that her former husband was attending services at the MCC, she prohibited him from taking their son to "that type of church."[10] At the time, she knew little about the MCC other than the fact that most attendees were gay. But for Jane, who did not want her son around gay people, that was enough. She therefore told her former husband that if he took Henry to his church again, she would not allow him to visit with their son.

This was not the first time that Jane had threatened to deny Daniel access to Henry. When the couple, two years earlier, divorced following Daniel's coming out as a gay man, Jane had demanded not only custody of Henry, but also that her ex-husband refrain from keeping the boy overnight during visitations. Jane had made it clear to Daniel that if he did not agree to her terms, she would not allow him to see his son. Fearing that his former wife would carry out her threat, Daniel agreed that the overnight visitation prohibition be included in the divorce settlement agreement.

That agreement stated that Daniel was to have the right of "reasonable visitation" with his son, but it did not specify when or how frequently the visitations should take place. After Jane's latest threat, this one regarding Daniel's attending his church with Henry, the father hired a lawyer and brought an action against his ex-wife in Missouri circuit court. Daniel asked the court to lift the overnight visitation restriction included in the original divorce agreement and to set a specific visitation schedule that would guarantee him the ability to see Henry for several hours every week.

For her part, Jane filed legal papers opposing the removal of the overnight visitation restriction. She also requested that three additional limitations be placed on her ex-husband's ability to visit with their son: (1) that no other gay people be present during visitations; (2) that Daniel not be allowed to take Henry to the MCC; and (3) that he also not take the boy to "gay activist social gatherings."[11]

At the hearing held to sort all this out, Buford Farrington, Jane's lawyer, contended that Daniel was improperly exposing his son to homosexuality. His evidence in support of this predictable allegation included the fact that Daniel had introduced his son to some of the approximately dozen men with whom he had had sexual relations in the two and a half years between the divorce and the hearing. In addition, Farrington pointed out that MCC attendees regularly greeted one another during the services with an embrace or a kiss instead of the more traditional shaking of hands. He also complained that the church "promotes a homosexual lifestyle by recognizing the commitment persons of the same sex might have for each other, which it calls 'a holy union.'"[12]

Other evidence of alleged "improper exposure" of the father's homosexuality included the fact that when Daniel, the previous year, had taken his son on a vacation trip to Houston, the two were shown around town by a gay friend of Daniel's. On another occasion, the father took his son to a birthday party at which five or six other gay men were present. Finally, Farrington made much of the fact that Daniel's roommate was gay, even though the two men were not sexual partners and each had his own bedroom. (During her testimony, Jane claimed that the mere fact that the roommate was gay—she had never met him and knew nothing about him other than his sexual orientation—was enough to justify her objection to her son staying with his father in his apartment overnight.)

While cross-examining Daniel, Farrington asked him whether he wanted his son to grow up gay. It is common for lawyers of straight parents in custody and visitation hearings to ask this question of lesbian and gay parents because it puts them in a no-win position. If the parents respond "no," they seem to be admitting that there is something wrong with being gay. And if they answer "yes," they can be accused of trying to pressure their child to be gay.

At first, Daniel answered that whether Henry grew up to be gay was not a decision for his father to make. But when Farrington pressed him to answer the question of whether he thought his son being gay would be "desirable," Daniel answered "yes." Later in his testimony he clarified that he did not care whether Henry turned out to be gay, that he could not do anything about his son's sexual orientation anyway, and that his focus was on the boy's well-being.

David Greis, Daniel's lawyer, pointed out during his closing argument to circuit court judge Fernando Gaitan that despite his opponent's best efforts, no evidence was introduced that his client had exposed his son to sexual matters or to a sexualized environment. Greis also emphasized that Daniel never took his son to meetings of gay organizations or to gay bars. In addition, no one ever tried to sexually molest the child and the boy never saw anyone having sex. Surely, Greis argued, the mere fact that the father attended a gay church, had a gay roommate, allowed a gay friend to show them around Houston, and once took his son to a party where other gay people were present was not enough to justify the draconian restrictions on visitation demanded by the mother.

Judge Gaitan, however, disagreed. The judge—who would later be appointed to the federal bench by President George H. W. Bush—concluded that Daniel thought it was in his son's best interests to be exposed to a "homosexual living environment." Gaitan also found that Daniel cared more about his sexual orientation than about its effect on the child. And, finally, Gaitan stated that the father's "behavior pattern" during visitation was "seductive in nature" and that it showed a purpose to encourage his son to become gay.[13] All of this led the judge to prohibit Daniel from having overnight visitations with his son, and to bar him from taking the boy to religious services at the MCC and to any "gay activist social gathering."

On appeal, Greis wrote an impassioned eighty-eight-page brief in which he made two basic points: First, that there was absolutely no evidence in the record to support the judge's factual findings regarding his client's alleged improper exposure of homosexuality to his child. Although it was true that Daniel on a few occasions introduced his son to other gay men whom he knew—including some who attended his church and others who were present at a birthday party—that by no means could be considered "seductive" activity. Greis's brief explained that "only if one assumes that the mere presence of gays is conducive to becoming gay (as if sexual orientation were a contagious disease) can these entirely normal father-son activities be twisted into something ugly."[14]

Second, Greis argued that the restrictions imposed by Judge Gaitan violated his client's rights to due process, equal protection, and religious freedom. In doing so, Greis explained that Gaitan had imposed limitations without any evidence of actual or potential harm to the child; that he imposed the restrictions based on Daniel's status as a gay man rather than on any particular conduct; that the term "gay activist social gatherings" was vague and might be interpreted as covering any event where there might be more than two gay people present; and that the ban on visits to the MCC with the child limited Daniel's ability to worship as he saw fit.

The Missouri Court of Appeals rejected all of Greis's arguments. It reasoned that there was more than sufficient evidence for the trial judge to have concluded that Daniel was potentially harming his son by living with another "avowed homosexual" and by openly associating with other gay men. The court then detailed just how disturbed it was by Daniel's conduct as an openly gay man who did not seem troubled by his sexual orientation:

> The whole tenor of the father's appeal and his conduct in the trial and appellate stages demonstrate that he is oriented towards the "cause" of homosexuality. Whatever the father's rights may be—an issue which this court does not address—concerning his own choice of "lifestyle," those rights do not extend to activities designed to induce in a child similar behavior. . . . It is not as the father insists a question of the court's involvement in the morality of such behavior, it is [instead] the court's concern for potential harm to the child which requires consideration of such conduct by a court charged with determining the best interests of the child.[15]

In upholding the restrictions imposed by Judge Gaitan on Daniel's ability to visit with his son, the appellate court cited several cases from across the country—including Bruce Voeller's New Jersey case—in which courts placed restrictions on the ability of lesbian and gay parents to visit with their children. The court finished its opinion with a warning to Daniel: if he persisted "in his vehement espousal to the child of the 'desirability' of his chosen lifestyle," he would face even greater restrictions on his visitation rights in the future. Although Daniel did not go back before the Missouri courts, those courts during the 1980s consistently ruled against lesbian and gay parents seeking to retain contact with their children following the dissolution of a heterosexual marriage.[16]

Daniel's case illustrates how for many early courts, the mere fact that a father was living openly as a gay person was enough to support a finding that his sexual orientation was harming his child. It was not necessary, in other words, for a gay father to be, like Bruce Voeller, a committed gay activist. The simple fact that a gay father was open about his sexual orientation and that he associated with other gay people was for many courts enough to place restrictions on his ability to see his children.

David Greis had argued in his appellate brief that the trial judge had treated his client's gay sexual orientation as a contagious disease that placed his son at risk of being "infected." Greis submitted the brief in the summer of 1982, before most people realized that there was an actual infectious disease being transmitted sexually (among other ways) throughout the country. Even though that disease would strike many different kinds of individuals, it quickly became thought of, in a society that was already deeply suspicious of gay men and their sexuality, as a "gay disease." Indeed, in the early days of the epidemic, scientists and public health officials called it Gay-Related Immune Deficiency (or GRID). As it happens, it was activists like Bruce Voeller who in the mid-1980s insisted that the disease be renamed Acquired Immune Deficiency Syndrome (or AIDS) to reflect the reality that the risk of acquiring HIV was by no means limited to gay people. It did not take long, however, for the specter of AIDS to make it into child visitation lawsuits involving gay men.

▲

Charles Conkel's story is similar to those of Bruce Voeller and Daniel Pearson. After a marriage that lasted almost ten years, in which he fathered two sons, Charles came to terms with his attraction toward other men and divorced his wife Kim in 1981. The separation agreement granted Kim custody of the children and Charles was awarded reasonable visitation. Eventually there were disagreements between the parents over how Charles was exercising his visitation rights (and over issues of child support), leading the couple to return to court in 1985. In his legal papers, Charles alleged that his wife was regularly denying him the opportunity to visit with his children.

The parties stipulated that Charles was a bisexual who was living in a two-bedroom apartment with a male friend and that, even though each man had his own room, they sometimes had sex with each other. The stipulation also stated that no sexual acts had taken place in front of the children and that no one had made any sexual advances on them.[17] After a hearing, an Ohio trial judge allowed Charles to see his sons several days a month, including overnight visitations on Friday nights, but ordered that none of the visits take place "in the presence of any male person."[18]

This restriction was broader than the ones upheld in Bruce Voeller's and Daniel Pearson's cases because it prohibited *any* man—regardless of sexual orientation—from being present during the visitations. Although Charles was not pleased with the restriction, he was willing to live with it. In contrast, Kim appealed the judge's ruling, insisting that her former husband should not be permitted to have overnight visitations with the children.

Like Voeller's and Pearson's former wives, Kim Conkel was troubled that her former husband was living with a gay man. Such a living arrangement, her lawyer explained in a brief to the Ohio Court of Appeals, "may trigger homosexual tendencies" in the young children. In addition, the brief made clear that the mother was "petrified that her children may contract AIDS."[19]

There was no evidence in the record that Charles Conkel was HIV positive. But for the mother, the fact that Charles was a bisexual man was enough to raise concerns about HIV transmission because, as her appellate brief put it, "if the children must have overnight visitation then they will be using common glasses, eating utensils and towels." The brief noted that HIV-positive children were being barred from schools across the country and that dentists were wearing gloves and masks while treating patients. Since others were taking precautionary measures, then she, too, was "entitled to the same safeguards" to protect her children from HIV.

In 1986 alone, there were several reported instances of restrictions imposed on fathers because of their HIV status. In Puerto Rico, a judge ordered an HIV-positive man not to kiss his children. A New Jersey court allowed an HIV-positive father to visit with his children but only under supervision. In Chicago, a court ordered that a gay man be tested for the virus before it would consider granting him visitation.[20] And most disturbingly of all, an Indiana trial judge ruled that a father who was HIV positive could never visit with his child again.[21]

Bruce Voeller and Daniel Pearson had the benefit of receiving highly competent legal representation as they battled their former wives in court over their right to visit with their children. The same cannot be said for Charles Conkel. The appellate brief filed by his attorney was only four pages long and did not cite a single case. And to make things worse, the brief promoted rather than undermined stereotypes on parenting and sexual orientation by claiming that if the Conkel children turned out to be gay, it would not be because of anything that the father had done, but instead would be because the mother was a "domineering female."[22]

As Bruce Voeller's and Daniel Pearson's cases showed, good legal advocacy did not guarantee gay fathers victories in court. But the opposite was also sometimes true. Even though Charles's lawyer undermined his client's case by suggesting that parents' traits determine their children's sexual orientation, the appellate court provided Charles with a resounding victory when it rejected the mother's effort to prohibit him from having overnight visitation with his children. On the issue of AIDS, the court noted that there was no evidence that Charles was HIV positive and that, in any event, medical experts had by then concluded that the virus was not transmitted through casual household contact.

The court also rejected the mother's argument that having more extensive visitation with the father meant that the children would likely suffer from what her brief described (quoting a 1981 opinion from the North Dakota Supreme Court) as "the slings and arrows of a disapproving society."[23] From the earliest custody and visitation disputes between gay and straight parents, lawyers for the latter frequently argued that the children needed to be protected from the social stigma that accompanies homosexuality. The North Dakota court had accepted that argument in granting custody to a straight father rather than to a lesbian mother who was living with her female partner. Although the court recognized that the children would have to cope with the disapproval of their mother's sexual orientation regardless of which parent had custody, it nonetheless reasoned "that requiring the children to live, day-to-day, in the same residence with the mother and the lover means that the children will have to confront the problem to a significantly greater degree than they would if living with their father."

The Ohio appellate court in Charles Conkel's case, however, ruled that it could not "take into consideration the unpopularity of homosexuals in society when its duty is to facilitate and guard a fundamental parent-child relationship."[24] In fact, the court analogized between the stigma faced by the children of a gay parent to that faced by the children of a divorced parent who later married someone of a different race. In that context, the U.S. Supreme Court had recently held that it was impermissible for courts to take into account racial prejudice in determining the extent of parental rights.[25] That same type of reasoning, the Ohio court explained, applied in the case of a bisexual father like Charles Conkel who wanted to have overnight visitation with his children over the objection of his former wife.

In the end, the court rejected Kim Conkel's request that it adopt a rule that a father's open bisexuality, by itself, justified the imposition of limitations on his visitation rights and that, as a result, no direct evidence of harm had to be introduced. In the strongest language of any appellate judicial decision up until then in a case involving a gay or bisexual father, the court made clear that the nexus test should be applied in these types of cases: "Before depriving the sexually active parent of his crucial and fundamental right of contact with his child, a court must find that the parent's conduct is having, or is probably having, a harmful effect on the child. In this case there is no evidence of any harmful effect."

The ruling in Charles Conkel's lawsuit was important not only because it clearly held that the nexus test was the correct legal standard to apply in these cases, but also because it blunted the precedential value of *Roberts v. Roberts*, a case decided two years earlier by a court from another Ohio appellate district. In *Roberts*, the court ruled that a gay father could visit with his children only on the condition that he agree not to reveal to them his sexual orientation. The court also ordered that the visitation take place either in the presence of the mother "or under other sufficiently controlled circumstances."[26] Interestingly, the trial court in *Roberts* had already held that visitations could not take place in the presence of any unrelated male person. But this was not enough for the appellate court. As it explained, "the state has a substantial interest in viewing homosexuality as errant sexual behavior which threatens the social fabric, and in endeavoring to protect minors from being influenced by those who advocate homosexual lifestyles."

The *Conkel* court clearly took a different approach in assessing a father's sexual orientation in a child visitation case. Rather than presuming the existence of harm and the need to protect children from their gay or bisexual parents, the *Conkel* court demanded that a straight parent who wanted to impose visitation limitations on an ex-spouse because of his or her sexual orientation and conduct introduce particularized evidence of harm. Resorting to vague arguments based on the dangers of homosexuality, the spread of HIV, and the social stigma faced by LGBT people was not enough to justify restricting the opportunities of parents and children to visit with one another.

The *Conkel* court's approach was the correct one because, in determining whether a father is a good parent to his children, the court rejected claims grounded in generalizations and assumptions based on sexual orientation. Instead, the court focused on the particular father before it and on the particularized evidence relating to his parental attributes and capabilities. Finding no evidence that the children were being harmed by Charles's parenting, the court rejected his former wife's misguided effort to limit his access to his children solely because of his bisexuality.

▲

Not all the early cases involving gay fathers were about the issue of visitation; a handful were about custody. One of those involved David Barker and his daughter Celeste. This case was unusual not only because it involved a gay dad fighting for custody of his daughter, but also because the trial judge hearing the dispute, unlike the trial judges who heard the cases of Bruce Voeller, Daniel Pearson, and Charles Conkel, ruled in favor of the gay father. As we will see, however, the Virginia Supreme Court later stepped in and held that David Barker could not keep custody of his daughter.

David and Catherine Barker were married in 1971. Their only child, Celeste, was born in 1974. The couple separated in 1975 and entered into an agreement that granted legal and physical custody to Catherine. That agreement was then incorporated into a final divorce decree issued by a Virginia trial court in 1976.

Two years later, Catherine was diagnosed with cancer, requiring surgery and extensive medical treatment. After the diagnosis, David took over caring for Celeste and in 1979 petitioned the court to grant him custody. At first, Catherine opposed the custody modification but later changed her mind, acknowledging that her illness prevented her from resuming full-time care of Celeste. The parents then entered into a new consent decree that awarded custody to David and reasonable visitation rights to Catherine.

The situation remained unchanged until the summer of 1983 when Catherine, shortly after learning that David was living with his gay partner, returned to court seeking a modification of the custody agreement. The principal bases for this request were that Celeste was living with her father and his gay partner, that the two men shared a bedroom, that the child had seen the two men "hugging and kissing and sleeping in bed together," and that David's gay friends visited the home and engaged in "similar behavior."[27]

During a one-day hearing held in August 1983 to consider Catherine's petition, Virginia circuit court judge Richard Jamborski heard testimony from several different witnesses, including Catherine, David, and David's partner. The judge also interviewed the nine-year-old girl. After the completion of the testimony, Judge Jamborski granted the parents joint custody. The order provided that Celeste was to live with her father during the school year and with her mother during summer vacations. Each parent was also awarded liberal visitation rights while the child resided with the other.

In refusing to strip David of custody of his child as Catherine demanded, Judge Jamborski noted that the father had done a wonderful job rearing his daughter "to the point that she is a lovely, outgoing, bright, and intelligent child."[28] In the five years in which Celeste had lived with her father, he was "always there like a rock" and had been "the one who . . . provided the love and nurturing of this child."

Judge Jamborski added that, except for the mother's concern over her ex-husband's homosexuality, "there would be no reason for all of a sudden taking the child from the parent who had met [her] physical, emotional, and financial . . . needs." Jamborski concluded that the father's homosexuality and his relationship with his partner had not had an adverse impact on Celeste and that, as a result, they constituted insufficient reasons to change the child's relationship with her father, especially since he had taken care of her for more than half of her life.

The only concession that the judge made to the mother's concern about her ex-husband's homosexuality was that he conditioned David's custody on his not sharing a bedroom with his partner while Celeste was in their home. This was not enough to satisfy Catherine. Since her objective was to deny her ex-husband custody altogether, she immediately appealed and was pleased when the Virginia Supreme Court agreed to hear the case.

The lawyers involved in the litigation knew that the court's ruling would depend on how it interpreted two of its previous decisions. One of those rulings was *Doe v. Doe*, the 1981 case discussed in the previous chapter in which the court had refused to terminate Marianne MacQueen's parental rights because she was a lesbian.[29] In Catherine's appeal of Judge Jamborski's ruling, her lawyer sought to distinguish *Doe* on the ground that it involved the question of whether a lesbian mother's parental rights should be terminated rather than that of whether a gay or lesbian parent should retain custody of a child. In contrast, David's lawyer argued that *Doe* was highly relevant because the court in that case had refused to engage in generalizations about the fitness of gay parents and instead had looked for evidence (and found none) that the mother's sexual orientation and same-sex relationship were harming her child.

The second crucial precedent was a 1977 case called *Brown v. Brown*.[30] In that case, the Virginia Supreme Court affirmed a lower court's order granting permanent custody to the father because the mother, who had temporary custody of the children, had lived with another man during the pendency of the divorce. In appealing Judge Jamborski's ruling, Catherine's lawyer analogized between the mother's adultery in *Brown* and David's homosexuality. Both adultery and sodomy, the lawyer noted, were prohibited by Virginia's criminal laws. (The lawyer added that sodomy was worse than adultery because the former was a felony offense while the latter only a misdemeanor.) In addition to being subject to criminal prohibitions, both types of conduct, the lawyer argued, raised questions about the moral climates of the homes where the children were being raised.

For his part, David's lawyer reminded the court that *Brown* had held that a trial court had the *discretion* of awarding custody based on a parent's sexual relationship with another adult. This did not mean, however, that a court was *required* to do so. The key issue was whether the sexual relationship at issue had a negative impact on the child's well-being. Judge Jamborski, after hearing testimony introduced by both sides, had concluded that there was no such impact. David's lawyer argued that the appellate court should respect that factual determination because it was not clearly erroneous.

In the end, the Virginia Supreme Court ruled on Catherine's behalf, concluding that the case was controlled by *Brown* and was distinguishable from *Doe*. Like in the adultery case, the court reasoned, David's "continuous exposure of the child to his immoral and illicit relationship renders him an unfit and improper custodian as a matter of law."[31] The court added that "the conditions under which this child must live daily are not only unlawful but also impose an intolerable burden upon her by reason of the social condemnation attached to them, which will inevitably afflict her relationships with her peers and with the community at large."

It bears emphasizing that the Virginia high court stripped a father of custody based solely on the fact that he shared a bedroom with his partner and that the two sometimes kissed and hugged in front of the child. There was never any allegation that the father, or anyone else for that matter, engaged in sexual conduct in front of the child. But for the court, the simple fact that David and his partner were in an open and affectionate relationship was enough to deny him continued custody of his daughter. As the court saw it, David was burdening Celeste "in exchange for his own gratification" by living with his partner. (The court would reach the same conclusion ten years later in the Sharon Bottoms case, involving a lesbian mother, profiled in the introduction.)

In addition, the court concluded that its ruling in Marianne MacQueen's case did not prevent it from stripping David of custody of his daughter. The court explained that although the child in the earlier case had sometimes visited with his lesbian mother and her partner in Ohio, that litigation had not dealt with "the question of the impact of a homosexual relationship upon a child in the context of day-to-day custody."

Even though the court seemed to believe that it was focusing on the *impact* of the father's gay relationship on the child, there was no individualized determination that the relationship actually had a deleterious effect on Celeste. Indeed, the trial court had concluded that the young girl was happy, outgoing, bright, and generally thriving in her father's home. Furthermore, there was no finding that the child had any discipline or emotional problems, or difficulties at school or with friends. The "harm" found by the appellate court, therefore, was abstract and generalized, and it would have applied to *any* child living with her openly gay father and his partner. The fact that David had taken care of the child when the mother had been unable to because of illness and that he had been her primary caretaker for years was, in the end, immaterial to the court because it cared only about the fact that he was living with his same-sex partner.

Despite the court's protestations to the contrary, it did in David Barker's case precisely what it had refused to do only a few years earlier in Marianne MacQueen's case—that is, it *assumed* that all children who observed their parents in same-sex relationships were harmed as a result. It was this thin reed that the court relied on not only to order that Celeste be removed from her father's home—where she had lived for the previous five years—but also to prohibit him from visiting with her child in his home as long as he continued to share it with his partner.

At the time the Virginia Supreme Court decided David Barker's case in 1985, the courts were about equally divided on whether being in an open same-sex relationship was enough to categorically deny custody to or restrict visitation by lesbian and gay parents. As we explored in the previous chapter, a growing number of courts around that time began rejecting the per se rule and embracing the nexus test. When properly applied, as we saw in the context of lesbian mothers, the test places the burden on parents who contend that their former spouses' same-sex sexual orientation and relationships are relevant in custody and visitation proceedings to prove that those factors have negatively affected the children in question. As the next case shows, courts have been increasingly willing to apply the nexus test not only in lesbian mother cases, but in gay father ones as well.

▲

For two years following the Georgia trial judge's ruling in his divorce case in 2007, Eric Mongerson was unable to introduce José Sanchez, the man he loved, to his children. Eric's lesbian and gay friends were also unable to attend his children's music recitals and Little League games. This was because when he divorced his wife of twenty years, the judge allowed him to visit with three of his children—a fourth child was too old to be covered by the order—once a week for four hours, on the condition that he not "expos[e] the children to his homosexual partners and friends."[32]

During those two years, Eric lived in fear that his former wife Sandy would return to court and ask that his already-limited visitation rights be further restricted. As a result, he did not bring his children to his Atlanta apartment, in order to avoid unexpected encounters with some of the other gay people who lived in the building. He also rarely socialized with his straight friends in front of his children—or asked them to babysit—because of the possibility that Sandy might accuse some of them of being lesbian or gay. As he would later tell the Associated Press, "I was always afraid of the 'What if?' I felt isolated, alone. Sandy could go get friends, have them watch the kids, but I could never because I was gay."[33]

At the same time that Eric was taking no risks that might lead his former wife to claim he was violating the court's order, he was cobbling together the more than $10,000 in legal fees required to appeal that order. He did this by regularly putting in thirteen-hour shifts at his job as a restaurant manager and by maxing out his credit cards.

In defending the trial court's order before the Georgia Supreme Court, Sandy Mongerson's lawyer argued that the visitation restriction was appropriate because Eric had had affairs with men during the marriage and because one of his children had once found a gay pornographic magazine in Eric's home. But in an amicus brief filed by the Lambda Legal Defense and Education Fund (now known as Lambda Legal) on behalf of Eric, the LGBT rights organization noted that there "was no support in law or in logic for the position that a parent's possession of adult pornography supports a ban on the presence of a demographic group depicted in the pornography (to say nothing of banning people, *i.e.*, lesbians, not depicted)."[34] The brief explained that prohibiting all of a father's gay friends from being present during visitation in a case like Eric Mongerson's made about as much sense as banning all heterosexuals from being present during visitation when a child inadvertently finds a *Playboy* magazine in her straight father's home.

The Lambda brief also pointed out that the Georgia Supreme Court only a few years earlier had struck down a visitation restriction precluding the woman with whom a father had had a relationship leading up to his divorce from being present during visitation. In that case, the court had demanded evidence that "exposure to [the woman] would adversely affect the best interests of the children."[35] Given that the trial court had made no factual finding of specific actual or potential harm to the children, the higher court overturned the visitation restriction. If the state supreme court in the earlier case had struck down a *narrow* restriction covering only the father's paramour, Lambda's brief sensibly argued, then the *broader* visitation restriction in Eric Mongerson's case—which applied to *all* lesbians and gay men in his social circle—also had to be struck down in the absence of evidence that their presence would harm the children.

It is likely that if Eric Mongerson's case had been litigated twenty years earlier, the appellate court would have been more receptive to the idea that a father's same-sex adulterous affairs during the course of a heterosexual marriage and the finding by a child of a gay pornographic magazine in that father's home would justify prohibiting him from visiting with his children in the presence of his partner or gay friends. Indeed, some of the gay father cases we explored earlier in this chapter upheld visitation restrictions on even more tenuous grounds.

But by the time the Georgia Supreme Court heard Eric Mongerson's case in 2009, the body of law, both from Georgia courts and from other states, requiring the application of the nexus test and the introduction of evidence regarding actual or potential harm to children had grown so large that it could no longer be easily ignored. It was not terribly surprising, therefore, when the state supreme court several months later ruled unanimously that the trial judge's imposition of a blanket rule keeping all gay and lesbian people known to the father (including his partner José) away from the children constituted an abuse of discretion. The court explained that "the prohibition . . . assumes, without evidentiary support, that the children will suffer harm from any such contact. Such an arbitrary classification based on sexual orientation flies in the face of our public policy that encourages divorced parents to participate in the raising of their children."[36]

The court issued its ruling several days before Father's Day. The first thing Eric Mongerson did after learning of the court's decision was call José to make plans for the two of them to spend the holiday with his children.

▲

This book has been concerned so far with the question of how courts have gone about determining whether having a same-sex sexual orientation and engaging in same-sex relationships affect the ability of parents to promote and protect their children's well-being. I have argued that courts should deem those factors irrelevant in determining whether the individuals in question are capable of being good parents to their children. Rather than focusing on the nature of litigants' sexual orientation and relationships, courts should look at their parental attributes and capabilities in deciding which custodial and visitation arrangements are most likely to advance the children's best interests. In doing so, I have contended that when parent litigants attempt to use their ex-spouses' sexual orientation and relationships to gain advantages in custody and visitation disputes, the courts should place on them the burden of introducing specific evidence showing a link between that orientation and those relationships on the one hand and actual or potential harm to the children on the other.

But parenting cases involving lesbians and gay men have not only raised the question of what makes a good parent; they have also raised the even more fundamental issue of who should be considered a parent to begin with. Interestingly, while the former question has arisen primarily in legal disputes between lesbian and gay parents on the one hand and their former heterosexual spouses on the other, the latter question has arisen primarily, as we will explore in the next two chapters, in litigation involving lesbian or gay individuals on *both* sides. It has usually been, in other words, lesbian and gay litigants, rather than heterosexual ones, who have argued in the courts that a particular lesbian or gay person should not be recognized as a parent for legal purposes.[37]

Who Is a Parent?

Breaking up Is Hard to Do

Alison Davis and Virginia Martin met in the fall of 1977 and quickly fell in love. Seven months later, they bought a house in Poughkeepsie, New York, and moved in together. Two years after that, they started discussing the possibility of having children. After many long conversations, and after consulting with friends, relatives, and a therapist, the couple agreed that Virginia would try to conceive and that if a child was born, the two would raise him or her together.

In the fall of 1980, the couple's physician successfully inseminated Virginia using an anonymous donor's sperm, leading to the birth of a baby boy. The couple named him Alex and gave him a last name that combined their surnames.

After Alex's birth, Virginia took a three-month leave from work, while Alison kept her job to pay for the family's expenses. Alison and Virginia shared in the daily care of the child, including everything from playing with him to arranging medical checkups to choosing the right nursery school. As Alex grew from a baby to a toddler, he started calling both women "Mommy." He also frequently visited with Alison's parents (whom he called "Grammy" and "Granddad") and grandfather (whom he called "Poppa").

In the fall of 1982, the two women decided to have a second child and that, this time, it would be Alison who would be inseminated. The insemination was successful and Avery, the couple's daughter, was born in the summer of 1983. As they had done with Alex, the couple began raising the baby girl together.

▲

Alternative insemination is the process by which a woman attempts to become pregnant through the introduction of sperm into her uterus via a means other than sexual intercourse. The first reported cases of alternative insemination in the United States took place in the years following the Civil War. During the next century, a small number of women, almost all of them married, relied on the procedure to get pregnant. It was not, however, until the medical establishment began embracing the procedure in the 1970s that its use started to grow significantly.

At first, most physicians were willing to help only married women with sterile husbands have children through alternative insemination. A 1979 survey published in the *New England Journal of Medicine* found that over 90 percent of doctors refused to inseminate unmarried women.[1] But except in cases when a woman's fertility was somehow physically compromised, the assistance of a physician was not actually needed in order to conceive a child through alternative insemination. Indeed, in the late 1970s, a growing number of unmarried women, including lesbians, began inseminating themselves at home with the aid of a baster or a syringe. By 1980, of the estimated 20,000 American women who were using alternative insemination to conceive every year, about 1,500 were unmarried. A *New York Times Magazine* article published that year estimated that 150 lesbians (most in the San Francisco Bay area) had so far used the procedure to become pregnant.[2]

The goal of making alternative insemination more widely available to unmarried women was an important part of the feminist movement's efforts, during the 1970s and 1980s, to expand the reproductive choices of women. In 1982, a group of women running the Oakland Feminist Women's Health Center opened the Sperm Bank of California with the explicit goal of helping both unmarried straight women and lesbians become pregnant through alternative insemination. In the first three weeks after the sperm bank opened, its operators received between seven hundred and eight hundred inquiries from women across the country, many of them lesbians.[3]

In the early days of alternative insemination, some lesbians also relied on informal networks of helpers who matched anonymous donors with women who wanted to conceive a child without having sex with a man. One woman described her efforts in Northern California in the early 1980s to assist lesbians with insemination as follows:

> I met sperm donors in parking lots, parks, and their homes, and relieved them of small containers that I placed immediately into the crook of my armpit. I handed cash to anonymous men, some of whose faces were still flushed, in exchange for a small warm vial. I pulled frozen semen vials from a tank, and thawed them in my hands until I could draw their contents into a syringe to present to a client. . . . I responded to late night phone calls from women whose ovulatory status required insemination the next morning. Sometimes I delivered semen "on ice" to clients who wanted to inseminate at home. Occasionally I drove for hours with semen

wrapped in a temperature-controlled gel pack to meet a woman waiting for me at her home. I drove many times with a fresh vial nestled between my legs, to keep it at the optimal temperature.[4]

By the mid-1980s, self-insemination had become less common because the advent of HIV led most women to want the sperm tested beforehand, a process that required the assistance of medical professionals. And many of those professionals continued to resist helping unmarried women with inseminations. Even in a relatively progressive city like Boston, for example, there were in the late 1980s only two medical offices that provided insemination services to lesbians. This lack of access to reproductive services was reflected in a 1987 government survey, which found that 63 percent of doctors who had performed at least four insemination procedures in the previous year had rejected (or were likely to reject) lesbians as patients.[5] It was not until around the mid-1990s that lesbians, particularly those living in urban areas, were able to have meaningful access to insemination services offered by licensed physicians and fertility clinics.

Many Americans first became aware of the use of alternative insemination by lesbians in 1979 when newspapers across the country published the story of an interracial female couple from Oakland. One of the women had had two children from a previous heterosexual marriage, but as one newspaper account put it, the couple found "the idea of having intercourse with a man in order to become pregnant . . . distasteful."[6] As a result, the two women began exploring the possibility of alternative insemination and were pleased to learn of a Berkeley doctor who was willing to assist lesbians with the procedure. But when they learned that the doctor charged fifty dollars for each attempted effort at conception, the couple decided to pursue a less expensive option by asking the brother of one of them to provide the sperm. He agreed to do so, and after only one try at home with the aid of a syringe, the other woman became pregnant.

The media portrayed the lesbian couple as two happy women who were in love and thrilled to be parenting together. There were, however, two important and largely unsettled legal issues lurking in the background of these types of stories. One issue, explored in the next chapter, involved the possible legal rights of the sperm donor. A second issue, explored in this chapter, involved the legal rights of the nonbiological mother.[7]

▲

In November 1983, several months after the birth of their second child, Alison Davis and Virginia Martin ended their relationship. Alison, who had found a new partner, moved out of the family home in Poughkeepsie. The couple agreed that Avery, their daughter, would live with Alison and that Alex, their son, would remain living with Virginia. The two women also agreed on a visitation schedule that permitted Alison to spend two or three nights a week with Alex in her new home, an arrangement that lasted until 1986. In addition, Virginia encouraged Alison to take Alex on vacations and to visit with her (Alison's) extended family.[8]

For more than two years after their relationship ended, Alison continued to pay half of the mortgage for the house that she and Virginia had bought and once lived in together. During that time, Virginia was unable to meet the mortgage obligation on her own. By early 1986, however, her financial situation had improved sufficiently that she was able to buy Alison's share of the house.

In 1987, Alison was offered a one-year job in Dublin, Ireland. Before she accepted the position, she sought to clarify with Virginia what type of contact she would be able to have with Alex while abroad. Although Alison suspected that Virginia was growing resentful of her continued relationship with the boy, Virginia seemed amenable to her sending letters to Alex and speaking weekly to him on the phone while she lived in Dublin. Virginia also seemed to agree that Alison could visit with Alex during her trips back to the United States, and that her parents and grandfather could continue to see Alex while she was in Ireland. With these apparent understandings in place, Alison accepted the temporary position and moved to Dublin with her partner Kimberly and daughter Avery.

But once Alison was out of the country, Virginia cut off all contact between her former partner and Alex. She changed her phone number to an unlisted one, acknowledging later that she had done so in order to prevent Alison from speaking with the child. Virginia also returned unopened Alison's letters and gifts for Alex. In addition, she prohibited Alison's parents and grandfather from visiting with the boy.

After Alison continued to write to Alex, Virginia hired a lawyer who wrote to Alison in Dublin demanding that she stop trying to contact the child: "I am returning your latest attempt to communicate with Alex. Please stop it. We will continue to return to you any such letters from you, directly or indirectly. You may believe this to be fun and games. It is not."[9]

Several months later, Alison traveled back to the United States, and without informing Virginia, visited Alex while the child was at home with a babysitter. Alison, accompanied by her partner Kimberly, took the six-year-old boy for a walk and gave him the letters and gifts that Virginia had not allowed him to see.

When Virginia got home that night and learned of Alison and Kimberly's visit, she contacted the police and filed a harassment claim against her former partner. In an affidavit she later submitted in support of the complaint, Virginia alleged that Alex was "upset and confused" by Alison's unannounced visit and that "for several weeks after, [he] was tearful and angry."[10]

Although the harassment charge was eventually dropped, Virginia continued to refuse Alison any contact with Alex. After Alison returned to Dublin, she wrote Virginia a long letter trying to find a solution to their growing dispute over Alex:

> I am very upset about how things are evolving . . . and I am writing to see whether there may be some basis for our working something out that we can all live with that would spare us any more hurt. I am very worried that things are at the point where each of us is on the verge of taking legal action. . . . I can't believe you wouldn't agree that this could only lead to more anger and conflict, and no real resolution. You cannot totally stop me from having a relationship with Alex, no matter to what lengths you go. . . . You know how much I mean to him. . . . All I want, and all Alex probably wants, is for us to be able to continue to see each other.[11]

Despite the letter, Virginia remained unmoved in her refusal to allow Alison to have any contact with Alex. This intransigence left Alison with no choice but to bring a legal action in the hope that a court might force Virginia to permit her to visit with her son.

▲

In 1973, the National Conference on Uniform State Laws issued a model Uniform Parentage Act (UPA) to assist state legislatures in enacting parenting laws. A UPA provision addressed alternative insemination, but only when it took place in the context of marriage. Specifically, the provision stated that if a married woman was "inseminated artificially with semen donated by a man not her husband" under the supervision of a licensed physician, the husband was deemed to be the legal father of the child as long as he consented to the insemination.[12] Since it was unclear at the time whether a child born to a married woman via alternative insemination using the sperm of someone other than her husband was a "legitimate" one, the main purpose of the provision was to clarify that such a child was a child of the marriage.

The measure's second goal was to encourage prospective mothers to seek the help of physicians rather than to self-inseminate. In the 1970s, alternative insemination was a highly controversial way of becoming pregnant and many policy makers believed it was best if it were conducted under the supervision of a licensed physician. (Indeed, some state legislatures went so far as to enact statutes making it illegal for anyone other than a licensed physician to assist with an insemination.)[13]

In 1974, the New York legislature enacted a law—titled "Legitimacy of Children Born by Artificial Insemination"—that was similar in crucial respects to the UPA provision.[14] Under that statute, if Alison had been a man and if she had been married to Virginia, she would have been recognized as Alex's legal parent despite having no biological link to him. (A licensed physician inseminated Virginia, so that statutory requirement was met.) Alternatively, if Alison had been Virginia's spouse, she could, prior to the end of their relationship, have brought a so-called stepparent adoption petition as a way of becoming Alex's second legal parent. In addition, if the two women had been married, the courts would have addressed issues related to custody and visitation as part of the legal dissolution of their relationship.

Alison, however, did not have any of these legal mechanisms available to her. The absence of a marital link to Virginia, and of a biological one to Alex, left her with no clear legal way of establishing that she, too, was Alex's parent. For the next few years, Alison argued before several New York courts that she should be legally recognized as Alex's parent even though she was not biologically related to him. The fundamental question that Alison's case raised was seemingly simple, but was in fact quite complicated: how does the law determine who is a "parent"?

American law has recognized for a long time that the biological connection between a mother and a child to whom she gives birth usually renders her a parent. (The law treats biological mothers differently than biological fathers. While the law almost always considers the bearing of a biological child by a woman as enough to grant her legal parentage, a father's biological contribution is not usually enough. As a result, a biological father must take an additional step—such as marrying the mother, caring for the child, or asserting his paternity—before the law deems him a parent.) In her eventual lawsuit, Alison never sought to question the point that a mother's biological connection to a child to whom she gives birth should be deemed *sufficient* for her to attain parentage status. Instead, her claim was that the biological link was not *necessary* to that status. Alison's legal position, in other words, was that even if most women acquire parentage status through biology, its absence should not categorically deprive her of the opportunity to seek parental rights by showing that she had served as a parent for several years with the biological mother's consent and encouragement.

▲

One of the lawyers whom Alison Davis contacted in 1987 seeking help with her case was Paula Ettelbrick, a staff attorney with the Lambda Legal Defense and Education Fund, a gay rights legal advocacy organization founded in New York in 1973. Although Lambda had filed its first amicus brief in a lesbian custody case in 1977, the group had traditionally not paid much attention to parenting matters. Ettelbrick, who was hired in 1986, set out to change that by focusing much of her advocacy on questions of family law.

Parenting issues are not always a top priority for those who work on law reform litigation because parenting law addresses private relationships and does so within an adjudicative context that is highly fact specific. As a result, it may seem that whether a particular litigant, for example, is granted legal standing to seek custody or visitation of a particular child is not an issue of great social concern. Ettelbrick understood, however, that behind that apparently narrow issue of standing lies the socially crucial question of who is legally entitled to be deemed a parent.

One of the complicating factors in cases involving nonbiological lesbian mothers was that if gay rights lawyers brought lawsuits on their behalf, they would have to sue LGBT individuals, something Lambda had never done before. But as Ettelbrick and others at the organization thought about these types of cases, they concluded that there was a clear pro-LGBT rights position to take in them. The law already recognized the relationships between lesbian mothers, such as Virginia, and their biological children. It was the relationships between lesbian co-parents like Alison and their nonbiological children that lacked legal protections. If the biological parents in these cases attempted to use the absence of a biological link between their former partners and the children to their advantage in visitation cases, then they were standing in the way of legal reform. As a result, by the late 1980s, a growing consensus emerged among LGBT rights advocates that it was necessary to start bringing legal actions against lesbian mothers who were preventing their former partners from having contact with children whom the partners had helped raise.

Ettelbrick and others at Lambda concluded that there were three aspects to Alison's case that made it a good one to test the courts' willingness to recognize the relationships between nonbiological lesbian mothers and their children. First, there was the issue of *intent* by both parties—Alison and Virginia had agreed, before Alex was born, that they would raise him together. Second, there was the issue of *consent* by Virginia—after Alex was born, Virginia had encouraged Alison to develop a parental relationship with Alex.

And third, there was the issue of *functioning* as a parent—for the two years before they broke up, Alison shared with Virginia the responsibility of caring for Alex.

After Lambda agreed to represent Alison in 1987, Ettelbrick filed a petition in New York State court seeking an order permitting her client to visit with Alex. The applicable statute allowed "either parent" to file such a petition.[15] The threshold legal question in the case, therefore, was whether Alison was Alex's parent. If the court said yes, then it would proceed to determine whether permitting Alison to visit with the boy was in his best interests. But if the court decided that Alison was not a parent, then she lacked standing to seek visitation and would, as a result, be denied the opportunity to prove that Alex would benefit from that visitation.

While Ettelbrick in her legal papers emphasized issues of intent, consent, and functional parenting, the main legal argument relied on by Anthony Maccarini, Virginia's lawyer, was that Alison was a legal stranger to Alex because she was not biologically related to him. Maccarini also questioned the notion that the two women had ever truly been a family unit. From the law's perspective, the lawyer contended, the two had simply co-owned their home, and "what right," he asked, "does the former co-tenant of a house have to see the child of the other?"[16]

Maccarini added that since the legislature had not explicitly defined "parent" in the visitation statute, the courts should give the word its ordinary meaning. Noting that the word comes from the Latin term "parere," which means to give birth or to produce, Virginia's lawyer claimed that, with the exception of the statutorily created right of adoption, one had to beget a child in order to be deemed a parent. "Putting other adjectives in front of it, like 'nonbiological,'" he argued, "does not change the facts of life."[17] From this perspective, it was the legislature, and not the courts, that had the authority to provide a more expansive definition of "parent."

As for precedents, Maccarini relied heavily on *Ronald FF. v. Cindy GG.*, a case decided only a few months earlier by New York's highest court.[18] In that case, an unmarried heterosexual couple was in a relationship for most of the period between 1979 and 1983, except for a few months in late 1981 when the woman dated another man and became pregnant by him. After the couple reunited in 1982, the man (Ronald) attended childbirth classes with the expectant mother, was present during childbirth, agreed to be listed as the father on the child's birth certificate, saw the child regularly for several months, and considered himself to be the child's father. The couple eventually broke up and Ronald sued for the right to visitation.

The New York Court of Appeals rejected that request, concluding that the mother had a constitutional right to determine with whom her child associated, a right that precluded interference by the state in the absence of evidence that the mother had neglected or abused the child, or was otherwise unfit.

Maccarini argued that his client's situation was the same as that of the biological mother in *Ronald FF.* In both instances, he claimed, the mother's constitutional right to decide with whom her child associated trumped whatever interests the former partner might have to spend time with the child against the mother's wishes.

For her part, Lambda's Ettelbrick insisted that Alison's situation was distinguishable in several crucial respects from that of Ronald in the earlier lawsuit. First, Alison, unlike Ronald, participated with the biological mother in the decision to have a child. Second, Alison assumed and exercised the role of a parent for several years. In contrast, while Ronald had contact with the child for a few months, he never functioned as a parent.

In addition to these fact-based distinctions, Ettelbrick relied on two legal arguments in contending that *Ronald FF.* did not control Alison's case. First, she argued that *Ronald FF.* did not preclude Alison from raising arguments based on the equitable doctrine of de facto parenthood (sometimes referred to as in loco parentis or psychological parenthood), which allows individuals who do not have a biological or adoptive relationship with a child to attain parentage status by establishing a parental bond with the child after caring for him or her for a significant period of time. Some courts across the country were beginning to recognize that heterosexual individuals—primarily stepparents—who had helped to care for children with whom they did not have biological or adoptive links should be permitted to seek visitation following the dissolution of their relationships with the legal parents.[19] Ettelbrick contended that the same legal doctrine should apply to a lesbian woman such as Alison who had functioned as a parent for years, both before and after her breakup with Virginia.

Second, Ettelbrick pointed to another equitable doctrine, that of estoppel. Grounded in fairness principles, this doctrine seeks to prevent individuals from asserting otherwise valid legal rights when they have consented to a restriction of those rights and someone else relies on that consent. Some courts from other jurisdictions had applied the doctrine to prevent biological mothers from denying the parental rights of men (usually former husbands) after the latter had established caring and ongoing relationships with children with whom they were not biologically related.[20]

Ettelbrick insisted that the estoppel doctrine was also applicable in Alison's case because Virginia had consented to and encouraged the relationship of love and care that developed between her former partner and Alex. It would be unfair to both Alison and the boy if Virginia were allowed, years later, to change her mind about the role that Alison should play in his life.

Three different New York courts entertained Ettelbrick's contentions and all rejected them. In 1987, the trial judge ruled from the bench after the lawyers made their arguments before him, taking less than five minutes to explain that, because of the absence of a biological link between them, Alison could not be deemed Alex's legal parent. Two years later, the intermediate appellate court reached the same conclusion by holding that *Ronald FF.* precluded a finding that Alison was Alex's parent.[21]

Ettelbrick had suspected that she would not prevail before the two lower courts because of the absence of clear law on her client's side. But she felt hopeful about Alison's chances of succeeding before the New York Court of Appeals. Two years earlier, that court had grappled with a case called *Braschi v. Stahl Associates* in which it had to determine whether a gay man who had lived with his same-sex partner for ten years was eligible for protection under a New York law that prohibited landlords of rent-controlled apartments from evicting family members of deceased tenants.[22] The court concluded in *Braschi* that two men in a committed and intimate relationship could constitute a "family" under the applicable regulation. In doing so, the court applied a functional definition of family that focused on the emotional and financial interdependence of the parties and rejected a formal definition that would have required ties of marriage, blood, or adoption.

This was the same approach that Ettelbrick was now urging that the New York Court of Appeals embrace in Alison's case. The Lambda lawyer urged the court to focus on whether her client had functioned as a parent with Virginia's approval, and on whether Alex considered Alison to be his parent, rather than on the absence of a biological link between the two. As she put it in her oral argument to the court, "it always has been the hallmark of courts [and] judges dealing with family relationships to have the flexibility to look at the family before [them] and do justice. The law should never be interpreted . . . in a way that results in harm or injustice. I am not sure that there is any way to use only a biological definition of 'parent' that isn't going to exclude a lot of children from the very important relationships that they share."[23]

The New York Court of Appeals, however, refused to adopt the position urged by Ettelbrick, noting in the very first sentence of its unsigned opinion issued in 1991 that Alison was "a biological stranger" to the child.[24] For the court, the most important aspect of the case was the need to protect the relationship between the biological mother and her child. As such, any award of visitation rights to Alison would impermissibly interfere with Virginia's "right to custody and control" of the child.

Since Alison did not allege that Virginia was an unfit mother, the court explained, she did not have standing to seek visitation with the child. The fact that Alison had for years, with Virginia's consent and encouragement, functioned as a parent proved legally irrelevant to the court. Indeed, whether it might have been in Alex's best interests to continue a relationship with someone whom the court conceded had "nurtured a close and loving relationship with the child" played no role in its decision.

Alison's request of the legal system had been a modest one. Although she wanted the law to recognize the reality of her parental relationship with Alex, she did not seek custody of the boy. Instead, she simply sought the opportunity to show that being permitted to visit periodically with Alex would be in his best interests. And yet, even this relatively modest request proved too much for the judges on the New York Court of Appeals, a majority of whom seemed to view Alison no differently than someone who was Virginia's roommate or Alex's babysitter—that is, someone who might have helped the biological mother care for the child but who had no right to see the child without the mother's consent. As a result, the bonds of love between Alison and Alex, forged through years of care and nurture, went entirely unrecognized by the law.

The fact that the statute at issue in Alison's case did not provide an explicit definition of "parent" meant that the New York Court of Appeals had no choice but to answer the question of whether it was possible for someone who did not have a biological (or adoptive) link to a child to be deemed his or her parent. Rather than recognizing the reality that children in many American families were not biologically related to all the adults who helped raise them, the court chose instead to apply a narrow and formalistic definition of parenthood.

The court's decision was misguided because it valued the rights of Virginia, as the biological mother, more than it did the well-being of the child. Alex was almost three years old when the two women ended their relationship. Most children know from a very young age who their parents are. Indeed, that understanding is in place well before they comprehend the implications (legal and otherwise) of biological connections. It should be obvious that to cut off all contact between a child and a person whom he considers a parent will almost always be harmful to him. Unfortunately, the court's normative prioritization of biology over all other considerations in determining what makes a parent blinded it to the harm inflicted on Alex when he was deprived of the opportunity of maintaining a relationship with one of the two women he considered a parent.

Despite Alison's loss in the courts, the question of the parental status of the same-sex partners of legal parents was not going away. By 1991, Lambda estimated that the number of children born through alternative insemination who were being raised by lesbians in the United States was over ten thousand.[25] Many, perhaps most, of those children were being cared for by lesbian *couples*. As the number of same-sex couples raising children grew, so did the number of such couples whose relationships ended due to irreconcilable differences. This correlation was hardly surprising given that same-sex relationships, like different-sex ones, sometimes dissolve. All of this meant that as the 1990s progressed, courts in just about every state were confronted with the question, in the context of dissolving same-sex relationships, of who is legally entitled to be recognized as a parent.

▲

Sandy Holtzman and Elsbeth Knott met in Boston in 1983, fell in love, and six months later bought a house together. In 1984, the two women participated in a commitment ceremony in which they professed their love for each other and exchanged rings. For years to come, they celebrated that date as their anniversary.

From early on in their relationship, the couple wanted to have children; first they considered adoption, but eventually they decided that Elsbeth would try to become pregnant through alternative insemination using sperm from an anonymous donor. The couple agreed that it should be Elsbeth who would be inseminated because Sandy had a job that paid well, allowing her to provide for most of the couple's financial needs, and because Elsbeth expressed a stronger desire to experience pregnancy.

After an early miscarriage in 1986, Elsbeth became pregnant again in 1988. Sandy accompanied her partner to every obstetrical visit and childbirth class. Together, they prepared the baby's room and bought furniture for it. They agreed on a first and middle name for the child that came from each of their respective families and a hyphenated surname that combined their last names.

On the day Elsbeth gave birth in December 1988, Sandy drove her to the hospital, was in the room during the delivery, and was the first one to hold baby Harrison in her arms. A few weeks later, the lesbian couple held a baby's dedication ceremony at their church; present that day were Sandy's parents, who flew in from Wisconsin and were recognized during the ceremony as the child's grandparents.

For the first four years of Harrison's life, Sandy and Elsbeth cared for him together. Although Sandy continued to be the source of most of the family's income, the two women shared parental responsibilities. Sandy taught Harrison how to ice skate, ski, ride a tricycle, and throw a baseball. She also enrolled him in swimming classes, took him to the zoo, and went trick-or-treating with him on Halloween. The boy's name for Sandy became "My San" and the family developed a tradition of celebrating "My San Day" every year on Father's Day. Both women provided for Harrison in their wills. They also established a trust for him, and Elsbeth named Sandy as the boy's legal guardian in the event of her death.

In the summer of 1992, the family moved from Massachusetts to Madison, Wisconsin, so that Sandy could fulfill a lifelong dream of attending law school. The couple sold their home in Boston and bought a new one in Madison. The fact that Sandy's parents also lived in Madison allowed them to develop an even closer relationship with Harrison.

In the fall of 1992, after the couple had been together for almost ten years, a growing tension developed in their relationship as Elsbeth coped with anxiety and depression. On January 1, 1993, Elsbeth informed Sandy that their relationship was over. She agreed, however, that Sandy could stay in their home for Harrison's sake and the two women continued to share parental responsibilities.

Six months later, Elsbeth moved out, taking Harrison with her. For a few weeks after that, Elsbeth allowed Sandy to visit with Harrison one night a week, but then she prohibited overnight visits altogether. A month later, Elsbeth abruptly cut off all contact between Sandy and her son, not even permitting the two to say good-bye to each other.

▲

By this time, Sandy had completed her first year of law school, meaning that she could read judicial opinions and understand their legal implications. She knew, therefore, that only two years earlier, the Wisconsin Supreme Court, like the New York Court of Appeals in Alison Davis's case, rejected a de facto parenthood claim brought by an adoptive parent's former same-sex partner, even though the couple had together decided that one of them would adopt and that the two of them would jointly raise the child.[26] If Sandy were going to prevail in possible litigation against Elsbeth, she would have to persuade the state supreme court to overrule this recent and seemingly unequivocal precedent. Although that seemed like a tall order, it was Sandy's only hope if she wanted to see her son again.

It turned out that Elsbeth sued first. Two days after she cut off all communication between her former partner and Harrison, Elsbeth sought a court order prohibiting Sandy from contacting her or the child, claiming that Sandy had threatened her. Prior to a hearing to consider Elsbeth's petition, the two women reached a resolution of sorts when Elsbeth agreed to dismiss her petition and Sandy agreed to refrain from contacting Elsbeth. Both women also stipulated that a guardian at litem would be appointed to represent the child, and that they would cooperate with a child placement study to be conducted by the family court's counseling services. But in the weeks that followed, Elsbeth refused to cooperate with the placement study, forcing Sandy to file a legal clam seeking the right to see her son.

The guardian at litem interviewed Harrison, who was now almost five years old. The child told the guardian that he considered Sandy to be his parent and that he wanted to continue seeing her even though he knew that Elsbeth opposed the idea. Harrison also told the guardian that he wanted to continue visiting with Sandy's parents, whom he considered his grandparents.

Interestingly, as she was denying Sandy all contact with her son, Elsbeth was trying to learn the identity of the anonymous sperm donor. During a deposition, Elsbeth stated that she believed it was important for Harrison to have a connection with the man who had donated the sperm that led to his birth.[27] Yet, paradoxically, she insisted that Harrison would not benefit from continuing his relationship with her former partner even though Sandy had helped raise him for most of his life.

A month after the deposition, an obviously conflicted trial judge dismissed Sandy's petition, noting that the state supreme court precedent of two years earlier required him to conclude, as a matter of law, that someone in Sandy's position could not be deemed a parent to a child like Harrison. The judge explained that he saw "this as a case where a family member ought to have the right to visit and keep an eye on the welfare of a minor child with whom she has developed a parent-like relationship. Unfortunately because the law does not recognize the alternative type of relationship which existed in this case, this court cannot offer the relief Sandy Holtzman seeks."[28] Noting that "bad law makes hard cases," the trial judge ended his ruling by urging the "appellate courts and the legislature to reexamine the law in light of the realities of modern society and the interests of its children."

The day after the trial judge issued his ruling, Sandy's lawyers appealed. They also filed a motion asking a Wisconsin intermediate appellate court to rule that Sandy should be allowed to continue visiting with Harrison while the case was under appeal. To Sandy, this motion was almost as important as the ultimate resolution of the case because she knew the appellate process might take several years, especially if the state supreme court decided to hear the case (as it eventually did). Even if she ultimately prevailed in her lawsuit, the passage of time might not permit her to reconnect with Harrison emotionally unless she were allowed to continue seeing him during the course of the litigation.

Two months later, the appellate court ordered that Sandy be permitted to visit with Harrison during the pendency of the appeal. The court's ruling came as a huge relief to Sandy because it allowed her to maintain a semblance of normalcy in her relationship with Harrison as she continued to battle with Elsbeth in the courts. It would be another two and a half years before the Wisconsin Supreme Court finally settled the matter of whether Sandy was legally entitled to visit with Harrison over Elsbeth's objections. During all that time, Sandy was able to visit periodically with her son.

▲

It is highly unusual for an appellate court to reverse itself, after only four years, on a legal question of great importance—such as who is eligible to be deemed a child's parent for purposes of visitation—but that is precisely what the Wisconsin Supreme Court did in 1995 as a result of Sandy's lawsuit. The court concluded that Wisconsin's visitation statute, which allowed a "person who has maintained a relationship similar to a parent-child relationship with the child" the opportunity to seek visitation, did not help Sandy because it applied only upon the dissolution of a marriage. But the justices also concluded that the legislature had not intended for the statute to serve as the sole means through which someone who was not a biological or adoptive parent could seek visitation. This meant that the court retained its equitable power to permit visitation by such an individual in appropriate cases. The key to the analysis, the justices explained, was a balancing of the constitutional rights of the biological (or adoptive) parents to decide how to rear their children against the interests of those children to maintain relationships with adults who had helped care for them and with whom they had developed a parent-child bond.

As the court admitted, the problem with its approach in the earlier case was that it had focused on the fact that the relationship between the legal mother and her child was still intact (thus ostensibly precluding the need for state involvement through a visitation order) without considering "whether the dissolution of the relationship between the mother and her partner might constitute a dissolution of a family."[29]

Sandy Holtzman with her son Harrison in the summer of 1994 after the Wisconsin Court of Appeals ruled she was entitled to continue visiting with him during the pendency of her appeal. Used with permission of Sandy Holtzman.

In overruling the earlier case, the court explained that a party petitioning for court-ordered visitation under the equitable doctrine of de facto parenthood had to demonstrate the existence of a parent-child relationship by proving four elements: (1) that the legal parent consented to and fostered the relationship between the petitioner and child; (2) that the petitioner and child lived together in the same household; (3) that the petitioner functioned as a parent "by taking significant responsibility for the child's care, education and development"; and (4) that the petitioner had a "parental role for a length of time sufficient to have established with the child a bonded, dependent relationship."

The sexual orientation of the parties was irrelevant to this test. As a result, the unmarried heterosexual partners of biological and adoptive parents who had helped to raise children would have the same opportunity, under the court's ruling, to continue seeing them after the dissolution of the adults' relationships. But the decision was particularly important to lesbians and gay men because they were ineligible either to marry their partners or to adopt their partner's children. (A year earlier, the Wisconsin Supreme Court had held that second-parent adoptions—which allow unmarried individuals to adopt their partner's children—were not permitted under the state's adoption statute.)[30] This meant that the only way that Sandy could be recognized as Harrison's parent was through the equitable doctrine of de facto parenthood embraced by the court.

The court's ruling transformed the legal status of lesbian mothers like Sandy in Wisconsin. Those mothers went from being, in effect, legal strangers to their children to at least having the opportunity to demonstrate to a court that their bonds of love and affection with their children merited legal recognition, so as to allow them to continue having contact with those children after their relationships with the legal parents dissolved.

The guardian at litem had explained in her brief in Sandy's case that young children do not understand the difference between a legal parent and a nonlegal one. What they know and feel is the sense of loss caused by the separation from someone they consider their parent. As the brief put it, Harrison's "trauma from losing his relationship with [Sandy] is no different from the trauma we presume for children whose parents are getting a divorce." And yet, the law in Wisconsin prior to the supreme court ruling did not "protect this child's relationship with the person who has historically acted as his parent and who he believes is his parent."[31]

Four months after the court's decision, the guardian at litem, concerned about Elsbeth's mental health, filed a petition asking that Sandy be named Harrison's permanent legal guardian. After holding a three-day hearing, a trial judge granted Sandy permanent guardianship of Harrison. Under the terms of a subsequent agreement reached between the parties, Elsbeth was permitted to visit with the boy for several hours every week. But in the end, it was Sandy, not Elsbeth, who got to raise Harrison in her home.

▲

The court's ruling in Sandy's case was the first time that a state's highest court provided former same-sex partners of biological (and adoptive) parents with the opportunity to demonstrate that it would be in the children's best interests for them to remain a part of the children's lives after the relationships between the adults ended. In properly taking an expansive view of what constitutes a parent, the court did not limit itself to formalistic ties, such as those of biology, but instead took a functional approach. The absence of the biological link, the court reasoned, should not categorically preclude an individual from attempting to show that she, too, was a parent because she had functioned as one, leading to the formation of a parent-child relationship. To put it succinctly, the court held that there is more to being a parent than successfully transmitting genetic material to one's offspring.

The Wisconsin Supreme Court opinion, perhaps because it was the first and because it was well reasoned, proved highly influential. Other courts around the country soon adopted its approach and applied similar tests to determine whether former partners of legal parents could seek parental rights over children they had helped raise.[32]

In the years following the Wisconsin ruling, many appellate courts have grappled with this issue. This is hardly surprising; although the law in all jurisdictions, either as a result of statutes or of case law, is clear that a husband who consents to his wife's insemination with sperm donated by another man is considered the child's parent, unmarried couples who conceive through alternative insemination are not entitled to the same kind of explicit protection under the laws of most states.[33] This has meant that nonbiological lesbian mothers who have been denied contact with the children by legal mothers following the dissolution of their relationships, have frequently turned to the courts asking that they be permitted to continue seeing their children.

Some appellate courts (including ones in Indiana, Maine, Massachusetts, North Carolina, Pennsylvania, and Washington State) have relied on the doctrine of de facto parenthood (or the analogous doctrines of in loco parentis and psychological parenthood) to give former same-sex partners of legal parents the opportunity to establish their parentage status upon the dissolution of the adults' relationship.[34] In addition, some legislatures, like those of Delaware and the District of Columbia, have enacted statutes allowing individuals who have functioned as parents to seek custody and visitation on the same terms as biological or adoptive parents.[35] The Delaware statute is particularly interesting because it was enacted as a legislative response to a ruling by the state supreme court denying the lesbian partner of a legal parent the opportunity to seek custody of the child after the couple separated.[36]

The view that LGBT rights advocates had been advancing since the 1980s, and that the Wisconsin Supreme Court embraced in Sandy Holtzman's case—namely, that intent and the functioning as a parent were important in determining who should be deemed a parent—received a considerable boost in 2002 when the prestigious American Law Institute (ALI) issued a set of principles for states to follow in their relationship dissolution laws. The ALI was founded in 1923 and is composed of leading judges, lawyers, and law professors. Its principal mission is to promote the clarification and simplification of American law and its adaptation to changing social needs and circumstances.

The ALI's 2002 relationship dissolution principles call for the granting of parentage status to individuals who reached co-parenting agreements with legal parents and who lived with and cared for the child.[37] Even in the absence of a parenting agreement, the principles call for the recognition of the parentage status of individuals who, with the consent of the legal parent, established a parental relationship with the child and lived with and cared for the child for at least two years.[38] The fact that the ALI embraced the approach followed by the Wisconsin Supreme Court in Sandy Holtzman's case, while rejecting the view advanced earlier by the New York Court of Appeals in Alison Davis's case (officially called *Alison D. v. Virginia M.*), shows the extent to which many legal decision makers, practitioners, and commentators have come to believe that there is more to determining who is a parent than asking whether a biological (or adoptive) connection with the child exists.

Nonetheless, several appellate courts (including ones in Florida, Illinois, Kentucky, Maryland, Missouri, and Utah) have agreed with the New York Court of Appeals' ruling in *Alison D. v. Virginia M.* by refusing to grant parentage status to the unmarried partners of biological and adoptive parents in the absence of explicit legislative authorization.[39] For its part, the New York court twenty years later reaffirmed its ruling in *Alison D.*[40]

Clearly, then, this is an area of the law that remains in considerable flux. Whether courts will grant the former same-sex partners of legal parents the opportunity to demonstrate that their having continued contact with the children is in the latter's best interests varies greatly by jurisdiction. Some courts continue to prioritize biology over all else, and are therefore unwilling, in the absence of explicit legislative authorization, to give former partners who are not biologically related to the children standing to sue for custody and visitation. In contrast, other courts have been willing to look beyond the absence of biological ties to assess whether the former partners, with the consent and encouragement of the legal parents, functioned as parents for sufficiently lengthy periods of time so as to allow them to form parental bonds with the children.

▲

In January 1998, the Boston-based LGBT legal advocacy group Gay & Lesbian Advocates & Defenders (GLAD) organized a series of meetings that brought together community leaders, social workers, lawyers, mediators, and parents to discuss how best to approach the dissolution of same-sex relationships that affected the well-being of children. The purpose of the meetings was twofold. First, organizers hoped to agree on a set of principles that would advise parents (and their lawyers) on how to minimize discord and acrimony during the separation process. Second, organizers wanted to strategize about how to prevent anti-LGBT judicial rulings in child-related litigation involving former same-sex couples. The attainment of these objectives, it was thought, would advance the interests of both the LGBT community and the children.

As GLAD's legal director Mary Bonauto explained it, the dissolution of same-sex relationships presented unique challenges to the LGBT community because, while the law prioritized biology, many LGBT parents were not biologically related to their children. In addition, separating same-sex couples could not avail themselves of legal divorce procedures that helped constrain emotional—and often harmful—responses to the end of relationships. While heterosexual divorces, of course, could also be quite fraught with tension and bitterness, divorcing heterosexual parents rarely contended that their soon-to-be former spouses were not their children's parents.

Bonauto noted that "the law fails lesbian and gay families by not helping them regain a more level-headed perspective on their children's needs during 'divorce.' Lesbians and gay men who formed families and made commitments should not adopt the law's inappropriate elevation of biology over the reality of relationships." She also warned "that the courts and many in our society are confused when they hear members of our community saying that our agreements don't count, our families never existed, and former partners are nothing more than 'legal strangers' or 'roommates.' How we end relationships is critical to our collective interests as well as to our children."[41]

After Bonauto helped to draft a set of principles that arose from the Boston-based meetings, she shared them with other LGBT groups across the country, seeking their input and suggestions. In 1999, GLAD published and disseminated the final document, which was titled "Protecting Families: Standards for Child Custody in Same-Sex Relationships."[42]

The standards called for LGBT parents and their lawyers to focus on the actual relationships between the parties and the children rather than on legal labels; to consider the dispute between the adults from the perspective of the children; to maintain as much continuity as possible in the children's lives; and to consider litigation only when alternatives (such as mediation) have failed. The document added that

> legal cases are often very damaging to our collective interests in addition to threatening deep injury to the individual families and especially to the children. A focus solely on the legal rights of the biological or adoptive parent ignores the real relationships of many parents, significant adults,

and children. It is extremely damaging to our community and our families when we disavow as insignificant the very relationships for which we are seeking legal and societal respect. Similarly, when an express agreement was entered into by the parties, it is very damaging later to turn around and claim that such an agreement has no validity simply because it has become inconvenient or [the] feelings among the adults have changed.[43]

Further elaborating on these points, the standards urged LGBT parents who believed they had to litigate to *never* argue in court that a former partner who had had a parent-like relationship with a child should not have standing to seek custody or visitation because he or she was not biologically related to the child.

▲

When Lisa Miller-Jenkins first asked a Vermont court in 2003 to dissolve her civil union with Janet Miller-Jenkins and to award her custody of their daughter Isabella, she seemed to be abiding by the GLAD standards. In fact, at a court hearing held a few months later, the judge explicitly asked whether Lisa was questioning Janet's parental status. Lisa's lawyer responded that her client was not. At that same hearing, Lisa testified that she wanted Janet to have liberal visitation rights with Isabella because that would be best for the girl.

The two women had met at an Alcoholic Anonymous meeting in northern Virginia in December 1997. Lisa, who was twenty-nine years old, had had a two-year relationship with another woman after she divorced the man she had married seven years earlier. At the age of thirty-three, Janet had recently ended a twelve-year relationship with a woman. Lisa and Janet fell in love, moved in together, helped each other stay sober, and started a child day-care business together.

In late 2000, the two women traveled to Vermont to enter into a civil union, an option the state had made available to same-sex couples a few months earlier. After returning to Virginia, the couple decided to have a child and that Lisa would be inseminated with an anonymous donor's sperm. They picked the donor together, one who shared several physical traits (like hair color and skin tone) with Janet.

After months of medical tests and procedures, Lisa became pregnant in September 2001. Janet accompanied Lisa to every prenatal visit with her physician and was present at the hospital when Isabella was born—it was Janet who cut the umbilical cord—in the spring of 2002. After the child's birth, both women shared parental responsibilities and caregiving. Isabella eventually learned to call Lisa "Mommy" and Janet "Mama."

A few months after their daughter was born, the couple moved to Vermont because they believed that that state was more hospitable to their family than was Virginia. Janet never sought to adopt Isabella—an option that was available to her under Vermont law—because it was her understanding that her civil union with Lisa accorded her parental rights. (Janet's failure to pursue adoption is not unusual. Sometimes same-sex partners of legal parents are not aware that they may have the option, as we will see in chapter 5, of adopting the children, depending on the state where they live. Others cannot afford the adoption-related expenses, while others conclude it is not necessary, especially when the relationship with the legal parent remains a happy one. And if the relationship sours as the adoption is sought, then the legal parent can prevent the adoption by withholding her consent.)

The couple bought a house together and attempted to have a second child by having Lisa again try to conceive with sperm from an anonymous donor. This time around, however, the insemination efforts were unsuccessful. The couple also started to grow apart emotionally, leading them to separate fourteen months after they moved to Vermont.

The separation was amicable at first. Lisa moved back to Virginia with Isabella but agreed that Janet—who stayed behind in Vermont—could visit with the child. For the next few months, Janet drove more than five hundred miles almost every weekend to visit with her daughter. She also, during this time, voluntarily paid Lisa child support.

Although Lisa, following her filing of the civil union dissolution petition, continued to be amenable to Janet's visitation with the child, she soon became resentful of her former partner's continued presence in Isabella's life. This led her to start seeking ways to limit Janet's contact with the child. When Lisa asked her lawyer, inconsistently with the GLAD standards, to argue in court that the absence of a biological or adoptive link between Janet and Isabella meant that the former was not the latter's parent, the attorney refused to continue to represent her. (Unbeknownst to Lisa at the time, her then attorney was a lesbian who several years earlier had successfully petitioned the Vermont courts to allow her to adopt her partner's biological children.)[44]

An increasingly determined Lisa then found another Vermont lawyer to assist her in trying to persuade the court that Janet should not be permitted to visit with Isabella without Lisa's consent. She also contacted a fundamentalist Christian legal advocacy organization by the name of Liberty Counsel, which agreed to help represent her pro bono.

After moving back to Virginia in 2003, Lisa had joined the Baptist Church in Lynchburg, Virginia, founded by the Reverend Jerry Falwell. Lisa also became a born-again Christian and denied that she was a lesbian any longer. "When I left Janet," she later explained, "I left the homosexual lifestyle and drew closer to God."[45] Lisa added that I do not "want to expose Isabella to Janet's lifestyle. It goes against all my beliefs. I am raising Isabella to pattern herself after Christ. That's my job as a Christian mom. Homosexuality is a sin."[46]

Lisa eventually came to believe, as she explained on a personal blog she named *Only One Mommy*, that God was using her "legal case as a warning of what will happen if Christians do not unite as the homosexuals groups have." She also complained that "I may lose my biological daughter to Janet, a practicing lesbian, because I have glorified God through obeying His commandment to bring up my child for the Lord."[47]

For Liberty Counsel, Lisa's case represented an opportunity to advance its views on the family through the courts. The organization, founded by attorney (and former Seventh-Day Adventist Church pastor) Mathew Staver in 1989, was one of the first Christian legal organizations in the country. For the first few years of its existence, Liberty Counsel, which was funded in part by Reverend Falwell and his church, focused exclusively on issues of religious liberty and on fighting abortion rights. In the mid-1990s, the organization started paying more attention to gay rights issues, and by the beginning of the new century it was actively involved throughout the country in legal efforts to prevent the recognition of same-sex marriages and to block the expansion of legal rights for LGBT parents.

In 2004, the same year he began representing Lisa Miller, Staver published a book titled *Same-Sex Marriage: Putting Every Household at Risk*. In that book, the conservative lawyer warned that "homosexual groups are aggressively targeting children and youth. If same-sex marriage was legalized, more children would be caught in the crosshairs of what amounts to a sexualized political revolution."[48]

▲

In the summer of 2004, a Vermont family court judge issued an order requiring that Lisa allow Janet to visit with Isabella. But a defiant Lisa refused to do so, cutting off all contact between her former partner and the child, leading the judge to hold her in contempt and to impose a daily fine until she obeyed his order.

Since Lisa's legal case was not going well in Vermont, Liberty Counsel advised her to file an action in the Virginia courts asking for a ruling that she was Isabella's only parent and that any claim by Janet of parental rights was "nugatory, void, illegal and/or unenforceable."[49] The conservative group believed Lisa would receive a more sympathetic hearing in the Virginia courts than she was receiving in those of Vermont, in part because Virginia had statutes in place rendering unenforceable same-sex marriages and civil unions entered into in other jurisdictions. Indeed, a few months later, a Virginia trial judge ruled that Lisa was Isabella's only mother and that she could therefore deny Janet access to the girl.

Meanwhile, back in Vermont, Liberty Counsel appealed the family court ruling recognizing Janet's parental rights to the state supreme court. The Christian organization argued to the high court that the couple's civil union was legally void because the two women were not residents of Vermont at the time they entered into the union. It also claimed that the absence of a biological or adoptive link between Janet and Isabella meant that the former had no parental rights over the latter. Finally, it was Liberty Counsel's contention that the Vermont courts had an obligation to honor the recent Virginia trial court's judgment denying Janet the ability to visit with Isabella over Lisa's objections.

▲

An important aspect of the litigation between Lisa and Janet implicated a statute enacted by Congress in 1980 called the Parental Kidnapping Prevention Act (PKPA). That law requires states to honor child custody and visitation rulings issued by other states' courts.[50] In doing so, the PKPA sought to prevent parents from engaging in "forum shopping"—that is, the filing of legal claims in a new state following the denial of the same claims by another state's court.

The possible impact of the PKPA in Lisa and Janet's case was procedural rather than substantive. The PKPA issue, in other words, did not speak to the merits of Lisa's contention that Janet was not Isabella's parent; instead, it involved the jurisdictional question of whether the dispute should be decided by the Vermont or the Virginia courts. It was clear to everyone involved in the case that Lisa's chances of prevailing were greater if the Virginia courts had the final say, because of the more conservative nature of its laws and its judges.[51]

If Lisa had originally filed for custody in Virginia rather than in Vermont, the Virginia courts would likely have been the ultimate arbiters of Janet's parental rights because they would have had jurisdiction over the case first. The PKPA was clear, however, that once the Vermont family court had proper jurisdiction over the lawsuit, Lisa could not seek to litigate the case in another state.

Liberty Counsel tried to get around the PKPA by pointing to language in the Defense of Marriage Act (DOMA), a statute enacted by Congress in

1996 that seeks to exempt states from an obligation to recognize "a relation-ship between persons of the same sex that is treated as a marriage" under the law of another state.[52] According to Liberty Counsel, DOMA's enactment meant that Congress did not intend statutes like the PKPA to apply in cases involving the dissolution of same-sex relationships. The problem with this argument was that DOMA addressed the question of whether a state had to recognize same-sex relationships (in particular marriages) solemnized in other states; the statute was silent on questions related to child custody and visitation.

In the end, the Vermont Supreme Court not only unanimously rejected Liberty Counsel's contention that the PKPA was inapplicable in this case, but it also upheld the trial court's conclusion that Janet was Isabella's parent. In doing so, the court explicitly dismissed Lisa's position that the lack of a bio-logical link between her former partner and the child meant that Janet could not, as a matter of law, be deemed a parent. The court noted that adopting such a rule would have drastic implications not only for same-sex couples who planned to raise children together, but for heterosexual married cou-ples as well. Since Vermont did not have a statute addressing the question of parental rights in the context of alternative insemination, Lisa's proposed rule would mean that not even the husbands of women who consented to their wives' insemination with the sperm of other men could be deemed legal parents of the resulting children. As the court explained, "such a hold-ing would cause tremendous disruption and uncertainty to some existing families who have conceived via artificial insemination or other means of reproductive technology."[53]

In ruling on behalf of Janet, the court gave considerable weight to the fact that the couple had entered into a civil union. That legally recognized union, which entitled the couple to all the marital rights and benefits avail-able under state law, was for the court "an extremely persuasive evidence of joint parentage." (The court also held that it had never been the legislature's intent to prohibit nonresidents from entering into civil unions. This meant that the women's civil union was legally valid even though they were Virginia residents at the time they entered into it.)

The court's emphasis on the legal union between same-sex partners is potentially significant as the number of states that recognize same-sex rela-tionships grows. When the legal dispute between Lisa and Janet began in 2003, Vermont was the only state that offered any significant form of legal recognition to the relationships of same-sex couples. In contrast, as of 2011, seventeen states make such recognition available.[54] If the courts in those jurisdictions follow the Vermont court's lead, it will be easier for lesbians and gay men who have entered into legal relationships with their partners—but who lack biological (or adoptive) connections with the children they have helped raise—to attain parentage status.

It is important to emphasize, however, that the Vermont court did not rely solely on Janet and Lisa's civil union to deem the former a parent. Instead, it pointed to three additional factors. First, the court noted that it was the couple's "expectation and intent," before the child was born, that Janet would be Isabella's parent. Second, Lisa treated Janet as a parent during the time they lived together with the child and identified her as such when she (Lisa) filed the civil union dissolution and custody petition. And, finally, a ruling that Janet was not a parent would leave the child with only one parent. As the court had concluded several years earlier when it recognized the rights of same-sex partners of legal parents to adopt the latter's children, the ability to have a second parent benefits children in many ways, including providing them with the right to inherit property from that parent and the opportunity to receive government benefits (e.g., Social Security and workers' compensation).

The Vermont Supreme Court took the correct approach in determining who is a parent. Rather than focusing only on biology, the court looked for other indicia of parenthood, which included not only the couple's civil union, but also their clear intention, expressed before the dissolution of their relationship, to raise Isabella together. The Vermont court was also properly cognizant of what it would mean to Isabella for Janet to be cut off from her life. At the end of the day, it made no sense for the law to ignore the parental role that Janet had played in Isabella's life, especially since the child's emotional and financial well-being was so closely tied to her having two parents.

Despite her failed efforts to have the Vermont courts deny Janet's parental status, Lisa remained hopeful that the Virginia courts would continue to side with her. Eventually, however, the Virginia Court of Appeals agreed that under the PKPA, it was the Vermont courts and not the Virginia ones that had proper jurisdiction over the case.[55] Despite Liberty Counsel's repeated attempts to have the United States Supreme Court hear Lisa's case, that Court refused to interfere with the rulings of either the Vermont or the Virginia courts.

After getting the case back from its state supreme court, the Vermont family court in June 2007 dissolved Lisa and Janet's civil union, awarded custody to Lisa, and granted Janet the right to visit with Isabella on alternating weekends and on some holidays. The judge also imposed a fine of $9,200 on Lisa for disobeying earlier rulings ordering her to allow Janet to visit with Isabella. (Although Lisa permitted Janet to visit with her five-year-old daughter twice in 2007, she had not, prior to that, allowed Janet to see Isabella since the summer of 2004.) In addition, the judge warned Lisa that he would reconsider his custody ruling if she continued to interfere with Janet and Isabella's relationship.

For the next two years, Lisa denied Janet regular access to her daughter. Indeed, during 2008 and 2009, Janet was able to see her daughter for a total of about forty-eight hours. This led the judge, in late 2009, to hold Lisa in contempt of court once again, but this time he also transferred custody of Isabella to Janet. The judge explained that the only way of ensuring that both mothers had access to the child was to switch custody. He added that the benefits to Isabella of having access to both parents outweighed the difficulties that came with modifying the earlier custody order. If Lisa had allowed Janet to visit with Isabella, she would have retained custody of her child. Instead, by disobeying the court's orders, she now had lost her custodial rights altogether.[56]

Following the court's ruling, a clearly desperate and distraught Lisa ceased all contact with the court and her attorneys and went into hiding with her child. In February 2010, the Vermont court issued a warrant for her arrest for contempt of court. Although the media has reported that Lisa may be living in Central America with Isabella, the authorities, as of this writing, have been unable to find either of them.[57]

For several years now, Lisa Miller has been viewed as a hero in some right-wing circles. In April 2009, a group called the Protect Isabella Coalition placed television and radio ads in Virginia complaining that "activist judges" had ruled that Isabella had two mothers and urging the public to contact legislators to rein in this latest example of "judicial tyranny." After Lisa disappeared with Isabella, some members of her Virginia Baptist Church compared her action to that of Harriet Tubman and the setting up of the Underground Railroad that helped blacks escape slavery.[58] (In 2011, federal authorities arrested a fundamentalist pastor and charged him with aiding in the "international parental kidnapping" of a child by helping Lisa take Isabella first to Mexico and then to Nicaragua in 2009.)[59] In addition, a leader of a group formed to help "ex-gays" renounce their homosexuality stated in a television interview with ABC News that Lisa was a victim of a legal system that discriminated against biological parents.[60]

The case, however, was never about discrimination against biological parents because Janet never sought to deny Lisa her parental rights. Even after

Lisa disappeared with Isabella, Janet made it clear that she would not interfere with her former partner's parental rights when she was found. During the five years of litigation in two different states, all that Janet had sought was simply the right to periodically see her daughter.

In contrast, it was Lisa and her lawyers who repeatedly questioned Janet's right to be involved in Isabella's life, trying to render legally irrelevant the fact that the two women had jointly decided to have a child and that they had together raised that child for almost two years. At one point, Mathew Staver, Lisa's Liberty Counsel lawyer, even went so far as to tell *Newsweek* magazine that to force Lisa to permit Janet to visit with Isabella was like being forced to hand "my child over to the milkman."[61]

The main point that Staver and the other lawyers representing Lisa made in their papers submitted to the Virginia and Vermont courts, as well as in their failed efforts to get the Supreme Court to hear their appeals, was that biology trumped all other considerations in determining who were Isabella's parents. But it was never clear why that should be the case. After all, a biological link does not guarantee an adult's commitment to a child; it is possible to have that link without any accompanying emotional or caregiving connection to the child.

All that Janet asked of the courts was that they look beyond her lack of a biological connection to Isabella and focus instead on the relationship that she had with both Lisa and Isabella before the lesbian couple separated. It was surely relevant to the issue of whether Janet was Isabella's parent that Lisa and she decided to enter into a civil union, a legal status that provided them with all the rights and benefits available to married couples under Vermont law. It was also highly relevant that the two women jointly decided to have a child and that the two were actively involved in the conception process. The fact that a physician placed the donated sperm inside of Lisa's body rather than inside of Janet's was significantly less important than the fact that the two women intended to become parents together and then jointly functioned as parents until they separated. And Janet would have continued to serve as a parent during the many years it took to litigate the case if only Lisa had allowed her to do so.

In the end, the Vermont Supreme Court—like the Wisconsin Supreme Court in Sandy Holtzman's case—held that the rights of biological parents in these types of cases do not trump all other considerations. The biological link that Lisa had with Isabella did not give her a unilateral right to cut Janet out of her daughter's life.

Lisa and her lawyers also made much of the fact that she and Janet had once been in a *same-sex* relationship. As they viewed the case, laws like the federal Defense of Marriage Act, along with Virginia's version of that law, prevented Janet from acquiring parental rights over Isabella. Neither of those statutes, however, limited the ability of a sovereign state like Vermont to enact civil unions, nor did it prohibit Lisa and Janet from entering into such a union, as they did in 2000. In addition, neither statute spoke to the issue of parent-child relationships and the question of who should be deemed a parent for purposes of visitation. Instead, the statutes addressed the extent to which same-sex relationships recognized in one state must be recognized by either the federal government or other states. For all these reasons, the Vermont Supreme Court appropriately refused Lisa's lawyers invitation to focus on Janet's sexual orientation in deciding whether she was Isabella's parent for purposes of seeking visitation.

The Vermont court's ruling reflects a proper and necessary acknowledgment that there are ways of forming families that go beyond the traditional manner of conceiving children. It simply makes no sense, at a time when there are tens of thousands of children born every year in the United States who are not biologically related to all the adults who intend to be their parents, and who will actually function as such, to hold that biology trumps all other considerations in determining parentage.

▲

The legal importance of biology continues to be felt even in jurisdictions that recognize the equitable doctrine of de facto parenthood and thus provide some protection to the relationships between nonbiological lesbian mothers and their children. Courts in most of those jurisdictions continue to prioritize biology by making it difficult for de facto parents to be awarded custody, essentially limiting their rights to those of visitation.

In Sandy Holtzman's case, for example, the Wisconsin Supreme Court held that, as the nonbiological mother, she could not seek custody of her son because she had not introduced sufficient evidence to prove that the biological mother was unfit or unable to care for the child.[62] And in Vermont, it took Lisa Miller's flagrant disregard of several judicial orders over a period of years before the family court finally decided that it had no choice but to take custody away from her and grant it to Janet Jenkins, the nonbiological mother.

Other courts have ruled similarly. For example, although the New Jersey Supreme Court in 2000 issued a decision recognizing the visitation rights of de facto lesbian mothers, it also held that custody was a different matter altogether. As the court explained, "the legal parent's [i.e., the biological parent's] status is a *significant* weight in the best interests balance because eventually, in the search for self-knowledge, the child's interest in his or her roots will emerge. Thus, under ordinary circumstances when the evidence concerning the child's best interests (as between a legal parent and psychological [or de facto] parent) is in equipoise, custody will be awarded to the legal parent."[63]

The problem with relying on these types of presumptions in favor of biological parents is that they are not sufficiently attuned to the needs of children who would benefit from living with their nonbiological parents following the dissolution of the adults' same-sex relationships. It is for this reason that the Pennsylvania case of Patricia Jones and Ellen Boring Jones is so interesting and potentially significant. Patricia, a community college professor, met Ellen, a writer of medical articles, in 1987. After a few months of dating, the two women began living together. More than eight years later, the couple decided to try to have a child.

It was Patricia who first attempted to conceive by using sperm provided by an anonymous donor, but those efforts failed. Ellen then tried to become pregnant in the same way, and she succeeded, giving birth to twin boys in 1996. Patricia was present in the delivery room and the birth certificates listed the children's last name as Jones, which was Patricia's surname. A year later, Ellen had her last name legally changed to Jones.

During the twins' first two years of life, Ellen stayed at home while Patricia taught at the community college. But Patricia did a lot of the child care in the evenings and on weekends. In 1999, Ellen started working again, and Patricia arranged her teaching schedule so that she could be with the children as much as possible.

The couple lived together with both children until they separated in 2001. At a custody hearing later that year, Ellen tried to minimize Patricia's parenting role, testifying that she considered her former partner to have been "merely a mother's helper with respect to the boys."[64] But the trial judge did not find her testimony credible, concluding that both women had shared child-care responsibilities for years and that they had been equally involved in making medical, educational, and religious decisions on the boys' behalf before the couple's separation.

The court granted both women shared legal custody but awarded Ellen, the biological mother, primary physical custody. (The court allowed Patricia to visit with the children in her home every other Tuesday and weekend, and during some holidays.) The judge never explained why she granted Ellen primary physical custody. There was no indication in the court's ruling that Ellen was a better parent than was Patricia. Instead, it appears that the judge implicitly relied on the biological link between Ellen and the children to grant her physical custody.

Four years later, however, the judge changed her mind after Patricia filed a petition seeking a modification of custody. During those intervening years, the court now found, Patricia showed great concern for the children's well-being, placing their interests above her own. She also demonstrated "excellent parental skills" and never attempted to interfere with the relationship between her former partner and the twins. In contrast, the judge found that Ellen "demonstrated a tendency to put her interests ahead of others, including her children," and showed "questionable parental skills."[65] Ellen also repeatedly sought to interfere with the relationship between Patricia and the boys, including twice attempting to move out of the area in order to make it more difficult for her former partner to see the children. All of this led the trial judge to modify the earlier custody judgment by granting primary physical custody to Patricia, subject to Ellen's right of visitation every other weekend and for five weeks during summers.

A few years earlier, the Pennsylvania Supreme Court had dealt with a custody contest between a stepfather and a biological father following the death of the child's mother. The court noted in that case that while two biological parents in a custody dispute share equally the burden of proving what is in the child's best interests, the burden between a biological parent and a third party (such as a stepparent) is not equally balanced. Instead, the court held that there is a legal presumption that the biological parent is entitled to custody unless there are convincing reasons why it should be granted to the third party. Although, under Pennsylvania law, that party does not have to show that the biological parent is unfit, he or she does have the burden of rebutting the presumption that awarding custody to the biological parent is in the child's best interests. In affirming the granting of custody to the stepparent, the court noted that, "while this Commonwealth places great importance on biological ties, it does not do so to the extent that the biological parent's right to custody will trump the best interests of the child."[66]

The issue in Patricia Jones's case was whether the law should treat her as it does stepparents by placing the burden on her to rebut the presumption in favor of primary custody afforded to biological parents, or whether she, in effect, stood as an equal to Ellen on the issue of custody. The trial judge noted that, unlike in the typical stepparent situation, Patricia and Ellen had decided to become parents together before the children were born. In addition, both women had cared for the children for several years from the time of birth. There was a good argument to be made, therefore, that Patricia and

Ellen should have been equally situated when it came to showing what type of custody arrangement was in the twins' best interests. But the judge felt it unnecessary to so hold in the case because, in her opinion, even if the rebuttable presumption in favor of primary custody in the biological parent was applied, Patricia overcame that presumption. An appellate court later affirmed the trial judge's ruling.[67]

The trial court's suggestion that de facto parents and biological parents should be equally situated in showing what is in the best interests of children for purposes of custody makes a great deal of sense. We should remember that before an individual can attain the status of a functional or de facto parent, the legal parent has to consent to that person serving as a parent. The constitutional rights of legal parents (who, in most instances, will be biologically related to their children) to determine what is best for their children, therefore, are protected, since they get to decide, as an initial matter, whether their partners should serve as an additional parent.

Furthermore, the partner must then actually function as a parent for a sufficiently long period of time to create bonds of dependency with the child. The fact that both of these criteria must be met before a legal parent's partner will be deemed a de facto parent provides significant protection to the legal parent against intrusion by third parties. But once the standard is met and the individual in question is deemed to be a *parent* (albeit a de facto one), there is no good reason to presume that one parent will be more capable in advancing the child's welfare than the other. The better rule is to treat both parents as similarly situated and let each try to persuade the court that granting custody to her would better promote the child's interests.

▲

All the cases explored in this chapter have involved disputes between former same-sex partners when only one of them is biologically connected to the children. But there are always, of course, *two* individuals genetically linked to any given child. In the legal disputes chronicled in this chapter, that second biological link was legally irrelevant because all the cases involved conception with sperm provided by anonymous donors. It has long been clear that such donors do not acquire parental interests over children conceived with their sperm.

As we will see in the next chapter, the question of who is a parent becomes (even) more complicated when the provider of gametes (whether of male sperm or of female eggs) is not anonymous. In such instances, the question requires more than determining how much weight to give to biology because, if the case ends up in court, it is likely that more than one party will be biologically related to the child.

4

Donate Here, Parent There

When Sandy Russo was fifteen years old, she went to see a psychiatrist and told him she might be attracted to women. The psychiatrist laughed, told her not to be concerned, and asked her "to come back to me when you have six children."[1] A quarter of a century later, and after two failed marriages to men, Sandy did have a child, one she conceived through self-insemination with the assistance of Robin Young, her lesbian partner.

Several months after their daughter Cade was born in 1980, the couple decided to have a second child and that this time it would be Robin, who was fifteen years younger than Sandy, who would try to conceive. And, as they had done the first time, they asked a gay man they knew to donate his sperm.

The couple flew to San Francisco from their home in Manhattan to meet with Tom Steel, a thirty-year-old civil rights and personal injury attorney who had been suggested by a mutual friend as a possible donor. Tom was well-known in San Francisco's gay community because of his legal advocacy on behalf of sexual minorities. While attending law school at the University of California's Hastings College of the Law during the early 1970s, he founded the Gay Caucus of the National Lawyers Guild, a progressive legal organization, and later became president of the guild's Bay Area chapter. He also later cofounded the Bay Area Lawyers for Individual Freedom, the nation's first lesbian and gay bar association. In 1978, Tom successfully helped to defend Huey Newton, a leader of the Black Panthers, who had been charged with criminal assault in Alameda County, California. A year later, he sued the city of San Francisco after one of its police officers, and a group of his friends, attacked patrons at a lesbian bar.

When Sandy and Robin met with Tom in his office to discuss their plans to have a second child, they explained that they wanted to raise their next child as they were raising Cade: jointly and without the assistance of the sperm donor. They specifically did not want the donor to think of himself as a father or to act as one after the child was born. Indeed, the women wanted to use a donor who lived far from New York to help avoid misunderstandings about his role in the child's life.

At the same time, the couple explained to Tom that they wanted their children to have the opportunity to know the identities of their biological fathers. After many frustrating years of searching for her biological father, Sandy—who was raised by her mother and stepfather—did not learn of his identity until after he died. The couple hoped to spare their children a similar ordeal by offering them the chance to meet their biological fathers when they grew older.

Tom, who had previously donated sperm to another lesbian couple, told Sandy and Robin that he understood their preferences and was willing to abide by them. Tom did not want to put their agreement in writing because he did not want the document to be used later on, by either the lesbian couple or the government, to extract child support payments from him. The lack of a written agreement was acceptable to Sandy and Robin; they, too, did not want a document that acknowledged Tom as the biological father. Furthermore, they did not believe that the agreement would be enforceable anyway.

A few weeks later, Robin returned to San Francisco and inseminated herself using a syringe filled with Tom's sperm. The following year, she gave birth to a baby girl whom the lesbian couple named Ry. During the first three years of Ry's life, the two women and their girls had almost no contact with Tom, even though the family spent part of that time in San Francisco, living only a few miles from him, after Sandy took a temporary job in that city.

In 1985, when Ry was three years old, and after the family had moved back to New York, her older sister Cade asked her mothers who her father was. As they had planned to do when they got this question, Sandy and Robin contacted Tom—and Jack Kolb, Cade's biological father—who agreed to visit with the girls. A few weeks later, the two women traveled with their daughters to San Francisco and introduced them to Tom (and to Jack, who also lived in the Bay Area). The visit was successful, leading to increasing contact between the lesbian couple, their daughters, and Tom. It was important to Sandy and Robin that Tom, during the family's visits with him, treat both girls equally by not showing favoritism toward Ry, his biological daughter. Tom was willing to do so, a gesture the mothers greatly appreciated.

Cade and Ry had ongoing contact with Jack as well, but he soon became ill and died of AIDS-related complications. In 1987, Tom also learned he was HIV positive, yet he remained otherwise in good health. Over the next few years, Tom—often accompanied by his partner Milton Estes, a San Francisco physician—visited with the family on several occasions. Sometimes he would go to New York; other times the women and the children would fly to California. Tom also exchanged many affectionate cards and letters with his biological daughter. And Ry sent Tom Father's Day cards in which she referred to him as her "dad."

At first, Tom did not mind meeting with Ry at the times and places chosen by her mothers. But as Ry got older, and as he grew more attached to her, he began to chafe against what he came to view as unreasonable restrictions in his ability to spend time with his biological daughter.

In early 1991, Tom asked Sandy and Robin whether Ry could spend part of the coming summer with him in California. (Perhaps sensing that the mothers were unlikely to send only Ry, Tom also invited Cade.) Tom hoped to introduce Ry to his parents and siblings, but he did not want the mothers to come along because he was not comfortable introducing the lesbian couple to his family.

To Sandy and Robin, Tom seemed to be envisioning a visit with Ry that was different from the ones in the past. Except on one occasion when Cade and Ry had traveled to California by themselves to stay with a friend of the family, the girls had never spent time with Tom without the mothers being around. It now seemed that Tom wanted her to split the coming summer (and presumably future ones) between her New York and California families. But as the couple saw it, Ry had only one family, consisting of her two mothers and her sister. Sandy and Robin were also troubled by the fact that Tom did not want his relatives to know they were lesbians.

After considering Tom's request, the mothers refused to send nine-year-old Ry to spend part of the summer with him, a decision that led to rancor and recrimination on both sides. At one point, Tom suggested they consult a family mediator, but the lesbian couple did not believe it was necessary to enter into a mediation involving their daughter with someone they considered a friend of the family.

With both sides at loggerheads, Tom hired a lawyer and, in August 1991, filed a petition in New York family court seeking an order of paternity naming him Ry's father and an order granting him visitation rights. In response to Tom's lawsuit, Sandy and Robin ended all contact between their daughter and him.

▲

In 1984, Donna Hitchens, a lesbian lawyer who cofounded the Lesbian Rights Project in San Francisco, wrote a short pamphlet titled *Lesbians Choosing Motherhood*. In that publication, Hitchens explained to lesbians considering alternative insemination some of the implications of using a known sperm donor as opposed to an anonymous one. The advantages of choosing the former included (1) the likelihood of learning more about his medical history; (2) the fact that his identity could be revealed to the child in the future; and (3) the possibility of him forming a meaningful relationship with the child. But this last potential benefit came with a possible significant downside: the donor spending time with the child, Hitchens wrote, "may lead to more 'paternal' feelings than he expected and, consequently, to more demands to be treated as a father than the mother ever anticipated." Hitchens warned her lesbian readers that there had been several recent cases in which a known donor, who had originally agreed to play a limited role in the child's life, "later began demanding the right to visitation, some control over the child's upbringing, and time with the donor's family."[2]

Hitchens added that the principal benefit of using sperm donated anonymously to a sperm bank or to a fertility clinic was that it prevented the donor from later claiming parental rights over the child. There were also, however, potential difficulties with this way of proceeding, starting with the fact that many doctors and fertility clinics refused to assist unmarried women, including lesbians, with insemination. (At the time, sperm banks dealt only with physicians and clinics; they did not ship sperm directly to women interested in conceiving.) In addition, there was usually significantly less information available about the personal and medical histories of anonymous donors. Furthermore, the identities of such donors could not be made known to the children. And, of course, the donors would not be available to have relationships with the children.

Whether to choose a known or an anonymous donor ultimately depended on the priorities and wishes of the prospective mothers. For some women, having the donor play a role in the child's life was not worth the risk that he might later claim parental rights. In contrast, some women were willing to take that chance in order to have the option of eventually letting the child know the identity of the biological father and permitting the two to develop a relationship.

The law made it difficult for prospective lesbian mothers who chose known donors to protect themselves against future legal claims brought by the men. Starting in 1973, states began adopting insemination parenting statutes based on (or influenced by) the Uniform Parentage Act, drafted by the National Conference on Uniform State Laws, which called for the termination of the rights of known sperm donors under some circumstances. The majority of those statutes applied only when the woman who was inseminated was (1) married to a man (other than the donor) and (2) the "sperm [was] provided to a licensed physician."[3]

Even though Sandy Russo and Tom Steel were both attorneys, neither of them knew that California was one of the few states with a statute making it possible for *unmarried* women to terminate the rights of known sperm donors as long as the sperm was provided to a licensed physician. But even if they had known about the existence of that law, there were few doctors in 1981, even in a progressive city like San Francisco, who were willing to assist lesbians with the insemination procedure. As a result, Sandy and Robin, like the majority of lesbians who pursued alternative insemination in the late 1970s and early 1980s, chose to do so without the assistance of a physician. (The self-insemination rate dropped significantly beginning around 1985 because the prevalence of HIV made it prudent to test the sperm prior to insemination.)

As a possible way of protecting themselves against future claims brought by known donors, lawyers advised prospective lesbian mothers to enter into written agreements making clear the intent and expectations of the parties regarding the type of relationship, if any, that the donor was to have with the child. There were no judicial precedents in the early 1980s, however, regarding the enforceability of such agreements, so no one knew for sure the extent to which they would successfully preclude parental claims by donors. In fact, as already noted, Sandy and Robin decided not to put in writing their oral agreement with Tom regarding the limited role he was to play in the child's life, in part because they did not believe it would be legally enforceable (a prediction that turned out to be accurate when the New York appellate court hearing their case years later ruled that even if the agreement had been in writing, it would have been unenforceable).[4]

In this environment of almost complete legal uncertainty, there were some practical advantages for lesbians in asking gay men to serve as known donors. One benefit was that if the gay donor later attempted to bring a parenting claim, he could not effectively use the mother's sexual orientation against her because he, too, was gay. In this sense, both biological parents would be equally disadvantaged by their sexual orientation. Furthermore, a gay donor was unlikely to marry a woman who might later try to assert, through her status as the biological father's wife, parental rights over the child.

In addition to these practical considerations, there was also the fact that using gay men as donors allowed lesbians to enjoy what one early writer on lesbian parenting called "the feeling of gay pride" that came with relying on someone from within the LGBT community to conceive children.[5] All of this meant that it was quite common for lesbian mothers like Sandy and Robin to turn to a gay man like Tom for sperm.

▲

Tom's decision to seek judicial orders of paternity and visitation left Sandy and Robin feeling both angry and scared. As lesbian mothers raising children together, they already felt vulnerable due to the lack of clear legal protection afforded to their family. And now Tom was reneging on his promise not to seek parental rights over Ry. The couple feared that if Tom won his lawsuit, they would have to send Ry to California regularly so that she could visit with a man who had betrayed them by dragging them into court. They were also afraid that if Robin died or became ill, Tom might seek custody of Ry. If he did so, the court was likely to grant custody to him, as the biological father, rather than to Sandy, who lacked a legally recognized relationship with the child despite having co-raised her all her life. (Although New York law eventually permitted individuals in Sandy's position to adopt their partners' biological—or adoptive—children, that opportunity was not available at the time of Tom's lawsuit.)[6]

Tom's petition was assigned to New York Family Court judge Edward Kaufmann. Between April and October 1992, Judge Kaufmann heard twenty-six days of testimony. During the trial, Tom's lawyer contended that her client was entitled to orders of paternity and visitation because of his biological connection with Ry. Biology mattered a great deal, the attorney argued, a proposition she supported by introducing into evidence social science studies reporting a strong link between children and their biological parents, and on how children can be harmed when that link is broken.

In addition to emphasizing his biological connection to Ry, Tom's case also focused on the relationship he had established with her during the 144 days he claimed to have spent with her over the previous six years. Tom testified that he believed Ry considered him to be part of her family, a sentiment she expressed in a letter in which she told him that "you have become a very important part of all our lives, we are so happy that we have grown together as a family."[7] Tom also introduced into evidence several letters in which Ry referred to him as "Dad" and expressed love for him.

For their part, the mothers emphasized during the trial that Tom had never spent an evening with Ry in which they were also not present, and that the total number of days Tom had actually spent with the girl was about a third of what he claimed (because he was either at work or Ry was in school during most of them). In addition, the mothers pointed out that Tom had never provided them with child support or helped make educational, medical, or religious decisions for Ry. Furthermore, they noted that Ry had also sent a Father's Day card to Jack Kolb, Cade's biological father. Finally, they pointed out that despite the fact that whatever relationship Tom had had with

Ry he also had had with Cade, he was not seeking visitation rights with the older child. To the mothers, this meant that what Tom valued most was his biological connection with Ry, rather than the bonds of affection he claimed were so important to him.

The main legal point that the mothers made during the trial was that as a sperm donor who had agreed not to seek parental rights, Tom was entitled to neither an order of paternity nor one of visitation. They further contended that Tom should be estopped from asserting parental rights because he had not claimed such rights for nine years, and because during that time he had not established a *parental* relationship with Ry. The mothers insisted that their family consisted of themselves and their two daughters, and that Tom had been a close friend, not a family member.

Both sides agreed to retain a psychiatrist to evaluate the girl and to make a recommendation to the court. Ry told the psychiatrist that she considered Robin and Sandy to be her parents and Cade to be her sister, despite the fact that she was not biologically related to the last two. Although Ry knew she was biologically related to Tom, she did not consider him to be her parent because he had not cared for her in the ways her mothers had.

Ry, who was by then ten years old, also told the psychiatrist that she viewed the court proceedings as an attack on her family. She had no interest in visiting with Tom any longer, and it was the psychiatrist's opinion that she would only do so "if she were dragged to him kicking and screaming."[8] After relaying all this information to the court, the psychiatrist recommended that there be no declaration of paternity and no court-ordered visitation.

Six months after the trial ended, Judge Kaufman issued an opinion denying Tom a paternity order, while adding that even if he had granted such an order, he would have proceeded to deny Tom the right to visit with Ry. The judge noted that Tom's conduct for most of Ry's life was consistent with his representation to Sandy and Robin, made when they first met, that he had no interest in seeking parental rights. Tom did not pay for pregnancy-related expenses and never provided financial support to the child. He also did not attempt to see Ry until the mothers contacted him when the girl was three years old. For years after that, Tom "outwardly supported" the "functional family relationships" that Ry had with both Sandy and her sister Cade. It was not until "Ry was almost ten years old, [that] he decided . . . to attempt to change the ground rules of her life."[9] As a result, Kaufmann concluded that Tom should now be estopped from claiming any parental rights over Ry.

Sandy Russo (*top right*), Robin Young, and their daughters, Ry
(*right*) and Cade, in 1992. Used with permission of Sandy Russo.

The judge added that Tom seemed to assume that because of their biological connection, Ry must feel "fatherly affection for him." But this was
not the case because Ry viewed Sandy and Robin "as equal mothers," and
Tom as a man who had become important in her family's life but who
remained outside the family. It was crucial to Kaufmann that Ry never
deemed Tom to be a parental figure, even though she understood that he
was biologically related to her. As the judge put it, for Ry to consider Tom
a parent "would have been disloyal to her family and inconsistent with the
reality of her life."

In the end, it was Judge Kaufmann's view that to permit Tom to exercise
legal rights over Ry after all these years would not be in her best interests.
Refusing to give up, Tom quickly appealed the judge's ruling.

▲

In all the legal cases profiled in this book so far, it has been clear on whose
side LGBT rights advocates have been. Thus, and most obviously, we saw in
the first two chapters how advocates sided with LGBT parents in their custody and visitation battles with their former opposite-sex spouses. We also
saw in chapter 3 how LGBT rights advocates consistently sided with nonbiological lesbian mothers in their legal disputes with biological mothers.

In stark contrast, Tom Steel's paternity case split the LGBT community in ways that no other family law litigation had ever done before and that few have done since. The divide became especially clear after New York Law School professor Arthur Leonard wrote a brief assessment of Judge Kaufmann's ruling in his monthly publication covering LGBT legal developments. In that account, Leonard opined that the decision could be viewed as a progressive one because it recognized a family unit consisting of a lesbian couple and their children. At the same time, however, Leonard analogized between Tom's legal defeat and the recent cases in which courts had denied lesbians the ability to visit with children they had helped to raise after their relationships with the biological mothers ended. Leonard added that "the decision may actually appear conservative in clinging to a view of families limited to a two-parent model and not accepting the possibility in the gay context of different kinds of parental relationships. Yet the opinion contains strong language recognizing the legitimacy of the non-traditional family unit Young and Russo had created."[10]

Leonard's two-paragraph treatment of the case led to a flurry of responses from readers, some of whom lauded the ruling as the greatest judicial victory for lesbian and gay families to date and criticized Leonard for suggesting that it was a defeat for the LGBT rights movement. These supporters of Sandy and Robin in the LGBT community were troubled that a sperm donor—who was not part of their family and who had agreed not to seek parental rights over the child—had turned to the judicial system to push himself onto a lesbian familial unit that did not want him as a member.

In contrast, several letters criticized Judge Kaufmann's opinion for failing to acknowledge the parental interests of a gay man who had been a part of the child's life for years. The judge was also criticized for failing, as one lesbian writer put it, "to envision any resolution of the case that looked like anything other than a traditional nuclear family."[11] From this perspective, the child's best interests had been undermined by the court's failure to recognize the loving, supportive, and long-lasting relationship that Tom had had with Ry, with the mothers' encouragement. To conclude that Tom was, in effect, a legal stranger to Ry was to prioritize form (i.e., the nuclear family headed by two parents) over function (i.e., the reality of Ry's close relationship with Tom).

In this debate, both sides tried to claim the mantle of progressivism and family diversity while accusing opponents of promoting conservative and outdated views. Those who agreed with Judge Kaufmann's ruling were thrilled with a judicial opinion that recognized, at least implicitly, that a child could have two parents, neither of whom was a man. Those who disagreed with the decision saw it as a missed opportunity to recognize either that a child can have more than two parents or that someone who has long-lasting and close ties with a child can have a legally recognized relationship with that child even if he or she is not deemed a full legal parent.

▲

It does not appear that the type of contact Tom had with Ry for more than six years rendered him a functional or de facto parent, as that term has been defined in some of the nonbiological lesbian mother cases explored in the previous chapter. For one thing, Tom never lived in the same household with Ry and he never provided ongoing care for her. In addition, unlike in many of the nonbiological lesbian mother cases, Robin—Ry's biological mother— never explicitly or implicitly consented to Tom serving as a co-parent.

Nonetheless, the legal action filed by Tom had the *potential* for expanding the legal definition of parenthood beyond the traditional two-parent model. Tom could have argued that the binary parent/nonparent legal framework that tends to view parenthood as an "all or nothing" proposition did not adequately reflect the structures and dynamics of some families, including some LGBT ones. It was possible, in other words, for Tom to take the legal position that, as someone who had had a loving and supportive relationship with the child for many years, he was entitled to some rights—including perhaps visitation rights—even if he were not deemed Ry's full legal parent.[12] It was also possible for Tom to argue that the law should recognize that a child could sometimes have more than two parents. Either position could have helped to move the law away from the traditional two-parent model, which was one of the reasons why some in the LGBT community approved of his legal claim.

The problem was that Tom, in framing his legal arguments, relied heavily on traditional views regarding the family, including (1) the dispositive role that biology should play in defining a family and (2) the need for all children to have contact with their fathers. This meant that there was a large disconnect between what many of Tom's supporters in the LGBT community hoped might be achieved through his case and what he was actually arguing in court.

It was also troubling that Tom contended throughout the litigation that Ry had only two legal parents: Robin, the biological mother, and himself. This position failed to acknowledge that Ry had a second mother, Sandy, who had helped raise the girl since her birth. Tom repeatedly claimed that his assertion of legal rights over Ry did not come at the expense of anyone else's rights. That claim, however, was belied by his effort to portray Sandy's role in Ry's life as legally irrelevant. (In fact, during the paternity trial, Tom permitted his lawyer to persuade Judge Kaufmann that Sandy should not be allowed into the courtroom to observe the proceedings because she did not have a legally recognized relationship with Ry. This meant that Sandy, who had co-parented Ry for ten years, was forced to wait outside the courtroom while her child's future was being decided.)

Furthermore, it was disconcerting that Tom argued on appeal that the doctrine of estoppel—which might prevent him, as the biological father, from seeking to exercise parental claims after agreeing not to do so, and after failing to have contact with Ry for her first three years of life—was only applicable in cases in which the mother was married to another man and the paternity order sought by the biological father would negate the child's "legitimacy." If accepted by the court, this argument would deny lesbian mothers the opportunity to raise estoppel claims against biological fathers because the mothers were not married to men. In other words, Tom's legal position—by making the applicability of the estoppel doctrine in paternity cases dependent on a woman's marriage to a man—would make it *more difficult* for some lesbian mothers in the future to establish and protect their parental rights.

For all these reasons, most gay rights organizations, including Lambda and the National Center for Lesbian Rights, sided with the lesbian mothers.[13] In an amicus brief submitted by several gay rights groups, American University law professor Nancy Polikoff argued that courts should abide by three basic principles in deciding cases involving lesbian and gay families: First, that biology was neither necessary nor sufficient to establish parenthood. Second, that agreements evincing the intent of parties—including biological parents—to share or not share parental responsibilities should be honored, particularly when reinforced by ongoing conduct. And third, that a child's understanding of which individuals make up her family is critical in determining the parental status of the adults in her life.

For lesbian parenting advocates like Polikoff, the concept of functional or de facto parenthood was helpful because it recognized the legal status of same-sex partners who had parented with the consent and encouragement of legal parents.[14] Yet to recognize parent-like rights in individuals (like Tom Steel) who had established relationships with the children but who were not part of the same-sex couples raising them was dangerous, because it might permit relatives and others to intervene in the child's life, as happened in the infamous *Bottoms* case explored in the introduction. As Polikoff put it in an essay written in 1986, "it is tempting to argue for expanded rights for nonparents. However, we must bear in mind that if we ask judges to stretch case law and statutes to reach such a result, those very [same] interpretations may be used against" lesbian mothers.[15]

Polikoff's amicus brief explained to the court that lesbians frequently create families in which the children know the identity of their biological fathers without considering them their parents. This was precisely, Polikoff argued, what had happened in this case since, as the trial court had concluded, Ry never thought of Tom as her parent, despite their biological connection. Instead, she viewed him as a friend of the family. And friends, no matter how close or loving, are not entitled to visitation over the objections of parents.

The ACLU also filed an amicus brief on Sandy and Robin's behalf. In that brief, the civil liberties group argued that preconception agreements—whether oral or written—in which sperm donors forego parental rights should be enforced. The brief added that sperm donors who entered into such agreements should remain free to argue that they qualify as de facto parents if they functioned as such for an extended period with the consent of the child's parents. It was the ACLU's position that Tom initially waived his parental rights when he entered into the oral agreement with Sandy and Robin, and that he then failed to establish a functional parenting relationship with Ry in the years that followed. For those reasons, the ACLU urged the appellate court not to overturn Judge Kaufmann's ruling.

▲

In November 1994, a divided panel of the New York intermediate appellate court issued an unsigned opinion in which it ruled that Tom should be legally recognized as Ry's father. The court also remanded the case for a determination of whether Tom was entitled to visitation. As the child's biological father, the court explained, Tom was entitled to his day in court. And the majority opined that Ry objected to having Tom in her life not because he was seeking to enforce his legal rights, but because of the mothers' "apparent manipulation of an innocent child's affections."[16]

As the court saw it, the case was one of discrimination against a gay man who was asserting his parental rights. "The notion," the majority explained, "that a lesbian mother should enjoy a parental relationship with her daughter but a gay father should not is so innately discriminatory as to be unworthy of comment." Furthermore, the court deemed the preconception agreement that Tom entered into with Sandy and Robin unenforceable because parental rights could not be waived via a contract, whether oral or written.

As for the mothers' argument that Tom should be estopped from raising a parental claim so many years after the child's birth, the court agreed with Tom's legal position that the use of estoppel against a biological father was only appropriate in cases involving the child's potential "illegitimacy." If Robin had married a man and Tom had not asserted parental rights for nine years, he would have been estopped from bringing a paternity claim because if he succeeded, he would render Ry "illegitimate." But since there was no other potential father in Ry's life, the court concluded that the estoppel doctrine did not preclude Tom's claim.

Instead, the court ruled that estoppel principles prevented *Robin*, as the biological mother, from defeating Tom's parental claim because she had purposefully encouraged a relationship between him and Ry for more than six years. Having done so, Robin was now precluded from seeking to terminate the relationship between the biological father and his daughter.

The court's decision left Tom—who had not seen Ry for four years—elated. The day after the court issued its opinion, he told the *New York Times* that the ruling was a win not just for him but also for everyone involved, because "it takes nothing away from Robin Young and Sandy Russo. It merely adds to the complement of people who are loving of and involved with Ry."[17] Despite the conservative arguments he had made in court about the importance of biology in parenting and the need for *all* children—even those raised by lesbian mothers—to have contact with their fathers, Tom sought to portray his victory as one that promoted diversity in familial arrangements. "It is so satisfying," he explained to the *Times*, "after all these years of struggle to maintain this relationship [with Ry] to see a court recognize the diverse nature of our families and honor the different relationships we create." He added that in 1981, when he had agreed to serve as a sperm donor, "there weren't that many role models [for planned LGBT families], and we didn't have a good or clear understanding of what everyone's role would be."

For their part, Sandy and Robin, terrified at the prospect of having to send Ry to California to visit with a man who had been battling them in court for more than three years, quickly appealed the case to the state's highest court. But after that court agreed to hear the appeal and oral arguments were scheduled, Tom ended the case by withdrawing his paternity petition because his health was beginning to deteriorate. Three years later, he died of AIDS-related complications.

Although he never saw Ry again, Tom did speak to her when the sixteen-year-old called him after she learned he was dying. During that phone conversation, Tom explained that he had always wanted to be her father and that he had not intended to cause her pain with his lawsuit. Six years later, in describing the last time she spoke with Tom, Ry still believed he had filed his legal claim to drive a wedge between her mothers and herself. At the same time, she acknowledged that she had once cared a lot for Tom, not as a father but more as "an uncle you love hanging around with."[18]

▲

The LGBT community remained as divided over Tom Steel's case after the appellate court's decision as it had been before. Although most gay rights organizations had supported the lesbian mothers in their legal fight against the sperm donor, Abby Rubenfeld, a former legal director of Lambda, and Dennis deLeon, a former openly gay New York City human rights commissioner, defended the court's ruling: "How ironic it is that in this day and age when the absence of parents from the family, both physically and spiritually, is so bemoaned, there are those who seem unable to recognize that the child in this case, in fact, is fortunate enough to have three parents, all of whom love her very much. . . . The court . . . embraced the reality of this extended family, [restoring] to the child the opportunity for a relationship with a loving and supportive parent and the only father she will ever have."[19]

In contrast, other LGBT advocates took strong issue with the court's decision. Polikoff, for example, complained that "Steel's victory was grounded not in respect for alternative gay and lesbian family structure but in the most rigid and patriarchal notion of family [in which] a man's biological connection confers [parental] rights."[20] There was also great concern among many in the LGBT community about the ruling's impact on the ability of lesbian mothers to choose the role that sperm donors should play in their children's lives. Indeed, Polikoff warned that in the wake of the decision, which remained good law in New York despite Tom's withdrawal of the underlying paternity claim, "selecting a known donor is a high-risk proposition."

Even though some of the media reporting on the ruling followed the appellate court's cue by suggesting that the crux of the case was whether a gay man could be a good father, that had never been an issue in the lawsuit.[21] Unlike the former heterosexual spouses in the cases profiled in the first two chapters of this book, Ry's mothers never suggested that Tom's sexual orientation was relevant to the dispute. Instead, the main issue in the case had been all along whether a known sperm donor who had had ongoing contact with his biological daughter for several years with the consent of her mothers acquired certain limited rights over the child.

Although the appellate court's ruling sang a false tune when it suggested that a failure to recognize Tom as a father was a form of discrimination against gay men, it stood on firmer ground when it noted the difficult position that known sperm donors like Tom sometimes found themselves in. For many years, Tom had respected the mothers' wishes by limiting his contact with Ry. And if he had attempted, when Ry was younger, to spend more time with her, Sandy and Robin would have likely balked. As a result, he would probably have been unable to establish a true parental relationship with Ry even if he had tried.

But ultimately, this difficult situation was of Tom's own making because he agreed for years to abide by Sandy and Robin's original request that he play a limited role in Ry's life. What ultimately should have been dispositive in the case was the intent and understanding of the parties both before conception and during Ry's first years of life. Lesbian mothers such as Sandy and Robin should be able both to choose a known sperm donor and to determine what role he will play in the child's upbringing. Sandy and Robin had made clear to Tom before the insemination, and for years after, that he should not think of himself as Ry's father, because their intent was to raise the girl in a two-mother household without the assistance of a male parental figure.

Almost a decade after Ry was born, this arrangement became problematic for Tom, largely because he had developed an understandably strong attachment to the girl. (As he would later put it, the emotions he eventually developed for Ry were "the strongest feelings I have ever known.")[22] But by then, Ry's understanding of her immediate family, which included a mother and a sister to whom she was not biologically related, was fully formed. It was ultimately unfair and harmful to Ry for Tom to change his mind by suddenly claiming that he had a legal right to be deemed a member of that family over the mothers' objections.

▲

In the late 1980s, several courts issued opinions sympathetic to the parental claims of known donors.[23] Even before the appellate court's ruling in the Tom Steel case, therefore, lawyers advising lesbian mothers interested in pursuing alternative insemination began suggesting more strongly that they rely on anonymous donors. For example, a highly influential 1993 handbook on lesbian and gay parenting warned its readers that "the only way to insure that a lesbian family will not suffer the disruption of a donor suing for parental rights is to use an anonymous sperm donor."[24] The author added that her two children were conceived through anonymous sperm donations because she and her lesbian partner had been unwilling to take the risk that the biological fathers might try to exercise claims over the children.

While many lesbians have since followed this advice and used anonymous donors, many others have continued to believe that, despite the risk of legal and emotional complications, their children are better off by knowing the identities of, and having relationships with, their sperm donors.[25] This has meant that courts have continued to grapple with the question of what parental rights, if any, should be conferred on known sperm donors.

One issue that arose in a Pennsylvania case from 2007 involving a known donor is whether it is possible for a child to have more than two parents. In that case, a sperm donor twice provided sperm to a friend so that she and her lesbian partner could have children. The lesbian couple separated after raising the children together for several years. A trial court granted joint legal custody to the mothers even though only one of them was biologically related to the children. It also granted the sperm donor visitation rights. A different trial court then refused to impose child support obligations on the donor. An appellate court later affirmed the joint custody ruling but required the biological father to pay child support.[26] The combination of all these rulings meant that the law ended up recognizing the parental status of three individuals, two who shared legal custody and a third who had visitation rights and child support obligations.

A review of the facts in this case suggests that the recognition of a third parent was unwarranted. There was evidence introduced that the mothers, as in the Tom Steel case, specifically asked the donor, before the time of conception, that he not play a parental role in their children's lives. Indeed, after the child was born, the donor visited the family only about once a month. This meant that the mothers and their children, as one of the mothers testified, did not consider the donor to be a parent, but instead "considered him to be an uncle [or] a friend."[27]

Although it was not true of the Pennsylvania case, it is true that some lesbian couples who seek to conceive through alternative insemination want the sperm donors—who continue frequently to be gay men—to play parent-like roles in their children's lives. The policy question becomes whether the law should be open to the possibility of recognizing parental rights not just in the nonbiological mother, but also in the biological father.

The first thing to note about these situations is that they are different from what happened in the Tom Steel case. In that case, the two lesbian mothers never intended that Tom assume parental responsibilities for their child. In contrast, it does appear that some lesbian mothers want donors to play parental roles in their children's lives. It appears, in other words, that there are some planned three-parent LGBT families. (It is also not unheard of for there to be planned four-parent LGBT families, which include the donor's male partner as an additional parent.)

Recent statutory changes can play an important role here. As noted earlier in this chapter, the 1973 Uniform Parentage Act called for the termination of a known sperm donor's parental rights only in instances in which the inseminated woman was married.[28] A revised version of that act, issued in 2002, no longer requires that the inseminated woman be married in order for the rights of the known donor to be terminated.[29]

Actual state laws have followed the shift in the UPA. While most states thirty years ago only permitted married women to terminate the parental rights of known donors, today most states have laws that terminate the rights of known donors without distinguishing between married and unmarried recipients. Even if many of these laws were not enacted specifically with prospective lesbian mothers in mind, their existence nonetheless helps lesbians who are interested in conceiving with the sperm of known donors and who do not want them to play parental roles in the children's lives.

But what about prospective lesbian mothers who *do* want known donors to assume parental responsibilities? There are statutes in place in some states that might help these women as well. These laws deem the sperm donor not to be a parent *unless the recipient and he agree in writing to the contrary*.[30] It is possible in these jurisdictions, in other words, for a sperm donor (including gay men) and a recipient (including lesbians) to agree in writing that the former will have parental rights over the child, an agreement that, when properly executed, must be enforced by the courts. When states with these statutes also recognize the biological mother's lesbian partner as a de facto parent, it makes it possible for a child to have three parents, all of whom (if the donor is a gay man) are lesbian or gay.

There has not been much litigation yet on the question of whether children can have more than two parents, so there is considerable uncertainty over whether courts will be willing to accept such planned three-parent families. But, in the same way that the familial arrangements of LGBT individuals have led some judges to reconsider the primacy of biology in determining parenthood, those arrangements may also lead future courts to reconsider the primacy of binary parenthood—that is, the notion that children can have only two parents.

It should also be possible for women who conceive through alternative insemination, as well as their partners if they have them, to choose to have the known sperm donor play a role in the child's life that, as one gay donor recently put it, makes him "more than an uncle and less than a father."[31] Indeed, some donors these days are significantly involved, with the mothers' consent, in the lives of the children—by, for example, routinely visiting with them and providing emotional and financial support—without assuming the ultimate responsibilities for the children's well-being or for the making of educational, medical, and religious decisions on their behalf.

The existence of these types of familial arrangements means that parenting does not have to be an "all-or-nothing" proposition. In fact, part of the difficulty that Tom Steel faced when litigating his case was that he essentially had to choose between contending that he was a full legal parent, with all the accompanying rights and obligations, and conceding that he was a legal stranger to his biological daughter. While a choice that is limited to those two options might be proper for some donors under some circumstances, such a limitation fails to account for the different degrees of involvement that known donors can have in the lives of children conceived with their sperm. This all-or-nothing view of parenthood is another element of American parenting law that, while long established, does not reflect the actual parental roles that some adults play in some children's lives.

In order to more accurately reflect the relationships of care and love that children have with the adults in their lives, courts should be open to the idea that more than two individuals can share parenthood. What is required of courts in these types of cases, above all else, is a sensitive and nuanced analysis that takes into account both the intent of the adults and the lived experiences of the children.

▲

It is not only lesbian women who have used alternative insemination and other forms of reproductive assistance to have children; so have gay men. But for the latter, of course, the process is complicated by the fact that they must rely not only on donated gametes (in their case, eggs or ova), but also on the assistance of a surrogate to carry the fertilized embryo to term.

There are two different types of surrogacy. The first, known as "traditional surrogacy," involves the use of sperm—from either the intended father or a donor—to inseminate the surrogate mother. In these cases, the birth mother is linked to the child both genetically and through gestation.

The second type of surrogacy, known as "gestational surrogacy," involves the retrieval of ova from either the intended mother or a donor. The ova are then fertilized in vitro (i.e., outside of the womb) with the sperm of the intended father or of a donor, after which the embryo is placed in the surrogate's womb. In these situations, the birth mother is linked to the child through gestation but not through genetics.

When surrogacy pregnancies first began taking place in the United States with some frequency—around the mid-1980s—in vitro technology was not very advanced and was quite expensive, making traditional surrogacy the only realistic option for most individuals interested in pursuing surrogacy as a way of becoming parents. In 1986, the country became riveted by the story of Mary Beth Whitehead, a married woman who agreed to serve as a traditional surrogate by being inseminated with the sperm of a married man so that he and his wife could raise the resulting child. But the day after the baby was born, Whitehead changed her mind, and a protracted and highly visible lawsuit—known as the *Baby M.* case—ensued over who was the child's mother. Eventually, the New Jersey Supreme Court held that the surrogacy agreement entered into by Whitehead and the child's biological father violated public policy because it effectively called for the sale of a child. As a result, the court held that Whitehead—and not the father's wife—was the child's mother.[32]

Shortly after the *Baby M.* case, several states enacted laws prohibiting surrogacy agreements. With time, however, the political opposition to surrogacy diminished, in part because advances in reproductive technology made gestational surrogacy easier (and less costly) to achieve. The fact that gestational surrogates are not genetically related to the children has meant that they have generally not been viewed as either victims or baby sellers. In fact, the media now routinely portray surrogate mothers in a positive light, highlighting their generosity in wanting to help prospective parents—both infertile heterosexuals and gay men—have children.[33]

In addition, legislators these days seem less interested in discouraging surrogacy than they are, as one commentator has put it, in "providing certainty about parental status and protecting all participants, especially children."[34] An example of this shift is a statute unanimously passed by the Illinois legislature in 2004 that creates a presumption in cases of gestational surrogacy that it is the intended parents and not the surrogate mothers who are the children's legal parents.[35] In other states, however, surrogacy of any kind remains strictly prohibited.

Although it is difficult to determine precise numbers, it appears that thousands of gay men in recent years have had children with the assistance of surrogate mothers. While the majority of these surrogacy arrangements seem to have gone as planned with the mother relinquishing parental rights after birth, some have ended up in litigation.

Several of the surrogacy cases in which gay men are litigants have involved relatively rare instances of traditional surrogacy where the issue is usually not whether the surrogate mother should be deemed a parent (she usually is), but is instead who should have custody of the child. In one case, a New York trial court concluded that the biological gay father should have sole custody over the objection of the surrogate mother, a former friend who had volunteered to help him have the child.[36] In another case, an Ohio appellate court ruled that a woman who was inseminated with the sperm of an anonymous donor did not have to share custody with her gay brother (and his male partner), even though there was evidence that she had agreed, prior to conception, that the brother could raise the child.[37]

There have also been some legal disputes between gay men and gestational surrogates. In 2009, a New Jersey trial court held that the *Baby M.* precedent also applied to gestational surrogacy. As a result, the court ruled that a gestational surrogate who had agreed to help a gay couple—one of whom was her brother—have children was a legal parent of the resulting twin girls.[38] But two years earlier, a Minnesota appellate court upheld the gestational surrogacy agreement between a gay man and his niece, holding that the former, and not the latter, was the child's legal parent.[39]

While the practice of surrogacy continues to generate some controversy, especially among some conservative and feminist critics, litigation involving gay men and surrogates has been relatively rare and has had little impact in the development of parenting law. Interestingly, the most important LGBT parenting case involving a gestational mother arose due to the efforts of a lesbian woman, rather than a gay man, to become a parent.

▲

In 1992, shortly after Elizabeth Gardner turned forty, she decided she wanted to have a child. A few months later, she met and started dating Karen Morris. Elizabeth told Karen early on in their relationship that she wanted to be a mother, and that she wanted to be her future child's only parent. In the months after they first became a couple, Elizabeth submitted an adoption application; she also went through thirteen alternative insemination procedures at a fertility clinic. When the insemination efforts proved unsuccessful, the clinic attempted in vitro fertilization with Elizabeth's eggs and sperm donated anonymously. But these efforts also failed because she was unable to produce enough eggs to successfully create embryos.

By this time, Elizabeth and Karen had moved in together and registered as domestic partners with the city of San Francisco. Karen accompanied her partner to most of the fertility appointments, offered her encouragement, and helped choose the sperm donor. Although Elizabeth appreciated Karen's assistance and support, she continued to make it clear to her partner that she wanted to be the child's only mother.

It so happened that the same medical practice that was helping Elizabeth become pregnant was also providing treatment to Karen for another condition. One day, Elizabeth's doctor suggested she might want to use eggs donated by Karen to attempt additional in vitro fertilizations. Elizabeth was at first reluctant to pursue this suggestion because the couple's relationship was still relatively new and because a mutual friend of theirs was in a custody dispute with her former lesbian partner, an experience that left Elizabeth fearful of having a similar battle with Karen in the future. Eventually, however, Elizabeth asked Karen to donate her eggs. Although Elizabeth again made it clear that she wanted to be the child's only mother, she added that she might be willing to consider a future adoption by Karen, but not before the child was five years old.

It is standard practice for fertility clinics to require egg donors to sign forms granting consent to the extraction procedure and waiving any claims to the children that might result from the subsequent fertilization. During the legal dispute between Elizabeth and Karen almost a decade later, Karen claimed that she received the four-page consent form the day of the procedure and was given only a few minutes to read it. In contrast, Elizabeth contended that Karen received the form in the mail several weeks before and that the couple discussed it at length before Karen signed it. The trial court eventually credited Elizabeth's version of what happened.

In any event, there was no dispute that Karen signed the form. After she did so, doctors retrieved her eggs and then fertilized them in vitro with sperm provided by an anonymous donor. The resulting embryos were implanted in Elizabeth's uterus, leading her to become pregnant with twin girls.

The children were born in December 1995, with Karen present in the delivery room. A few days later, Elizabeth asked Karen to marry her, and the couple exchanged commitment rings on Christmas Day. But Elizabeth was the only parent listed in the girls' birth certificates, and she alone added them to her health and life insurance policies. And, as they had agreed to do, neither woman revealed to family and friends that Karen had provided the eggs that made the births possible.

For the next six years, the lesbian couple and the two girls lived together as a family in a home jointly owned by the two women. Karen shared child-care responsibilities with Elizabeth, including staying at home with the children when they were sick and taking them to their pediatrician appointments. Karen also helped choose their nursery and kindergarten schools, and she was listed on school forms as a co-parent. The twins viewed both women as their mothers, giving both Mother's Day cards and including the couple in drawings they made at school of their family.

In 1998, tension developed between the two women over the issue of whether and how to tell the girls that Karen had provided the eggs that led to their birth. Elizabeth asserted that the children should not be told and insisted that she was their only mother. When Karen replied that she, too, was the children's mother, Elizabeth reminded her partner about the consent form she had signed several years earlier waving all parental claims.

As already noted, Elizabeth early on in their relationship raised the possibility of Karen adopting the children, but when the latter now expressed an interest in doing so, Elizabeth was no longer sure that was a good idea. Their relationship had grown strained, and Elizabeth wanted to move to Massachusetts, while Karen did not. In 2001, the couple separated; Elizabeth filed a notice of termination of their domestic partnership, and Karen filed a court petition seeking parental rights and an order prohibiting Elizabeth from moving the twins out of the state. A few months later, Karen voluntarily dismissed her petition when the couple reconciled and attempted to resolve their differences. But the rapprochement lasted only a few months, after which Elizabeth moved with the children to Massachusetts and Karen filed a new petition seeking the right to visit with the girls.

▲

It is not unusual for lesbian couples these days to engage in the type of "ovum sharing" that took place in Elizabeth and Karen's case. This is particularly true among lesbian couples for whom it is important that both women have a biological connection to their children, with one mother sharing a genetic link and the other a gestational one. The legal implications of ovum sharing are unclear, and this case sought to clarify them. The crux of the legal dispute was whether Karen had intended *to donate* her ova to her partner or whether she instead provided them with the understanding that both women would raise the children together.

During a seven-day trial in which the two women testified at length, Karen contended that she and Elizabeth had intended, early in their relationship, to have children together and that they specifically discussed how they would both be parents of children born through the fertilization of Karen's eggs. Karen conceded, however, that when she met Elizabeth, the latter had already filed an adoption petition and was trying to get pregnant through alternative insemination. Karen also acknowledged that Elizabeth, at the very beginning of their relationship, was reluctant to have Karen join her as a parent because their relationship was still new.

After the trial's conclusion, the judge ruled that Karen had knowingly relinquished all her parental claims when she signed the fertility clinic's consent form, and that both women had agreed that Elizabeth would be the only parent, an agreement that was not modified by their subsequent conduct. The court therefore held that Karen did not have standing to sue for visitation and dismissed her claim.

The California Court of Appeal affirmed, ruling that Karen's legal status was analogous to that of a known sperm donor whose clear intent, prior to conception, is to waive any parental claims over the child.[40] According to the appellate court, since Karen made that intent clear—and since the eggs were provided to a licensed physician, as called for by the California Uniform Parentage Act—the only way in which she could have established a parental claim over the twins was by adopting them. Karen appealed that decision to the state supreme court, which agreed to hear the case.

▲

The question of what role intent should play in determining who qualifies as a legal parent has been at issue in most of the cases explored in the last two chapters. A biological parent's intent that her same-sex partner serve as a co-parent, when coupled with the partner's intent to assume that role, has been a crucial factor in the willingness of some courts to recognize as parents individuals who lack a biological (or adoptive) connection to the children in question. In addition, the lesbian mothers in the Tom Steel case argued (ultimately unsuccessfully) that their original intent (and that of the sperm donor) that he not serve as the child's parent meant that the court should not grant him a paternity order.

Similarly, the crucial legal issue in the dispute between Elizabeth and Karen involved the question of intent. A few years earlier, the California Supreme Court, in a case called *Johnson v. Calvert*, had grappled with the issue of intent in another case involving two women, one who had provided an egg and another who had served as a surrogate mother by carrying it to term after it was fertilized in vitro.[41] Unlike Elizabeth and Karen, however, the two women in *Johnson* were not in a lesbian relationship.

Mark and Crispina Calvert were a married couple who wanted to have a child and started considering surrogacy after doctors performed a hysterectomy on Crispina. Despite having gone through that procedure, Crispina's ovaries were still capable of producing eggs. When Anna Johnson heard about the couple's predicament from a coworker, she agreed to serve as a gestational surrogate for the Calverts.

Anna signed an agreement with the married couple relinquishing all parental rights in return for the Calverts' promise to pay her $10,000 and buy her a $200,000 life insurance policy on her life. After Anna became pregnant with one of Crispina's eggs fertilized with Mark's sperm, tension between the parties developed when the Calverts learned that Anna had failed to disclose that she had a history of miscarriages and stillbirths. For her part, Anna felt that the Calverts were backpedaling on their financial commitments to her. After Anna threatened to keep the child once it was born, the Calverts sued her, seeking a judicial declaration that they were the child's only parents. In response, Anna claimed that she, and not Crispina, was the child's legal mother.

Although lawyers in the field recognized the importance of the *Johnson* lawsuit, the general public paid little attention to the case, reflecting the relative lack of controversy generated by gestational surrogacy cases in the 1990s. This was in stark contrast to the media frenzy engendered by the New Jersey *Baby M.* case in the 1980s.

At issue in *Johnson* was whether the child could have, in effect, two mothers, one who was genetically related to the child and the other who gave birth. The California Supreme Court eventually ruled that the parties' intent determined who qualified as a parent. The court held that the child could not have two mothers because the Calverts had not intended to donate their ova and sperm to the surrogate mother; instead, they had consented to the placement of the fertilized egg in Anna's uterus so that she could give birth to a child whom they intended to raise. Similarly, at the time of conception, Anna intended to serve as a gestational surrogate and not as the child's parent after birth. As a result, California's high court concluded that Crispina, and not Anna, was the child's mother.

In her legal battle with her former partner Karen, Elizabeth Gardner argued to the same court that its earlier ruling in *Johnson* controlled her case. The trial court, after all, had made a factual finding that the two women had agreed, at the time of conception, that Elizabeth would be the sole parent of any child conceived with Karen's eggs. In the same way that intent had proven to be the "tiebreaker" in a dispute between a genetic mother and a gestational mother in *Johnson*, Elizabeth argued, the parties' preconception intent should prove dispositive in her case.

For her part, Karen's legal arguments placed great weight on her biological connection to the children. She also sought to distinguish *Johnson* by noting that Elizabeth and she, unlike the recipient and the donor in the earlier lawsuit, were a couple who together raised the children for more than five years.

From Karen's perspective, it was highly relevant that Elizabeth had permitted Karen to establish parental bonds with the children. Indeed, the conduct of both her partner and herself through the years reflected their joint intent to raise the children together.

The California Supreme Court ultimately sided with Karen, concluding that, as in *Johnson*, there had not been in this case a true *donation* of eggs because Karen did "not intend to simply donate her ova to [Elizabeth], but rather provided her ova to her lesbian partner with whom she was living so that [Elizabeth] could give birth to a child that would be raised in their joint home."[42] The high court rejected the analogy, accepted by the lower courts, between Karen and known sperm donors whose parental rights are legally terminated when they provide their sperm to a licensed physician. Sperm donors, the court noted, are not usually in relationships with the recipients and rarely plan on living with them in the same home where the children will be raised. All of this meant that Karen's genetic link with the children made her a legal parent to them.

▲

As we have seen, LGBT parenting advocates have consistently urged courts to move beyond considerations of biology when determining who qualifies as a parent. It is somewhat ironic, therefore, that the court in Karen Morris's case relied heavily on *biology* to grant parental status to a lesbian over the objections of her former partner. It is important, however, to distinguish the argument that biology should not be solely determinative of parenthood from the contention that biology should be irrelevant to that question. Supporters of lesbian and gay parenting have never made the latter claim.

It was indeed legally relevant that Karen provided her eggs for the in vitro fertilization, because having a biological link is *one* of the ways that an individual can *begin* to establish a parental relationship with a child. The crucial point made by LGBT parenting advocates over the last three decades is that having a biological link should be neither necessary nor sufficient to claim parentage status. If it were sufficient, then it would be impossible, for example, to extinguish the parental rights of known donors in alternative insemination cases. If it were necessary, then it would be impossible to legally recognize as parents individuals who have functioned as such for years despite the absence of a biological connection to the children.

Whether the biological link is relevant in determining parenthood depends on the context, a view that was accepted by the California Supreme Court in Karen Morris's case. If Karen had truly been an egg donor without any expectation that she would play an ongoing role in the lives of the recipient and the children, then her biological connection with the twins would not have been enough to confer on her parentage status. But for the court, it mattered a great deal that Karen and Elizabeth were partners who shared the home where they planned to raise the children.

Like with biology, the role that *intent* plays in determining parenthood should also depend on the context. It is not enough to contend that intent trumps all other considerations because the parties' intent can change over time, requiring a determination of whether a later-expressed intent on the question of parenthood (one revealed, for example, after the children are born) should modify an intent expressed prior to conception.

Elizabeth Gardner, relying heavily on the trial court's factual finding that both women, at the time of conception, intended for Elizabeth to be the sole parent, argued that once there is agreement between the parties on who will be the parent(s), there should not be a redetermination of parental status. Indeed, she claimed in her brief to the state supreme court that "it would be destabilizing for both child and parent if parentage could be redetermined over time, based on changes in domestic partners' relationships to each other or to the children, changes in domestic partners' intentions, or parents changing partners."[43]

Although this argument is not without some merit—one can imagine, for instance, a parent with consecutive domestic partners all of whom may potentially raise parentage claims—it ultimately calls for a legal definition of parenthood that is unduly rigid. In framing her case, Elizabeth essentially argued that the parties' original intent (i.e., the intent evinced prior to conception) should prevail in every instance. But as with biology, context is crucial in determining the role that intent should play in assigning parental status. Even if Karen and Elizabeth's original intent was that the latter would be the sole parent (a claim that Karen fiercely disputed, but which was found to be true by the trial court), that should not have precluded Karen from raising a parental claim if, as actually happened, she later functioned as a parent with the consent and encouragement of Elizabeth. Even if Elizabeth, while she permitted Karen to function as a parent, still held fast to the view that she was the only legal parent, the important point is that the twins, because of that permission, came to view Karen as a parent. The law should not allow a parent to rely on original intent to sever a later-established parental bond between her then partner and the children, any more than it should permit a parent to rely on the absence of a biological link between her former partner and the children to achieve the same goal.

The complexity of the legal issues surrounding the two main lawsuits explored in this chapter is evident not only from the role that biology and intent played in the determination of the parties' parentage status, but also from the ways that *all* the parties used the concept of estoppel to support their legal claims. The normative underpinning of the doctrine of estoppel is one of fairness—it is premised on the idea that once someone makes a decision that is relied on by others, it is unfair for that person to change her mind, even if initially she would have been legally entitled to make a different decision. Cases involving the provision (or donation) of sperm or eggs are particularly vexing because both sides often can raise plausible fairness arguments.

Estoppel plays a relatively straightforward role in cases, not involving donors, in which the former partner of a legal parent seeks to exercise parental rights. In those cases, as we saw in the previous chapter, the doctrine is relied on by only one side—that is, by individuals who contend that legal parents who consented to and encouraged their functioning as parents should be estopped from seeking to deny them parental rights. But in Karen and Elizabeth's case, both sides relied on the doctrine of estoppel to try to advance their legal claims. Karen argued that Elizabeth should be estopped from *trying to deny* her parental rights after the latter allowed her to develop a parental relationship with the children. For her part, Elizabeth contended that Karen should be estopped from *trying to claim* parental rights after the latter initially agreed that Elizabeth would be the sole parent.

Similarly, in the Tom Steel case, the sperm donor argued that the lesbian couple should be estopped from *trying to deny* him parental rights after they encouraged him to develop a relationship with the child. At the same time, the lesbian mothers argued that the sperm donor should be estopped from *trying to claim* parental rights after he initially agreed that they would be the child's only parents. In both cases, then, the courts had to grapple not with the question of *whether* the doctrine of estoppel applied, but with the issue of which party had the *better* estoppel argument.

The cases explored in this chapter show how complex the analysis can be in LGBT parenting cases involving the provision (or donation) of sperm or eggs. It is important to acknowledge that the complexities of these cases comes with a certain cost: the outcome of parenting litigation would undoubtedly be more certain if courts applied categorical rules (e.g., "biological links always trump other considerations" or "the original intent of parties trumps later expressed intent"). The advantage of such predictability is that it allows the adults to more easily know where they stand legally, which in turn reduces the need for litigation.

But the costs that accompany the application of categorical rules in these types of cases outweigh the benefits. To rely on categorical rules to determine parentage status fails to account for the multiple ways in which it is possible to construct and structure familial arrangements involving children. Categorical rules, in other words, ignore the reality of the lives of many children who are raised outside of households led by two married heterosexuals. A diminished degree of certainty and predictability is the price that we have to pay for avoiding formalistic and rigid parenting rules that do not account for the particular and differing contexts in which children are raised today.

▲

Planned LGBT families are formed in two principal ways. One, explored in this and in the previous chapter, involves the use of reproductive assistance, primarily alternative insemination and in vitro fertilization. The other main way is through regulatory mechanisms created and administered by the state, such as adoption and foster care.

The role played by the state in the cases discussed in this book so far has been generally an adjudicative one, as judges make individualized determinations regarding who is a parent and who is entitled to custody and visitation. In the context of foster care and adoptive parenting, the state plays the additional roles of regulator and administrator. This means, as we will see in the next chapter, that lesbian and gay litigants in foster care and adoption cases have sometimes found themselves in court battling government officials seeking to deny them the opportunity to become parents.

5

When the State Discriminates

In 1984, Don Babets and David Jean, a gay couple living in Boston, asked a friend to contact the Massachusetts Department of Social Services (DSS) to inquire whether their sexual orientation rendered them ineligible to serve as foster parents. After officials assured their friend that it did not, the couple attended a six-week foster care training program. They were also visited at home several times by a social worker who interviewed them for hours on end.

For most individuals, approval by the social worker after a home visit would have led to their certification as foster parents. But because Don and David were a gay couple, their application was forwarded to the department's headquarters in downtown Boston for special review. After several months went by, and after Don called on a weekly basis inquiring about the application's status, DSS finally issued them foster parent licenses.

Don, who was thirty-six and worked as an investigator for the Boston Fair Housing Commission, and David, who was thirty-two and worked as a nursing home administrator, had met nine years earlier on a blind date as Don was finishing an eight-year stint with the army. The two men hoped to adopt children some day but wanted to start with foster parenting as a way of proving to themselves, and to the Commonwealth of Massachusetts, that they could be good parents.

In April 1985, DSS placed two brothers in Don and David's care; the older boy was three years old, the younger one twenty-two months. The boys' mother, who was going through difficult times but hoped to regain custody of her sons later that year, consented in writing to the state's placement of her children with the gay couple.

For Don and David, the first two weeks with the boys in their home were nothing less than blissful, as the two men happily adjusted their routines to care for the energetic toddlers. But one day, as David was giving a friend a ride in his car, he shared with her the happy news that the state had placed two foster children in their home. To David's surprise, the friend, who was the wife of a local community activist by the name of Ben Haith, advised him to be careful because some neighbors might not approve of children living with a male couple.

Don and David had considered Ben Haith a friend; they had had him over for dinner several times, and David had given his daughter piano lessons. But a few days after David's conversation with Haith's wife, the community activist (who was planning on running for city council) contacted editors at the *Boston Globe* to complain that DSS had placed two young boys with a gay couple in his neighborhood.

The day after Haith contacted the newspaper, the *Globe* published a story on the foster care placement that focused mainly on the negative reactions by some of the gay couple's neighbors. Haith—who later ended his efforts to seek elected office after being criticized for contacting the newspaper in order to bring attention to his political aspirations—told the reporter that he was "completely opposed" to the placement, and that he saw "it ultimately as a breakdown of the society and its values and morals." Other neighbors, after being told of the placement by the *Globe*'s reporter, were also troubled. One person, described in the article as a "prominent lawyer," referred to the placement as "crazy," while another opined that "this situation falls below what is normal and healthy."[1]

On the morning the story appeared, the DSS commissioner called Don and David to assure them that the newspaper article would not lead the agency to take the children back. That commitment lasted about five hours. After Governor Michael Dukakis later that day ordered that authorities remove the boys, two government social workers showed up at the gay couple's doorstep—TV cameras in tow—and removed the crying and startled children from the home. The gay couple later explained in a statement that to see the children "leave us—angry, confused, and in tears—was one of the most difficult moments of our lives."[2]

The state placed the children with a (heterosexual) foster mother living in a town outside Boston. A few months later, the local district attorney announced that he was investigating a social worker's report that the boys may have been sexually abused by someone living in their new foster home.[3]

▲

In 1973, the National Gay Task Force—the organization cofounded by Bruce Voeller, a gay father profiled in chapter 2—began working with private child welfare agencies to find foster placements for gay teenagers in the homes of gay men in New York City. By the time the *New York Times* published a story describing the program in May 1974, about thirty boys aged twelve to seventeen, who described "themselves as homosexuals and who [were] unwanted by or unable to adjust to youth homes," had been placed under the program's auspices.[4]

In the early 1970s, gay organizations in several other cities, including Chicago, Los Angeles, and Minneapolis, worked with child welfare officials to place gay youth in the homes of gay men. There were also reported instances of foster care placements with lesbians, including one in Philadelphia in which "a 15-year-old transvestite male youth" was placed in the home of a lesbian couple.[5]

In 1974, the *Advocate*, a national gay magazine, reported that the publicity engendered by the custody case of Sandy Schuster and Madeleine Isaacson—lesbian mothers profiled in chapter 1—led several lesbians and gay men in Washington State to seek foster care licenses. The applications, in turn, produced a backlash as conservative activists urged the state to adopt a regulation prohibiting lesbians and gay men from serving as foster parents. One of those activists, who led an effort to gather more than seven thousand signatures in support of the regulation in a little over two weeks, claimed that gay people wanted to serve as foster parents to get state money to "support their lifestyle," and to make "contact with the youth of our country [in order to] drag them down to their sordid and sinful way of life."[6]

Although a coalition of progressive child advocacy organizations successfully lobbied against the proposed regulation, they could not prevent some judges from refusing to approve foster placements in gay households. This happened in Vancouver, Washington, in 1975, when child welfare authorities attempted to place a sixteen-year-old gay youth with a gay couple after the boy had spent two years living in institutions. When a judge found out about the proposed placement, he called for a hearing in his courtroom to consider the matter.

The administrators at the institution where the boy was living, as well as his social worker and a psychiatrist, testified that the child would benefit from the placement because the gay couple would be good foster parents and because there was no other family willing to take the openly gay boy into their home. In contrast, the local prosecutor's office, which opposed the placement, repeatedly suggested to the court that there was a real risk that the gay couple would "role-model [the] child into homosexuality" by, among other things, having sex in front of him.[7]

Several weeks after the trial ended, the judge issued an opinion ordering that the teenager be placed in the custody of the county juvenile detention facility until another family—a heterosexual one—could be found for him.

The opinion explained that "it is not a proper function of the state to encourage and foster deviant behavior. If this [proposed placement] were followed to a logical extreme, state action could be rationalized in placing promiscuous girls with prostitutes or psychopathic youths with the mentally ill."[8]

Despite judicial rulings such as this one, the placement of foster children in lesbian and gay households continued through the late 1970s and 1980s. Supporters of these placements received a considerable boost when the American Psychological Association in 1977, and the National Association of Social Workers a decade later, issued statements urging child welfare authorities not to discriminate based on parents' sexual orientation in making foster care placement decisions.

▲

In May 1985, Don Babets and David Jean, still reeling from the events of a week earlier when the state abruptly removed two foster children from their home, granted the *Boston Globe* an interview in which they criticized DSS for its actions. To the men, it made no sense for the agency to issue them foster care licenses after spending months evaluating their application only to then remove the children "hours after the media learned of the placement."[9] This suggested to the couple that the decision to take the boys away was driven by politics rather than by what was best for the children.

Ten days later, the Massachusetts House of Representatives approved a bill, by a vote of 112 to 28, that would ban the placement of foster children with lesbians and gay men. The provision stated that "a homosexual preference shall be considered a threat to the psychological and physical well-being of a child."[10] The bill was sent to the state senate, which never approved it because DSS soon announced that it had made changes to its foster care placement policy. From now on, the state would seek to place children only in "traditional family settings."[11] As part of this new policy, child welfare officials would ask everyone applying to serve as foster parents about their sexual orientation. Those who responded that they were lesbian or gay would be placed at the bottom of a priority list that had married heterosexual couples at the top. In addition, the agency announced that existing placements with lesbian and gay foster parents would be subject to a special, biannual review to determine whether the children should be removed from the homes.[12]

The new policy, which was drafted and instituted in a little over two weeks under the direct orders of Governor Dukakis, led to an outcry from the LGBT community, in Massachusetts and elsewhere. Activists in Boston formed a Gay and Lesbian Defense Committee to agitate against the changed policy, while the Civil Liberties Union of Massachusetts and the Gay & Lesbian Advocates & Defenders threatened a lawsuit. Several large demonstrations were held in front of the state capitol. Governor Dukakis found himself the subject of frequent protests—some outside his office and others outside his home—starting in 1985 and going all the way through 1988, when he secured the Democratic Party's nomination for president.

But the administration's new policy had powerful institutional supporters, including the Catholic Church and the *Boston Globe*. Archbishop Bernard Law—who would later be removed by the Vatican from his Boston post for failing to protect children from sexually abusive priests—urged that children be placed only with married heterosexual couples. In an editorial published two days after DSS announced its new policy, the *Globe* warned that "the state's foster-care program is not a place for social experimentation with nontraditional family settings. It should never be used, knowingly or unknowingly, as the means by which homosexuals who do not have children of their own . . . are enabled to acquire the trappings of traditional families."[13] Even Ellen Goodman, the stalwart liberal *Globe* writer who was otherwise critical of the decision to remove the children from Don and David's home, complained in her nationally syndicated column that "I have never understood the need of gay couples to define their relationships as 'family.'" She added, for good measure, that she was "uncomfortable with those gay women who deliberately go out to 'get' children on their own through artificial insemination."[14]

In early 1986, Don and David filed a lawsuit against the state claiming that the new foster care policy violated their rights to equal protection and privacy. In September of that year, a trial court judge found the policy unconstitutional. The litigation dragged on for three more years, in part because the state refused to turn over documents describing internal discussions during the days following the publication of the initial *Globe* story. In 1988, the state supreme court ordered government officials to make the documents available to the plaintiffs.[15] Those materials showed that Governor Dukakis and his staff had been driven by political considerations in drafting the new foster care policy.[16] Eighteen months after the high court issued its ruling, the state reached a settlement with Don and David, agreeing to change its foster care policy so that parenting experience—rather than sexual orientation or marital status—would be the most important factor in making foster care placement decisions.

In late 1990, the gay couple, elated by their victory but exhausted by their five-year battle with the Commonwealth of Massachusetts, moved to a rural part of the state, seeking peace and quiet. Less than two years later, that peace

Protestors in Brookline, Massachusetts, demonstrating near the home of Governor Michael Dukakis on Father's Day, 1985, against the state's antigay foster care policy. Photo by Ellen Shub. Used with permission.

and quiet came to a joyful end when they adopted four siblings simultaneously, all under the age of eight.

▲

The foster care controversy in Massachusetts led neighboring New Hampshire to enact a law in 1987 prohibiting lesbians and gay men from serving as foster care or adoptive parents. On the day the measure became law, state representative Mildred Ingram, who had been the main supporter of the bill, stated that "I'm not against homosexuals. They are adult people. They made their own choice and the only one they have to answer to is their maker. They can go on their merry way to hell if they want to. I just want them to keep their filthy paws off the children."17

New Hampshire was not the first state to enact a law prohibiting gay people from adopting. That distinction went to Florida ten years earlier. The Florida ban had its genesis in January 1977, when Dade County became the first southern municipality to enact a gay rights law. The ordinance, which prohibited employers, landlords, and places of public accommodation from discriminating based on sexual orientation, was hailed by the local gay community.

Many social conservatives, however, soon began pushing for its repeal, an effort that was led by Anita Bryant—a singer, a former runner-up to Miss

America in the 1950s, and a born-again Baptist. This apparently wholesome, all-American figure ended up conducting an antigay crusade driven by a vitriolic brand of rhetoric that had never been heard before and has rarely been matched since.

Bryant and her allies centered their campaign in favor of the ordinance's repeal on the need to protect children from gay people. Indeed, opponents of the law formed a group called "Save Our Children," which published ads in newspapers contending that "the recruitment of our children is absolutely necessary for the survival and growth of homosexuality—for since homosexuals cannot reproduce, they *must* recruit, *must* freshen their ranks."[18] During the repeal campaign, Bryant referred to gay people as "human garbage," while criticizing the ordinance as an attempt to "legitimize homosexuals and their recruitment of our children."[19]

Gay rights opponents collected more than sixty thousand signatures—six times the number required by law—in order to place a repeal referendum before voters in June 1977. The conservative activists also succeeded in assembling a broad coalition in support of the repeal, which included different religious denominations. The Roman Catholic archbishop of Miami, for example, distributed a pastoral letter urging parishioners to vote against the gay rights law, while some local rabbis signed a statement in support of the repeal. Bryant's success in mobilizing opposition to the ordinance also caught the attention of social conservative leaders across the country eager for national exposure—including a minister from Virginia by the name of Jerry Falwell—who descended into South Florida to assist in the repeal effort. In the end, the gay rights forces were overwhelmed by their opponents. On Election Day, county residents voted by a two-to-one margin to void the ordinance.

The political campaign in South Florida presenting homosexuality as a threat to children led the Florida legislature, that same year, to pass the nation's first statute prohibiting gay people from adopting. At the time the law was enacted, there had been only a handful of reported instances in the entire country of an openly lesbian or gay person adopting a child, and none of those had taken place in Florida. The statute, therefore, was not so much aimed at "protecting" children from gay people as sending a message of disapproval of homosexuality. As one of the measure's strongest supporters in the Florida legislature explained at the time, the law was meant to say to gay people that "we're really tired of you. We wish you would go back into the closet." The same legislator added that "the problem in Florida is that homosexuals are surfacing to such an extent that they're beginning to aggravate the ordinary folks, who have rights of their own."[20]

While Florida (in 1977) and New Hampshire (in 1987) enacted statutes banning gay adoption, the laws in the other states remained silent on the issue.[21] (One exception was New York, which in 1978 issued a regulation stating that adoption "applicants shall not be rejected solely on the basis of homosexuality.")[22] This regulatory void provided lesbians and gay men, especially those living in relatively tolerant parts of the country, with the opportunity to pursue adoption as a way of becoming parents.

One of the earliest reports of an adoption by an openly gay person in the United States appeared on the front page of the *Advocate* in August 1974. The article reported that a twelve-year-old boy, whom the social worker described as having "effeminate tendencies" and whose placement had been rejected by a married heterosexual couple, was adopted by an openly gay man in Southern California.[23]

In 1979, the gay media wrote about a gay couple in San Francisco—one a physician and the other a minister with the Metropolitan Community Church—that had jointly adopted a two-year-old boy.[24] This appears to have been the first time that a same-sex couple adopted a child anywhere in the country. Also that year, the *New York Times* reported that a gay minister in Catskill, New York, who lived with his partner, was permitted to adopt a thirteen-year-old boy.[25]

During the 1970s and early 1980s, there were other gay men, as well as lesbians, who adopted children, but many of them appear to have done so without revealing their sexual orientation. Since in most jurisdictions, prospective adoptive parents were not asked about their sexual orientation, it was possible for lesbians and gay men to refrain from volunteering information about their personal relationships without having to make false statements.

Instances in which officials denied the adoption applications of openly gay people served as clear disincentives for others to come out of the closet while seeking to become parents. In 1975, after Draffan McBride, a Scottish immigrant and a physician living in Arizona, applied as an openly gay man to adopt a child, child welfare authorities turned him down. He reapplied three years later, this time with his same-sex partner of eight years. That petition went before an Arizona trial judge who denied it because of the men's relationship. McBride later surmised that if he had not mentioned his homosexuality when he had applied as a single man, he would likely have been allowed to adopt. But he chose not to pursue that route, explaining that if "I keep things aboveboard and don't try to hide anything, then I have nothing to feel guilty about." In 1979, the state did permit a sixteen-year-old boy—

whose parents had thrown him out of their home after he told them he was gay—to live with McBride and his partner until the teenager enlisted in the army when he turned eighteen.[26]

A few years later, another Arizona court considered an adoption application submitted by a bisexual man. The application had been endorsed by his social worker and by the appropriate state agency. The court of appeals, however, affirmed a trial judge's denial of the application, in part because of the man's bisexuality. The court, after noting that the petitioner had testified that he might have a sexual relationship with a man in the future, pointed out that sodomy was a crime in Arizona. It then went on to conclude that it "would be anomalous for the state on the one hand to declare homosexual conduct unlawful and on the other [to] create a parent after that proscribed model, in effect approving that standard, inimical to the natural family, as head of a state-created family."[27]

But four years later, another court, this time the Ohio Supreme Court, became the first appellate court in the country to hold that the sexual orientation of an openly gay man did not legally preclude him from adopting.

▲

Lee Balser, a psychological counselor, first met a four-year-old boy by the name of Charlie when the Licking County (Ohio) Department of Human Services (DHS) in 1986 referred the child to his office. Up to that point, the little boy had had a difficult life. The previous year, his biological parents had voluntarily transferred custody of him and his two sisters to the county because they were unable to care for the children. In addition, Charlie had been diagnosed with leukemia, though the disease was then in remission after lengthy radiation and chemotherapy treatments. Furthermore, Charlie had learning disabilities, a speech impediment, and facial features that suggested he suffered from fetal alcohol syndrome.

Starting in July 1986, Lee met with Charlie during weekly counseling sessions aimed at helping the child deal with issues of anger and low self-esteem in preparation for a future adoption. Although Charlie responded well to the sessions, Lee was concerned that, every few months, DHS moved the boy from one foster home to another. It did not take an expert to see that what Charlie needed most was a stable home life, something that the foster care system seemed incapable of providing. It was then that Lee—who was becoming quite attached to the boy—started considering the possibility of adopting him.

Even though DHS had placed Charlie in its adoption registry shortly after his biological parents gave up custody of him the year before, no one had stepped forward expressing interest in adopting him. When Lee first started thinking about the possibility of doing so, he discussed the matter with his partner Tom Kuzma, a research scientist with a Ph.D. in astronomy, with whom he shared a home in Columbus. At first, Tom was unsure about whether he wanted to help raise a child. But after many conversations with Lee and after Tom started spending time with Charlie—in February 1987, DHS agreed that Charlie could visit regularly with the gay couple—he came to support the idea of Lee adopting the boy.

A few weeks later, Lee informally let officials at DHS know that he would be interested in adopting Charlie and suggested that the agency conduct a study of his home. Rather than doing so, DHS became more proactive in trying to find a permanent (heterosexual) home for the boy. In May 1987, it located a married, straight couple who expressed interest in adopting Charlie. But after the agency began taking steps to place Charlie with them, the couple changed their mind and decided not to go through with the adoption.

In the meantime, DHS moved Charlie yet again to a new foster home after he had difficulties in the home of a foster mother—who had fostered more than two hundred children for the county through the years—because her rigid parenting style did not mesh well with Charlie's behavioral problems. Knowing that he could provide the loving and stable home that the boy so desperately needed, and tired of waiting around for the agency, Lee in January 1988 filed a court petition seeking to adopt Charlie.

Since DHS had legal custody of the boy, it had to consent to the adoption. Every week following the filing of his petition, Lee called the agency to inquire whether it would provide its consent. And every week he was told that the matter was under advisement. Three months later, and only one day before the scheduled court hearing on Lee's adoption petition, the agency's executive director announced that it would oppose the adoption.

At the hearing, two psychologists testified on Lee's behalf. The first told the court that sexual orientation was irrelevant to the question of whether someone could be a good parent. The second testified that Lee and Charlie had developed a tight bond and that given Charlie's medical and emotional issues, he needed the stability, care, and love that Lee was willing and able to provide. After stating that Lee would be a good parent and that he could handle Charlie's behavioral problems, the expert witness added that "my concern isn't so much that Mr. Balser gets Charlie, but that Charlie gets Mr. Balser."[28] In addition, the guardian at litem assigned to represent Charlie recommended that Lee's adoption petition be granted.

The government's only witness was a DHS administrator who told the court that the agency had developed a profile of the type of family that it believed would be best suited to adopt Charlie: one that consisted of two parents who had prior parenting experience, a proven ability to deal with behavioral issues, and "a child-centered lifestyle."[29] The agency's position was that Lee did not meet most of its criteria. For example, the DHS administrator told the court that Lee did not lead "a child-centered lifestyle" because he had been a single man—his five-year relationship with Tom apparently did not count—all his adult life. She also expressed concern that "society's view of a homosexual family may make it difficult for homosexual parents to access and receive" the type of medical and educational services that a special needs child like Charlie required.[30] Finally, the witness testified that the agency had contacted other child welfare agencies in Ohio and elsewhere, only to learn that none of them had ever approved an adoption by an openly gay person.

It was not clear how the judge was going to rule on the adoption petition, especially after he asked Lee at one point whether "if you adopt Charlie, are you going to turn him into a homosexual?"[31] (Lee answered that the boy's sexual orientation would be something for him to figure out on his own when he grew older.) But several weeks after the hearing, the judge issued an order approving Lee's adoption petition. The government immediately appealed and successfully got a stay of the trial court's ruling.

▲

The law in Ohio, like that of most states, was silent on the question of whether gay people could adopt. The Ohio adoption statute permitted both married couples and unmarried persons to adopt. Since Lee was not married, and since the statute did not address the question of sexual orientation, it seemed clear that he was not, as a matter of law, prohibited from adopting. But the Ohio Court of Appeals, in a poorly reasoned opinion, overturned the lower court's ruling after concluding that Ohio law, in fact, categorically prevented gay people from adopting children.[32]

The court provided two rationales in support of its *reading into* the statute a gay adoption ban that had not been enacted by the legislature. First, the judges opined that "homosexuality and adoption are inherently mutually exclusive" because "homosexuality negates procreation." The relevancy of this observation, however, was not clear since adoption and procreation are two *different* ways of becoming a parent. In fact, many heterosexual couples who choose to adopt do so precisely because they cannot procreate. The ability to procreate, therefore, does not distinguish those couples from lesbians and gay men interested in adopting.

Second, the court noted that a child raised by "announced homosexuals" will not be able "to pass as the natural child of the adoptive 'family' or to adapt to the community by quietly blending in free from controversy and stigma." According to the court, "adoption imitates nature," which meant that "a fundamental rationale for adoption is to provide a child with the closest approximation to a birth family that is available."

The court's understanding of adoption, while once widely shared, had by the late 1980s become dated and anachronistic. By then, few in the child welfare and adoption fields still believed that it was crucial for adopted children to "blend in" with their adopted families so that outsiders would not know that they had been adopted. The Ohio Supreme Court had itself made this point clear when it ruled in 1974 that a white couple could adopt an African American child, a decision that was consistent with one from twelve years earlier in which the court permitted a white man and his Asian wife to adopt a Latino child.[33]

As suspect as the court's reasoning was, its ruling meant that Lee would not be able to adopt Charlie unless the Ohio Supreme Court reversed. In arguing its case before that court, the government contended that it would not be in Charlie's best interests "to be adopted into the home of two male homosexuals living as husband and wife in a relationship they consider a marriage." The government lawyers insisted that gay people were not the kinds of "parental role models" that children needed.[34]

But for the Ohio Supreme Court, the legal issue was straightforward: it was up to the legislature to decide whether gay people were eligible to adopt. The legislature had not explicitly prohibited lesbians and gay men from adopting; instead, it had expressly concluded that *any* unmarried adult could file an adoption petition, one that should be approved if doing so was in the child's best interests. As a result, the state high court ruled that the court of appeals had erred when it categorically prohibited an entire group of individuals from adopting in the absence of a legislative mandate.[35]

The law required adoption petitions to be considered on a case-by-case basis depending on the particular circumstances of both the child and the prospective parent. Since Lee was not, as a gay man, legally precluded from adopting, and since the trial court had found that the adoption would be in Charlie's best interests, the state supreme court ordered that the adoption decree be issued.

It bears noting that not every justice on the Ohio Supreme Court joined the majority opinion. The sole dissenting justice would have sided with the government, but would have relied on a different—though not any less problematic—rationale than the one embraced by the court of appeals. This justice would have denied the adoption petition because Lee Balser was a gay man who, despite being HIV negative, was at risk (the justice believed) of being infected with the virus in the future, which in turn supposedly placed Charlie at risk of getting AIDS. The dissenting justice noted that the boy's immune system was already compromised because of the leukemia treatment. Acquiring HIV, the justice feared, would only further compromise the boy's immune system.

Although the dissenting opinion did not carry the day, it is nonetheless indicative of the extent to which some judges were willing to go to deny LGBT people the opportunity to become parents. By the time the Ohio Supreme Court issued its opinion in 1990, it was widely understood that HIV was not transmitted through casual household contact. Yet, this did not prevent the dissenting justice from concluding that a gay man—even one who was HIV negative—should be prevented from adopting a child.

▲

After the Ohio Court of Appeals reversed his ruling allowing Lee to adopt Charlie, the trial judge granted temporary custody of the boy to Lee's sister Edna Balser until the state supreme court could review the case, a wait that lasted fifteen months. The court of appeals' ruling had been so adamant in its opposition to the idea that gay people should be permitted to adopt that Lee, Tom, Edna, and Lee's mother spent many hours discussing how it might be possible to keep Charlie in the family if that ruling was upheld. The only way of achieving that goal seemed to be for Edna to adopt Charlie. So a month after the court of appeals' decision, Edna filed a petition to adopt the seven-year-old boy.

In the end, that adoption was not necessary because the state supreme court ruled that Lee's sexual orientation was not a legal impediment to his adopting the child. The court's decision cleared the way for Lee (and Tom) to take the boy into their home to care for him permanently while experiencing the unique joys and satisfactions of parenthood. As an emotional Lee put it at the time, "there's something special about a kid putting his arms around you and kissing you and saying, 'good night, daddy.'"[36]

▲

Although everyone involved in assessing Lee Balser's adoption petition, from the trial judge to the county welfare officials, knew his partner would play an important (even parental) role in Charlie's life, Tom did not join Lee's petition. That Tom did not also seek to adopt the boy was hardly surprising: it was difficult enough in the 1980s to get courts to approve an adoption petition brought by an openly gay man; to add his same-sex partner to the petition diminished the likelihood of approval even more, since the issuance of the adoption decree might be perceived as judicial condoning of the same-sex relationship.

Joint adoptions by lesbian and gay couples were rare before the mid-1990s. ("Joint adoptions" are those in which two individuals, neither of whom is already a legal parent of a child, become his or her parents simultaneously. Such adoptions should be distinguished from "second-parent adoptions." In those cases, there is already a legal parent and the question is whether the parent's unmarried partner can become a second parent through adoption.) But as a growing number of child welfare officials, social workers, and judges grew more comfortable with adoptions by individual lesbians and gay men, the push soon came for the recognition of joint adoptions. One of the earliest and most important joint adoption cases took place in New Jersey.

When Michael Galluccio and Jon Holden, a gay couple in their early thirties, first decided to try to become parents in 1994, they were advised by a child placement specialist with the New Jersey Division of Youth and Family Services (DYFS) to settle for being foster parents because state officials would never allow a same-sex couple to adopt together. Since this was not a problem for the couple—the two men were unsure whether they wanted to commit to permanent parenthood anyway—they went ahead and enrolled in the state's foster care licensing program. During that process, in response to inquiries by officials, the couple made it clear that they would gladly accept a child with special needs.[37]

Six months later, after they were certified as foster parents, DYFS placed a twelve-week baby boy by the name of Adam in their home. The identity of the child's father was not known. The mother was a heroin and cocaine user who was HIV positive. Adam was born prematurely and spent the first few days of his life in an intensive care unit after testing positive for HIV antibodies. He also had respiratory problems, cardiac arrhythmia, and a hole in his heart's left ventricle (a condition that doctors believed would heal on its own). For the first six weeks of his life, Adam was given the AIDS drug AZT with the hope that the virus would not take hold in his little body. He was also on several other medications, including one that helped him cope with the tremors and seizures caused by the withdrawal from heroin and cocaine that he experienced once he was no longer connected to his mother's bloodstream.

Although Michael and Jon had thought, before Adam arrived in their home, that being foster parents would be enough for them, once they started caring for and bonding with the baby, they quickly decided that they wanted to keep him permanently. Concerned about what the placement specialist had told them the year before about their ineligibility to adopt, they made inquiries with Adam's social workers and other state employees involved in overseeing his care. This time, they were assured by everyone at DYFS with whom they spoke that both men would be able to adopt Adam together.

But after they officially requested that DYFS consent to the adoption so that they could file an adoption petition in court, the agency informed them that its employees' prior statements had been mistaken because agency policy prohibited unmarried couples from adopting jointly. State officials were willing to consent to Michael's adoption of Adam, but not to Jon's.

DYFS's sudden reversal left the gay couple with an excruciatingly difficult decision to make. They could proceed with a single-parent adoption, which would provide many benefits to Adam, including making it much more difficult for state officials to remove the boy from his home. It would also permit Adam, who needed constant medical treatment and attention, to be added to Michael's generous employer-provided health insurance. (As a child in the foster care system, Adam was covered by Medicaid, but as Michael and Jon learned soon after the boy was placed in their home, many of the doctors with the best reputations did not accept Medicaid patients because of that program's low payment rates.)

While there were good reasons for proceeding with Michael's adoption of Adam, it was also the case that the two men had jointly cared for the boy for almost a year while nursing him to good health. They both considered themselves Adam's parents, and it seemed like a betrayal of the boy for Jon not to join in the adoption petition. In addition, they were worried about what would happen to Adam if Michael, after adopting him on his own, died suddenly. There would be no guarantee that the state would then permit Jon to continue raising the child.

The couple did have the option of adopting Adam consecutively. Michael, in other words, could file an adoption petition on his own first, and if it was granted, Jon could file his. This was possible because New Jersey courts had recently started approving second-parent adoptions.[38] But there were significant drawbacks to this option: not only would doing a second adoption be more expensive, but the problems associated with the failure to recognize Jon as a legal parent would remain in place for the several months—and perhaps longer—that it would take to complete the second-parent adoption. After giving the matter much consideration, the couple decided to pursue the joint adoption by trying to persuade the agency, through letters and phone calls, to change its mind and allow both men to adopt together.

Around this time, Michael and Jon received the terrible news that Adam's biological mother had died of a drug overdose. Only a few weeks later, DYFS proposed that the couple take in another baby boy by the name of Andrew. Andrew's mother—who, like Adam's late mother, was HIV positive and a drug user—had given birth to the premature baby and then checked herself out of the hospital, leaving the child behind. The baby was now ten weeks old, still in the hospital, and had not been visited by any family members.

By now, Adam was almost a year old and his health was finally stable. Michael and Jon worried that they might not be able to cope physically and emotionally with taking in a second child, especially one who was just as sick as Adam had once been, while at the same time trying to pressure DYFS to allow them to adopt Adam together. It was clear, however, that Andrew desperately needed a home. As a result, despite their qualms, the couple accepted the placement.

In the end, Andrew remained in their home for only two months because the child's grandmother stepped forward and requested custody of the boy. The agency's mismanagement of the case—it had not known there was a grandmother who might be willing to take the boy—created further emotional turmoil for the gay couple. But as foster parents, they could not refuse the state's demand that they turn the child over. The whole incident only reinforced in their minds the need for *both* of them to adopt Adam as soon as possible.

The gay couple continued making inquiries of the agency regarding whether it would make an exception to its policy and permit them to adopt together. Every time they were turned down, the couple moved up the bureaucratic ladder another notch, until finally they heard back from the commissioner of the Department of Human Services, who (like every other state official before him) gave them the same answer: no.

It was now clear that if Michael and Jon were going to be able to adopt Adam, they would have to take the state to court. The couple contacted the ACLU seeking its assistance, and the organization agreed to represent them. The ACLU lawyers promptly wrote DYFS, warning officials that they would have a lawsuit in their hands if they insisted in prohibiting the two gay men from adopting jointly.

Incredibly, at the same time that DYFS was refusing the men's requests to allow them to adopt Adam together, it continued its efforts to try to place additional foster children—all of them HIV positive—in their home. The agency's requests exposed the contradictions of its own policies: on the one hand, it would not allow the men to adopt jointly; on the other, its officials knew perfectly well that they were providing excellent care to Adam, and that they could do the same for other children in need. The problem was not that the agency had doubts about Michael and Jon's ability to be good parents—instead, the problem was that child welfare officials did not want to be perceived as condoning adoptions by gay couples.

In the months that followed, Michael and Jon refused three additional placements of baby boys after concluding that they needed to settle the matter of Adam's adoption before accepting new children. But their resolve gave way when the state came back with another proposed placement, this time of a baby girl. The child's name was Madison; she was born prematurely and had tested positive at birth for the HIV antibodies and for heroin. The prospect of raising a baby girl, along with the little boy who was already in their home, proved too irresistible for the two men to turn down.

A few months after taking in Madison, the couple was elated to learn that Adam, as HIV-positive children sometimes do, had seroreverted to being HIV negative. While the boy had had HIV antibodies in his bloodstream for many months after his birth, they were there in response to his mother's HIV. Adam, it turned out, did not have the actual virus.

In the spring of 1997, the New Jersey attorney general sent the couple's lawyers a letter stating that the government was now willing to make a one-time exception to its policy regarding adoption by unmarried couples by not objecting to Michael and Jon's petition to jointly adopt Adam. The letter went on to explain that, although the state would not stand in the way of this particular adoption, it would not affirmatively support the petition either, thus leaving it to a judge to approve or disapprove of the adoption without a state recommendation.

The state's decision on how to handle Adam's adoption left Michael and Jon with another difficult decision to make. They could accept the attorney general's offer and proceed with what they had wanted all along, which was to file an adoption petition jointly, in the hope that a judge would approve it. Or they could continue with their plan of suing the state. If they won the suit, not only would they be able to proceed with their adoption of Adam (and later of Madison), but it would also mean that unmarried couples, both gay and straight, across the state would be able to adopt jointly.

After mulling it over, the two men decided that there was more at stake than just their adoption of Adam. The state's policy of prohibiting unmarried couples from adopting jointly was hurting children because it unnecessarily denied countless foster children the opportunity to be adopted by two parents who could provide stable and nurturing homes for them. As a result, Michael and Jon decided to sue.

In their dealings with the state up to this point, the couple had engaged in quiet, behind-the-scenes efforts to try to persuade DYFS to change its policy. But the time for discrete lobbying was over. It was now necessary to publicize their fight with the state, which the couple did by holding press conferences, granting media interviews, and telling anyone who would listen that New Jersey's restrictive adoption policy was harming children.

In the meantime, the ACLU filed a class action lawsuit, with Michael and Jon serving as lead plaintiffs, challenging the constitutionality of the state's adoption policy. The gay couple also filed a separate petition in court seeking to adopt jointly. The former, more complicated, legal case claimed that the policy violated the constitutional rights of unmarried couples, both gay and straight, to the equal protection of the law. The issue in the latter case was the more straightforward one of whether the adoption of Adam by both Michael and Jon was in his best interests. Both cases were assigned to superior court judge Sybil Moses.

Everyone involved in the case knew that if Moses ruled favorably on the adoption petition, she might be open to the possibility of later striking down the state's policy as unconstitutional. In contrast, if she ruled against Michael and Jon on their adoption petition by concluding that it would not advance the child's welfare, it was unlikely that she would rule against the state in the class action suit.

In October 1997, Judge Moses ruled that Michael and Jon could jointly adopt Adam. Although that ruling focused on the specific circumstances of the proposed adoption and did not address the constitutionality of the state's policy, the judge was now on record in holding that a joint adoption by a gay couple was in the best interests of a child. This made it entirely possible that she would proceed to strike down the policy after concluding that there was no valid justification for excluding all unmarried couples from the pool of individuals eligible to adopt.

Fearing that possibility, the state decided two months later to settle the class action lawsuit by agreeing to revise its adoption policies to allow unmarried couples to adopt jointly. In doing so, New Jersey became one of the first states in the country to institute an explicit policy providing same-sex couples equal standing with heterosexual married couples when it came to adopting children.

On the day that Judge Moses issued her ruling approving their joint adoption of Adam, Jon had told the gathered media outside the courtroom—with Michael by his side, holding their son in his arms—that "we are so grateful for what has happened today. We're a family now."[39] But the struggle by both

Jon Holden (*right*) and Michael Galluccio with their son Adam at a press conference in 1997 announcing the settlement of their adoption lawsuit against the state of New Jersey. Used with permission of the *Star-Ledger* (Newark).

men to adopt their son had always been about more than just their family. As Michael said at a press conference held two months later to announce their settlement agreement with the state, "this is a victory about goodness and equality. It is a victory for all families."[40]

▲

In the early 1980s, as the number of lesbians having children through alternative insemination started growing, lawyers working with lesbian mothers—including Donna Hitchens in San Francisco, Allison Mendel in Anchorage, and Nancy Polikoff in Washington, D.C.—began discussing among themselves how to help the female partners of biological mothers attain equal parental status. As the lawyers brainstormed about how to accomplish this, they kept coming back to the law of adoption.

When the lawyers reread adoption statutes with lesbian couples in mind, they identified some potential difficulties. The adoption laws of all the states required that the rights of the legal parents be terminated before a child could be adopted. This presented a problem for the lawyers because their clients did not want the biological mother's parental rights terminated; instead, the goal was *to add* her partner as a second parent.

There was one exception to the termination requirement, one that allowed the parents' *spouses* to adopt their children without first terminating their parental rights. Although it was possible to argue that courts should treat same-sex couples who were raising children together as if they were spouses for purposes of adoption law, it was highly unlikely that courts in the 1980s would do so. Indeed, lawyers working with lesbian and gay parents from the 1970s on generally sought to separate parent-child issues from relationship-recognition ones. This allowed the attorneys to emphasize to judges that the cases were about protecting the relationship between adults and children rather than about the legal validation or recognition of relationships between adults.

Faced with the challenges presented by the wording of the adoption statutes, Hitchens, Mendel, Polikoff, and a handful of other lawyers came up with a potential solution: what if the biological mother, in effect, sought to adopt her own child at the same time that her partner filed an adoption petition? Although this would mean that the biological mother's rights would be terminated, she would then be immediately recognized, along with her partner, as an adoptive parent of the child.

But there were also difficulties with this way of proceeding, starting with the fact that there were no precedents for the proposition that parents could adopt their own children. Furthermore, although all jurisdictions allowed married couples to adopt, and many permitted single people to do the same, it was unclear under the laws of most states whether unmarried couples could adopt together. In the end, all these complicated legal issues would have to be worked out, case by case and jurisdiction by jurisdiction, in the courts.

▲

One of the first times that a judge recognized a second-parent adoption, and wrote an opinion backing it up, was in the case of Laura Solomon and Victoria Lane.[41] The two women, both of whom were professional educators working with disabled and emotionally troubled children in Washington, D.C., met in 1979 when Laura was twenty-seven and Victoria twenty-nine. The following year, they moved in together, and in 1983, before a large gathering of family and friends, they participated in a commitment ceremony.

The two women, early on in their relationship, decided they wanted children. They at first tried to adopt a child, but when that effort proved unsuccessful, they decided that Laura would be inseminated with sperm from an anonymous donor. In 1985, Laura gave birth to a baby girl, whom the couple named Tessa. The two women gave the child their combined surnames to reflect the fact that they both considered themselves to be her parents and they wanted others to do the same. After Tessa was born, the couple began raising her together, dividing child-care responsibilities between themselves and jointly making all decisions about her welfare.

When Tessa was four years old, the couple decided to bring a second child into their home. In 1989, Victoria traveled to Nicaragua and adopted a baby girl, whom the coupled named Maya. As with Tessa, the two women gave Maya each of their surnames and began raising her together.

One concern that all couples in this situation have is what would happen if one of them were to die suddenly. Only a surviving legal parent is presumptively entitled to custody. This means that if a child has one legal parent and that parent dies, it makes the child a legal orphan. The only way of assuring that the child will be able to continue living with the surviving member of the couple is if he or she adopts the child.

All of Laura and Victoria's family members were supportive of their relationship and of their decision to raise children together. As a result, Tessa and Maya were fully integrated into the women's extended families, with no one differentiating between them according to biology, adoption, or which mother was the legal parent. It was therefore unlikely that a family member would petition the court for custody if one of the women were to die. Furthermore, the couple had entered into a parenting agreement, which in addition to expressing their intent to raise the children together, also named each other as their legal child's guardian in case of death. Nonetheless, there was a peace of mind that would come only with knowing that they were both the legal parents of both their daughters.

Other benefits would follow if the law were to recognize the relationship that the lesbian couple had with both girls. Each child would be able to inherit property from both mothers (as well as from the families of both women.) Each child would also be eligible to receive Social Security survival benefits and health insurance coverage from both women. In addition, third parties (such as schools and hospitals) would have to honor decisions made on their behalf by both women. Finally, if the mothers' relationship were to end, the children would benefit from rights of access to and support from both parents.

It was also the case that, as matters stood then, Tessa and Maya were legal strangers to each other. This was so despite the fact that they were being raised in the same home as sisters by the same two parents. Only the recognition of parental rights over both children by both women could avoid the confusion and uncertainty that the two girls would experience when they grew older and learned that the law did not recognize their relationship as sisters.

In 1982, before Laura and Victoria had children, they joined a group in Washington, D.C., consisting of lesbians who were considering having children. There they met and befriended Nancy Polikoff, a lesbian lawyer who had been a founding member of the Washington, D.C., Feminist Law Collective and was among the earliest legal advocates for lesbian mothers. Several years later, after the couple started raising their two daughters, they asked Polikoff to draft and file second-parent adoption petitions on their behalf. Polikoff—who was by then a law professor at American University—believed that Laura and Victoria's case would be a good second-parent adoption test case because the two women were so clearly committed to each other and to their children.

In the summer of 1990, Polikoff filed two petitions with the Superior Court of the District of Columbia on behalf of her clients, one to jointly adopt Tessa and another to jointly adopt Maya. The district's Department of Human Services (DHS), after speaking to references and conducting a study of the couple's home, found that the two women "are caring persons who express interest in the overall well-being of the adoptees and who are providing them with good care."[42]

Despite this finding, DHS recommended to the court that the adoption petitions be denied based on its lawyers' view that the granting of an adoption petition filed by a party who was not married to the legal parent required the termination of the latter's parental rights. In other words, under the lawyers' interpretation of the District of Columbia's adoption statute, the only way for each woman to adopt the other's child was if her partner's parental rights were first terminated. The lawyers also believed that the adoption petitions could not be granted because the adoption statute did not contain an explicit provision authorizing an adoption by two individuals of the same sex.

After DHS came out against the proposed adoptions, Polikoff wrote directly to Mayor Sharon Pratt Dixon urging her to review the issue personally. In the letter, Polikoff explained that her two clients had been together for more than ten years and were raising the children jointly. Polikoff added that if DHS's position on her client's adoption petitions did not change, it would reflect poorly on the mayor, who had recently been elected after campaigning as a strong supporter of gay rights. Although Polikoff was not asking that Dixon endorse all adoptions by lesbians and gay men, she did request that her administration support a reading of the adoption statute that would permit judges to grant adoption petitions filed by unmarried couples if doing so was in the best interests of the children.

The letter worked. Several weeks later, after the mayor's office asked DHS to reconsider its position, it filed a supplemental report with the court in which it recommended that the adoption petitions be granted.

▲

The facts in second-parent adoption cases are rarely in dispute, and Laura and Victoria's case was no exception. The record in the case was replete with evidence regarding the lesbian couple's committed and stable relationship and their ability to provide the girls with much love and good care. There is also usually little dispute that the children in question would benefit from having two legal parents. As trial judge Geoffrey Alprin eventually concluded, the couple's claims that Tessa and Maya would benefit legally and emotionally from the court's approval of the adoption petitions had "overwhelming record support."[43]

Instead, the issues in most second-parent adoption cases are almost always purely legal ones of statutory interpretation. Although DHS had originally contended that the adoption statute did not permit two individuals of the same sex to adopt the same child, Polikoff noted in her legal papers that the only explicit restriction in the law itself was a provision that prohibited married individuals from adopting a child unless their spouses joined in the petition. There was no explicit provision prohibiting two unmarried individuals, regardless of their sex, from adopting together. And in the absence of such a provision, there was no statutory impediment to Laura and Vanessa's filing adoption petitions that would make both of them the legal parents of both girls.

Potentially more problematic for Polikoff's clients was the termination of parental rights provision in the D.C. adoption statute. That provision stated that after an adoption decree is granted, "all rights and duties . . . between the adoptee [and] his natural parents . . . are cut off."[44] In dealing with this provision, Polikoff argued that its application was discretionary rather than mandatory, because the legislature could not have intended for the rights and obligations of the "natural" parent to be terminated in every adoption case regardless of whether doing so was in the best interests of the children. The provision in question, Polikoff explained in her legal papers, protected the welfare of children in cases in which the "adoptive parents and the adoptee will be forever strangers with the biological parents."[45] But this was clearly not the case in a proposed adoption of children by two individuals who intended for the same family unit that existed before the adoption to remain in place after the adoption.

Judge Alprin eventually agreed with Polikoff's analysis, noting in an opinion issued in August 1991 that "it would be unfortunate if the court were compelled to conclude that adoptions so clearly in the best interests of the prospective adoptees could not be granted because of a literal reading of a statutory provision obviously not intended to apply to the situation presented in these cases."[46] The judge also pointed out that the "cut-off" provision, according to the statute itself, did not apply to adoption petitions filed by stepparents. Alprin concluded that it would be as inappropriate to require the termination of the "natural" parent's rights in a case involving a lesbian couple in a committed relationship as it would be in a case in which a stepparent sought to adopt the child of his or her spouse.

With their legal victory in hand, Laura and Victoria now had the peace of mind in knowing that they were each the legal parents of both of their daughters. Unfortunately, that sense of security was tested in the most tragic of ways two years later. One day, while Victoria was driving her car with her two daughters in the backseat, a sudden and violent rainstorm hit. The fierce winds caused a large tree limb to fall, smashing through the windshield and striking Victoria with great force. Although the children were not harmed, Victoria was severely injured. She survived many hours of surgery but died two weeks later of an infection.

Victoria's tragic death would have left four-year-old Maya an orphan, an unsettling possibility that was avoided only because Laura had adopted her. That adoption also meant that Tessa (and not just Maya) received Social Security death benefits after Victoria's death. This provided Laura with additional funds to take care of the girls' needs after the loss of Victoria's income. As difficult as it was for Laura and her two daughters to cope with Victoria's death, the second-parent adoption worked as intended by providing stability, continuity, and economic benefits to the survivors. As Judge Alprin put it after Victoria's death, "it is tragic that we had to have such obvious and direct evidence of the need" for the second-parent adoption.[47]

▲

Since the government had not objected to the granting of the adoption petitions, there was no one to appeal Judge Alprin's ruling in Laura and Victoria's case. A possible appellate opinion on the question of second-parent adoption was a double-edged sword for LGBT rights advocates in the nation's capital. On the one hand, if the District of Columbia Court of Appeals were to approve such adoptions, trial judges in the city would be required to evaluate second-parent adoption petitions as they did all other adoption petitions—that is, by keeping the best interests of the children in mind. (As it stood now, although other trial judges could follow Alprin's ruling if they found his legal analysis persuasive, they were not required to do so.) On the other hand, an appellate ruling prohibiting second-parent adoptions would mean that such adoptions would not be available to any same-sex couples living in the district unless—and this was highly unlikely in the early 1990s—the legislature (either Congress or the city council) got involved by amending the statute to make the adoptions possible. The opportunity for appellate review arose in 1994 when District of Columbia trial court judge Susan Winfield ruled that the members of a gay couple could not both be recognized as the legal parents of a child whom they were jointly raising.

Bruce Moffit and Mark Dalton, both lifelong Catholics in their late twenties, met in 1990 at a church service sponsored by Dignity, an LGBT Catholic organization. After dating for a few months, they moved in together and began thinking about becoming parents. In 1991, the couple placed an advertisement in a newspaper announcing that they were looking to adopt, an ad that was read by Sylvia Leffs, a young African American woman who was several months pregnant. Sylvia arranged to meet with the two white gay men and liked them immediately. After several meetings, she told them that she would give them her child to raise after she gave birth. She also moved in with Bruce and Mark for the last few months of her pregnancy because she was not getting along with her mother at home.

Sylvia gave birth to a baby girl she named Hillary in August 1991. Three months later, she signed a form consenting to the adoption of her child. (Hillary's biological father could not be found and his consent was waived.) A day after that, Bruce filed a petition in court to adopt the girl. After a favorable recommendation by the Department of Human Services, Judge Winfield in 1993 granted the adoption, knowing that Hillary would be raised by both Bruce and his partner Mark in their home.

Since the gay couple had always intended to raise a child together, they jointly filed a petition to adopt Hillary two months after Judge Winfield granted Bruce's petition. But this time around, the judge denied the petition. Judge Winfield recognized that the second-parent adoption would be in the girl's best interests. She also acknowledged that Hillary would continue to live with, and be cared by, the two men regardless of whether she granted the adoption petition. But in her view, the adoption statute did not permit two unmarried individuals to adopt the same child.

While Judge Alprin had held that the statute's failure to explicitly address whether an unmarried couple could adopt together meant that such an adoption was not prohibited by law, Judge Winfield reached the opposite conclusion by holding that the absence of an explicit statutory authorization meant that the adoption petition could not be granted. Winfield reasoned that since adoption had not existed at common law and was entirely a legislative creation, the adoption law had to be read narrowly. Otherwise, she believed that the court, in effect, would be improperly legislating by expanding the scope of the statute. She added that "the Legislature could not have foreseen the occurrence of the societal changes which have drastically altered our notions of what constitutes a 'normal' family. To hold that the Adoption Code provides a remedy for petitioners' problem is to impute an intent to the Legislature that it is highly unlikely to have held."[48]

When Bruce and Mark decided to appeal Winfield's ruling to the court of appeals in 1994, they turned to Polikoff to handle their case. In her brief to the appellate court, Polikoff made the same arguments that she had successfully raised more than three years earlier in Laura Solomon and Victoria Lane's case. In doing so, she urged the court to reject Judge Winfield's narrow and formalistic interpretation of the statute, one that required that the legislature have specifically contemplated the issue of second-parent adoptions before Bruce and Mark could both become Hillary's legal parents. Polikoff asked the court to instead focus on the statute's overarching purpose, which was to advance the best interests of the children.

The appellate court did precisely that a few months later when it issued a thirty-page opinion rejecting Winfield's restrictive interpretation of the statute.[49] Noting that it had in the past called for a liberal construction of the adoption law in order to effectuate its purposes, the court held that the appropriate approach was to interpret the statute in ways that would advance Hillary's best interests. Those interests, the court concluded, would not be promoted through the judicial imposition—in the absence of an explicit statutory provision—of a rule barring all unmarried couples like Bruce and Mark from adopting a child like Hillary. Instead, Hillary's welfare would be better promoted if the law recognized what was already in fact the case: that the young girl had two fathers who cared for her and who loved her very much.

Bruce and Mark's victory before the court of appeals caught the attention of conservative members of Congress, the body that has ultimate legislative authority over the District of Columbia. Beginning in 1995, some members of the House of Representatives tried to attach an amendment to the district's appropriation bill that would prohibit unmarried couples from adopting together. For several years in a row, Polikoff worked with the Human Rights Campaign and other LGBT rights groups to defeat the amendment. Those efforts helped to keep it from being voted out of committee and onto the floor of the House.

But in 1999, amendment supporters brought the measure directly to the floor and it passed the House. The Clinton administration, however, made it clear behind the scenes that it opposed the provision, and it was dropped from the final district appropriation bill when the House's version was reconciled with that of the Senate. This meant that same-sex couples raising children together in the nation's capital continued to have the option of strengthening and protecting their families through second-parent adoptions.

▲

By the time the court of appeals issued its ruling in Bruce Moffit and Mark Dalton's case in 1995, the highest courts of Massachusetts and Vermont had already authorized second-parent adoptions.[50] But some courts had refused to do so. The year before, the Wisconsin Supreme Court had held that a same-sex couple could not adopt the same child.[51] The court reasoned that since the legislature had explicitly created only one exception, that of stepparents, to the requirement that the rights of all legal parents be terminated before an adoption petition could be approved, it must have intended for that exception to be exclusive of all others. As a result, the lesbian partner of a legal parent was not allowed to adopt the latter's child even though everyone involved with the case, including the trial judge and the supreme court justices, recognized that the adoption would have been in her best interests.

But most appellate courts that have since grappled with the issue of second-parent adoptions have approved them.[52] And in two states (Colorado and Connecticut) in which appellate courts refused to recognize second-parent adoptions, the legislatures later enacted statutes explicitly doing so.[53] This means that, as of 2011, appellate court rulings prohibiting second-parent adoptions stand in only three states (Ohio, Nebraska, and Wisconsin).[54]

While some legislatures have enacted statutes explicitly allowing second-parent adoptions, others have passed laws explicitly prohibiting them. Mississippi, for example, has a law that prohibits same-sex couples from adopting.[55] And Utah has a statute in the books that prohibits cohabiting couples from adopting jointly.[56] But the most infamous gay adoption ban is the one whose history we explored earlier in this chapter, that of Florida.

▲

When a state social worker asked Steven Lofton and Roger Croteau in 1988 to serve as foster parents for an eight-month-old baby boy by the name of Frank, they were at first unsure what to do. The reason for the gay couple's uncertainty was not that the child had tested positive for HIV antibodies;

both men were pediatric nurses at a Miami hospital (in fact, Roger worked in the hospital's pediatric AIDS unit). It was just that the two gay men in their early thirties had never envisioned themselves as parents. What in the end convinced them to take Frank into their home was his mother's personal request that they do so as she lay dying in a hospital bed of AIDS-related complications.

In the months after Steven completed the necessary foster care training and received his license, the state placed not only Frank in Steven and Roger's home, but also two other HIV-positive children—Ginger, a six-month-old who was in relatively good health, and Tracy, a one-year-old who barely weighed twelve pounds, could not hold a formula bottle in her hands, had been hospitalized a dozen times, and suffered from such a severe sinus condition that the men for more than two years had to suction her several times a night to keep her breathing while she slept.

Because of the challenges that came with caring for HIV-positive children, the state insisted that Steven quit his job so that he could be with the children all day. Roger continued working as a pediatric nurse while also helping with the child care at home. As the two gay men settled into raising the three children whom the state placed in their care, they committed themselves to providing them with as much love as they could muster, while aggressively pursuing every medical option available to keep them as healthy as possible at a time when most children with AIDS did not live past the age of two or three.

All three children placed by the state in Steven and Roger's home were African American, while the two gay men were white. Children from racial minority groups are overrepresented in the country's child welfare system, and Florida's is no exception. It is therefore not unusual for state agencies to place minority children with white foster parents, including lesbians and gay men.

There are not many individuals who would volunteer to raise three young children with serious medical issues, but Steven and Roger carried out their parental responsibilities with a sensitivity and an aplomb that left even the most jaded social workers amazed. Eventually, the state child welfare agency that placed the children in their home created an "outstanding foster parent of the year" honor, named it the Lofton-Croteau Award, and gave the first one to Steven and Roger.

In July 1991, Steven got a call from a social worker asking him to accompany her to a private hospital to help her assess the needs of a biracial nine-week-old infant. The boy, whose name was Bert, had tested HIV positive at birth and had been placed in a shelter home after his substance-abusing mother refused to care for him. A few weeks later, the state placed him in a foster home, but caring for the sick baby proved too much for the foster parents. Feeling desperate and not knowing what else to do, the couple had dropped the child off at the private hospital.

When Steven and the social worker arrived at the hospital, they were told that Bert was in an isolation unit and was being visited only by staff wearing masks, gowns, and latex gloves. The two visitors, however, refused to put on the protective gear and instead took turns holding the baby in their arms, sensing that the child needed direct contact with human skin.

As they were evaluating Bert's condition, a nurse walked into the room and said that the baby was ready to go. The perplexed visitors explained that they were there to assess the child's needs rather than to take him with them, but the nurse insisted that the boy could not remain in the hospital.

Not knowing what else to do, Steven ended up taking Bert home that night. The following day, the social worker called and suggested that Steven and Roger add the baby to their bevy of foster children. After having Bert home for only a few hours, the couple was already smitten with love for him, and they quickly agreed to care for the boy.[57]

A few months later, Steven and Roger enrolled all four of their foster children in a medical study of AZT, the first government-approved AIDS medication, at the National Institutes of Health (NIH). During the following four years, the family took more than two dozen weeklong trips to the NIH campus in Bethesda, Maryland, where the children received comprehensive medical testing and evaluations.

Despite Steven and Roger's best efforts, they were unable to keep all of their children alive—in 1994, Ginger died when her fragile immune system was unable to cope with a bout of measles. Although the death of their six-year-old daughter was devastating to the couple, they were to some extent comforted by the fact that a few months before her death they had learned that Bert had seroreverted to being HIV negative. But once that happened, according to Florida regulations, Bert became eligible for adoption. And when Steven applied to adopt the boy, the agency denied his application because state law prohibited gay people from adopting.

After officials began taking steps to find an adoptive family for Bert—including showing up unannounced at his school to take pictures of him to show prospective parents—Steven filed a federal lawsuit, with the assistance of the ACLU, arguing that Florida's adoption ban violated the U.S. Constitution.

▲

There had been earlier unsuccessful challenges to the Florida law, but they were grounded in state constitutional claims.[58] In contrast, Steven's lawsuit contended that the adoption ban violated his federal constitutional rights to due process and equal protection. The former claim was based on the notion that the state had encouraged him to establish a parent-child relationship with Bert—at the time the lawsuit was filed, Bert had been living with Steven and Roger for almost nine years—and that the relationship was now subject to constitutional protection. The latter claim was grounded in the idea that it was irrational for the state to render all gay people—regardless of background, experience, and personality—ineligible to adopt.

In defending the law, the state argued that children were better off when raised by a married mother and father. This arrangement was particularly beneficial to children, Florida contended, because it allowed for proper "gender role-modeling." Only heterosexual couples, the state explained, permitted children to learn from both a male and a female parent.

Steven's ACLU lawyers responded to the state's claims by noting that even if the court were to assume that it was optimal for children to be raised by a mother and a father who were married, denying gay people the opportunity to adopt did not in any way help the state achieve that goal. This was because there were many more children in the Florida foster care system waiting to be adopted than there were married heterosexual couples willing to adopt them. In fact, at the time the lawsuit was filed in 1999, there were more than 3,400 children in Florida without permanent homes. And their wait for such a home was long—almost 40 percent of the children in foster care waited more than four years before being placed for adoption, while 80 percent waited more than two years. All of this meant that denying Steven the opportunity to adopt Bert because he was gay did not mean that the nine-year-old would be adopted any time soon by a married heterosexual couple. (A study conducted several years later concluded that Florida's gay adoption ban prevented an estimated 165 children in the state's foster care system from being adopted.[59] Ironically, this was the same number of Florida foster care children who "aged out of the system" in 2006—that is, who became too old to be adopted.[60])

The state's claim that it took seriously the purported benefits for children of being raised by a married mother and father was also undermined by the fact that 25 percent of adoptions statewide (and 40 percent of adoptions in Dade County) were done by single people. (Nationally, single individuals adopt about one-third of foster care children.) And single people, of course, were unable to provide the dual-gender parental role modeling that the state contended was so essential to the well-being of children.

The inconsistencies in the state's positions were further evident from the fact that it permitted gay people to serve as foster parents and as legal guardians. (One of the other plaintiffs who joined Steven in his lawsuit was a gay man who several years earlier, with the state's approval, had been named a young boy's legal guardian at the request of the child's biological father.) Clearly, Florida did not really believe that placing children, sometimes for years, in the care of gay people was harmful to them. Indeed, the state seemed to reserve that contention for when it found itself in court defending the constitutionality of its gay adoption ban.

Florida's adoption law targeted gay people while not denying any other group, not even convicted felons or perpetrators of domestic violence, the opportunity to file adoption petitions. The fact that the state evaluated the adoption petitions of *all* Floridians *except* for gay ones on a case-by-case basis showed that the real purpose of the ban was to send a message of disapproval of homosexuality rather to advance the best interests of children. This seemed particularly true in Steven's case, since state officials acknowledged that he had done an admirable job raising the foster children whom they had placed in his care.

None of Steven's legal arguments, however, was enough to persuade the federal district court judge who heard the case. In August 2001, that judge issued an opinion upholding the statute's constitutionality.[61] Despite the fact that the state had placed several children with Steven for years on end, the judge concluded that foster care placements were not permanent enough to merit constitutional protection. Since the state had almost unlimited discretion in deciding when to terminate foster care placements, the type of due process constitutional protection usually afforded to parent-child relationships did not apply to the relationship between Steven and Bert.

The court also held that the adoption ban withstood the equal protection challenge, concluding that the state had a rational reason for instituting it. After finding that lesbians and gay men are not a "suspect class"—which would have required Florida to defend its policy by showing the existence of an important state interest (as it must, for example, with policies that make distinctions based on gender)—the court went on to agree with the government that it was reasonable to believe that children benefit from being raised by a married mother and father.

▲

The disconnect between Florida's contention that its only interest was in promoting the well-being of children and what was happening in the real world

Steven Lofton (*left*) and Roger Croteau in 1992 with their foster children (*clockwise*): Bert, Tracy, Ginger, and Frank. Photo by Tomas R. Gaspar. Used with permission.

outside the courtroom became apparent for everyone to see in the months following the federal judge's ruling. In 2002, the state's Department of Children and Family's (DCF) came under national scrutiny and criticism after it conceded that it did not know the whereabouts of a five-year-old girl who had been missing from her foster care home for fifteen months. (The child's foster mother was eventually charged with murdering her.) Rather than an isolated incident, DCF admitted a few months later that seven children had died while missing from their foster care homes in the previous three years.[62]

In order to try to address this disturbing pattern of neglect, Governor Jeb Bush a few weeks later ordered DCF child protection workers to visit all the children who were then under the state's care. Two months after the governor issued his order, DCF had failed to contact more than 1,800 children. Incredibly, a year later, the state conceded that there were still 500 foster-care children whose whereabouts were unknown.[63]

Losing track of those whom it was supposed to be protecting was not the only way in which DCF failed to keep children from being harmed. A disturbing number of children under DCF's care were also found to be victims of abuse inflicted by adults. In fact, two studies released in 2002 found that the number of children in foster care in Florida who were subjected to physical or sexual abuse increased significantly in the previous two years.[64] Another survey found that the number of children suffering repeated incidents of abuse increased from 7.3 percent to 9.7 percent between the first and second halves of 2002.[65]

It is striking to compare this pattern of neglect and abuse of children entrusted to the care of the state of Florida with the quality of care and nurture provided by gay foster parents like Steven Lofton. As part of the litigation papers filed in his lawsuit, Steven explained how, for almost ten years, he had done his best to care for his son Bert and to meet all his needs:

> I have been his parent in every way. For example, every day, I wake him up in the morning and help him get dressed and ready to go to school; I help him with his homework when he comes home from school; we have a family dinner together every night, cooked by Roger; and we spend our evenings engaged in a variety of family activities. I take care of Bert when he is sick. I make sure all his vaccinations are up to date. I am a parent volunteer in Bert's class once a week and an active P.T.S.A. member. I try to expand his horizons by taking him on trips. I encourage him to pursue the positive, healthy activities that he enjoys, such as swim team and drama. I provide a child-friendly home. I include Bert's friends in our family, inviting them over for dinner and having them join us on family outings to the beach or park. Roger and I teach Bert household responsibilities such as yard work, car maintenance and cooking. I discipline him appropriately when he misbehaves. I hug and comfort him when he is upset. I teach him manners, respect and other values that I consider important. I make sure he is safe. He calls me "Dad."[66]

Steven and his partner Roger were by no means the only gay people in Florida providing loving and caring home environments for foster children. There are many other stories of gay foster parenting successes in Florida, including that of Curtis Watson and his partner Scott Elsass. In 2003, a DCF caseworker was desperately trying to find a home for a young girl whose behavior, according to a newspaper account, was "so violent and temperamental that she had been *in 17 different foster homes in two months.*"[67] Through the years, Watson and Elsass had taken more than two dozen foster children into their home, so when the state asked, they agreed to care for this troubled girl as well. The gay couple soon provided the child, for the first time in her life, with the necessary combination of love and discipline that allowed her not only to stop acting in self-destructive ways, but also to begin to thrive. The transformation in the girl's behavior was so remarkable that a trial judge issued an order awarding the two men long-term custody of the girl while adding that the state owed them "a debt of gratitude" for the way they had cared for the child.[68]

There is also the story of Wayne Larue Smith and his partner Dan Skahen, a gay couple that joined Steven as plaintiffs in the federal lawsuit challenging the gay adoption ban. Wayne and Dan took care of twenty-three foster children between 1999 and 2005. One of them was Charlie, a three-year-old whose caseworker categorized him as "retarded" because he rarely emitted a sound. But it took only a few weeks of living in the men's home for Charlie to begin speaking in complete sentences. As a magazine article later put it, "Charlie wasn't retarded. He had simply withdrawn from a world that until then hadn't given him much reason to be engaged with it."[69]

It is deeply disturbing that, in the end, neither DCF's inability to protect hundreds of children from actual harm inflicted by poorly trained and supervised (heterosexual) foster care parents, nor the proven ability of many gay Floridians to do remarkably well raising children entrusted into their care by the state, made a difference to the federal courts. In 2004, the U.S. Court of Appeals for the Eleventh Circuit issued a ruling upholding the constitutionality of the gay adoption ban. The court reasoned that since most children grow up to be straight, it was reasonable to believe that heterosexual parents are better able "than homosexual individuals to provide adopted children with education and guidance relative to their sexual development."[70] A judge who later dissented from a decision not to rehear the case dismissed the court's reasoning as ludicrous. "There is . . . no evidence," she complained, "that the ability to share one's adolescent dating experiences (or lack thereof) is an important, much less essential, facet of parenting. . . . It is downright silly to argue that parents must have experienced everything that a child will experience in order to guide them."[71]

The court also, in discounting the constitutional relevance of the years that many of Florida's foster care children had to endure before being adopted, contended that it was reasonable for the state to keep children in foster care longer in order to eventually place them in the types of homes that it believed were optimal for them. Finally, the court accepted the state's claim that children were better off raised by a married mother and father by noting that no family arrangement "has proven as enduring as the marital family structure, nor has the accumulated wisdom of several millennia of human experience discovered a superior model." The court added that "against this 'sum of experience,' it is rational for Florida to conclude that it is in the best interests of adoptive children, many of whom come from troubled and unstable backgrounds, to be placed in a home anchored by both a father and a mother."

The state never found another adoptive family for Bert. Before the end of the litigation, DCF granted Steven and Roger permission to move to Oregon with their three foster children. A few months after moving to Portland, social workers there, having heard about the gay couple as a result of the publicity engendered by the lawsuit, asked them to take into their home two brothers (Wayne, aged five, and Ernie, aged two) who were HIV positive and who had been through a long history of severe abuse and neglect. Less than a year later, Steven and Roger adopted the two boys with the full support of Oregon child welfare officials.

▲

Less than a year after the federal court of appeals upheld the constitutionality of Florida's gay adoption ban, state officials asked Martin Gill and his partner Tom Roe, a gay couple living in North Miami, to care for two brothers, one a baby and the other four years old. Although Martin and Tom had fostered several children before, they initially told officials they could not take the brothers in because they were planning to move to Georgia. But after the state agency's representatives assured them that the placement would be temporary, Martin and Tom agreed to take the children into their home.

When the brothers first arrived, they both had bald patches on their heads caused by ringworm. The younger boy was also in severe pain from an ear infection that had gone untreated. The older child was silent and sullen, apparently traumatized and depressed after being taken away from his biological family. He did not speak for several weeks, and when he did finally start to do so, it was difficult to understand what he was saying. The four-year-old also "had never seen a book, could not distinguish letters from numbers, could not identify colors, and could not count."[72]

Martin and Tom quickly grew attached to their foster sons, happily giving up their plan to leave the state in order to continue caring for them. The baby also quickly bonded with the two men, but it took the older child some time to do so. Eventually, however, his depression lifted and he became a happy and talkative child who refused to go to school in the mornings without first hugging his "daddy" and his "papi." He also went from being behind educationally—he had to repeat the first grade—to making significant progress in school. A court would later conclude that the children had healed—both physically and emotionally—in the men's care and that they were thriving in their home environment.[73]

The boys became eligible for adoption in 2006 when a court terminated the biological parents' rights. A year later, after no one else had come forward expressing an interest in adopting them, Martin filed an adoption petition. And, with the assistance of the ACLU, he requested that the court rule that the gay adoption ban violated the state constitution.

One of the differences between the federal litigation in Steven Lofton's case a few years earlier and the state litigation in Martin Gill's case was that a trial was held in the latter instance. This provided the ACLU with the opportunity to inform the court, through expert witnesses, of the extensive social science research that, over several decades, had studied the children of lesbian and gay parents and concluded that they were as well-adjusted psychologically and socially, and did as well academically, as the children of heterosexuals.

For its part, the state contended during the trial that lesbians and gay men threatened the well-being of children because their relationships were more unstable and they suffered from greater psychiatric disorders and rates of substance abuse than did heterosexuals. The sole witness the state called to testify in support of these controversial contentions was Dr. George Rekers, a clinical psychologist and an ordained Baptist minister.

The state paid Rekers, a fierce opponent of gay rights, over $120,000 for his work on the case. Rekers had come to the attention of the state's lawyers because he had previously testified in other proceedings involving the constitutionality of bans on gay marriage and adoption. As the New York Times reported, Rekers had become well-known for testifying in court that "gay men and lesbians lead parlous lives and raise troubled children."[74] Less than two years after making the same claims during the Florida adoption trial, the media reported that Rekers had recently traveled to Europe with a male prostitute whom he had met through a website called "rentboy.com."[75] This led the state attorney general's office to announce that it would no longer use Rekers's services in the litigation.

The ACLU lawyers did not have much difficulty rebutting Rekers's inflammatory contentions about LGBT parenting through expert witnesses. Those witnesses noted that gay people are no more susceptible to psychological disorders, relationship instability, or domestic violence than are heterosexuals. That testimony, when coupled with the extensive evidence introduced during the proceedings regarding the ability of lesbians and gay men to be good and effective parents, led the trial court, in November 2008, to strike down the gay adoption ban.

Almost two years later, a Florida appeals court upheld that ruling by also concluding that the ban violated the state constitution's guarantee of equal protection. The state appellate court, unlike the federal courts in Steven Lofton's case a few years earlier, rejected the notion that there was any plausible justification for a policy that prevented all lesbians and gay men, and no others, from the opportunity to show that they could be good adoptive parents. In so doing, the court noted the extensive reports and studies from social scientists finding "that there are no differences in the parenting of homosexuals or the adjustment of their children. . . . Based on the robust nature of the evidence available in the field, this Court is satisfied that the issue is so far beyond dispute that it would be irrational to hold otherwise; the best interests of children are not preserved by prohibiting homosexual adoption."[76]

Shortly after the court's ruling, the state announced that it would not appeal the case to the state supreme court. This meant that, for the first time in thirty-three years, lesbians and gay men were eligible to adopt children in Florida. One of them was Martin Gill, the gay man who (along with his partner) had six years earlier opened his home to two scared and neglected little boys and provided them with the kind of happy and safe home environment that all children are entitled to have.

Despite the long-delayed victory by LGBT parenting advocates in Florida, other states continue to restrict the ability of lesbians and gay men to become parents. One of them is Arkansas. In 2006, the state supreme court struck down a regulation that prohibited lesbians and gay men from serving as foster parents.[77] Conservative activists then persuaded Arkansas voters to approve a ballot measure that would prohibit cohabiting couples from adopting or serving as foster parents. But in 2011, the Arkansas Supreme Court once again intervened by holding that the proposed law, which never went into effect, would have impermissibly interfered with the constitutional right of individuals to sexual privacy.[78] The measure, the court explained, was constitutionally deficient because it asked prospective parents to choose between the protected right to engage in sexual conduct in the privacy of the home and the opportunity to foster or adopt a child.

As courts continue to grapple with the constitutionality of parenting restrictions that affect lesbians and gay men in some states, adoption and foster care remain viable parenting options for prospective lesbian and gay parents in many other states. A study published in 2007 found that there were sixty-five thousand children nationwide living with lesbian and gay adoptive parents, and that there were fourteen thousand children being cared for by lesbian and gay foster parents.[79] The existence of this large number of families is in part due to the actions of those individuals, several of whom we have profiled in this chapter, who refused to give up their dreams of becoming parents even after being told by child welfare officials that their same-sex sexual orientation and relationships rendered them incapable of being good parents.

It has not only been lesbians and gay men who have found themselves in court battling for recognition of their parental rights. As we will see in the next chapter, the intersection of parenthood and gender identity has also been the subject of litigation as courts have grappled with how the law should respond to the transsexuality of some parents.

PART III

Can Transsexuals Be Parents?

6

Gender Does Not Make a Parent

In 1981, shortly after doctors told Suzanne Daly that she was eligible to have sex reassignment surgery, she spoke to her eight-year-old daughter Mary about her transsexuality. Suzanne had a good relationship with her daughter and the child seemed to understand, after asking many questions, that her father would be happier living as a woman. Since Suzanne's biggest concern was not how Mary would react, but instead how her ex-wife Nan would respond, she asked her daughter not to share the news of her upcoming operation with Nan so that she could later break the news herself.

After high school, Suzanne enrolled in the United States Army and later attended the University of California at Berkeley. Suzanne (who then went by the name of Tim) and Nan were married in 1969, and the two bought a home in Oakland after Suzanne got a position as a science researcher at the University of California's prestigious Lawrence Berkeley National Laboratory.

Their only daughter, Mary, was born in 1973. The couple separated in 1979, after which Nan moved to Reno, Nevada. Two years later, the couple divorced and the court awarded custody to Nan; it also granted Suzanne visitation rights and required her to pay child support. For the next two years, Suzanne visited with Mary about once a month.

Shortly after the separation, Suzanne consulted with Lynn Frazier, a Bay Area psychotherapist who specialized in the treatment of transsexuals. Dr. Frazier evaluated Suzanne and determined that she met the medical guidelines for a person who had gender identity disorder—that is, someone whose psychological gender identity as a female did not match her male anatomical sex. Dr. Frazier recommended that Suzanne begin hormone therapy with the goal of developing some female physical characteristics and that she then live openly as a woman for a year. After that, Suzanne would be eligible for sex reassignment surgery.

For eight months after Suzanne revealed to Mary that she was a transsexual, the girl kept the information to herself. But in February 1982, Mary told her mother that her father would soon start to live as a woman. A few weeks later, Suzanne traveled to Reno for her regular monthly visit with her daughter, without knowing that the girl had shared the news with her mother. As she waited in the car for Mary to come out of Nan's house—which was the usual way she began her visits with her daughter—she was suddenly confronted by two sheriff's deputies, who demanded that she leave the area. The officers explained that Nan had a court order prohibiting Suzanne from visiting with Mary because of her transsexuality. It turned out that Nan had no such order and instead had called the sheriff's office after unilaterally deciding to deny Suzanne the ability to visit with her daughter, in violation of the divorce decree. Not wanting to make a scene, a dispirited and saddened Suzanne returned to Oakland without seeing Mary.

Early the following year, after Suzanne began taking female hormones and after she acquired her new female legal name to replace her male birth name, she returned to Reno in another attempt to visit with her daughter. This time, Nan's mother met her at the door of the house, rifle in hand, warning her that she was not welcome inside. Several weeks later, Nan filed a petition in a Nevada court seeking to terminate all of Suzanne's parental rights on the ground that she was a transsexual.

▲

It is settled constitutional law that a court may not terminate a parent's relationship with his or her child except under extraordinary circumstances, such as, for example, when the parent has abandoned the child or when leaving the child under the care of the parent would cause the minor to suffer serious physical or emotional injury.

The extent of the constitutional protection afforded to legal parents when it comes to the termination of their parental rights is reflected in the fact that, after the mid-1970s, lesbian and gay parents have rarely been the subjects of termination proceedings for reasons related to their sexual orientation. Even the most conservative of courts would likely recognize that it is impermissible to terminate parental rights on those grounds. In fact, the Virginia Supreme Court in 1981—the same court that in 1985 took custody away from a gay man because of his sexual orientation (as explained in chapter 2), and in 1995 took custody away from a lesbian mother for the same reason (as chronicled in the introduction)—drew the line at the *termination* of the parental rights of Marianne MacQueen (as we saw in chapter 1). In MacQueen's case, the court refused to terminate the rights of a lesbian mother, who lived with her female partner, so that the husband's new wife could adopt her son.

Unlike custody and visitation decisions, which are always subject to later modification based on changed circumstances, a termination of parental rights, if upheld on appeal, is final. Once an individual's parental rights are terminated, she becomes a legal stranger to the child, without the right to have any contact with the child over the objection of the other parent. If the latter refuses to grant access to the child, the parent whose rights were terminated must wait until the child reaches eighteen and can decide for herself whether to resume contact.

▲

In February 1983, a hearing was held in a Nevada courtroom to determine whether the parental rights of Suzanne Daly should be terminated. Both Suzanne and Nan testified at the hearing. The court also heard from Ira Pauly, a psychiatrist and expert on transsexualism who wrote some of the earliest articles on the subject and who collaborated closely with Harry Benjamin, the German doctor who in the 1950s and 1960s was a pioneer in the medical treatment of transsexuals. Dr. Pauly explained to the court that Suzanne fit the diagnostic model of a transsexual because she self-identified, in a strong and unequivocal way, as a woman despite her male anatomical characteristics. (Suzanne did not have sex reassignment surgery until later in 1983.) The court also heard from a psychiatrist hired by Nan to evaluate Mary. That expert told the court that the girl would suffer emotional harm if she were required to spend time with her transsexual father.

Two months later, the trial court issued a ruling terminating Suzanne's parental rights, concluding that she had acted selfishly by putting her needs as a transsexual person ahead of the child's interests. Rather than viewing the medical treatment sought by Suzanne as Dr. Pauly did—that is, as a way of successfully addressing the distress and internal conflict that she felt over her gender—the judge used the very fact that she was seeking medical treatment for her gender identity disorder as the main reason for terminating her parental rights.

After Suzanne appealed to the Nevada Supreme Court, Nan continued to take the legal position that Suzanne was, in effect, no longer entitled to be a parent because of her transsexualism. Part of this argument was based on the contention that Suzanne wanted Mary to "accept her lifestyle." As proof of this, Nan's brief to the appellate court noted that Suzanne volunteered at a Berkeley LGBT community center and that one of the witnesses who testified on her behalf was a lesbian. The brief added that Suzanne had invited this lesbian friend to dinner at her home, and that this friend had "admitted" on the stand that she would return to Suzanne's house if invited again. The brief then complained that it was this environment (i.e., where there were lesbians present) "to which [Suzanne] intends to bring Mary. . . . We are dealing here with the mind of a 9 year old . . . not with the selfish desires of appellant."[1]

In March 1986, the Nevada Supreme Court, focusing exclusively on Suzanne's transsexuality, upheld the termination of her parental rights. In doing so, the court credited Nan's claim that when the child returned from visiting Suzanne for the last time in 1981—the visit in which Suzanne revealed her transsexuality to her daughter—Mary seemed depressed and lethargic. As the dissenting judge pointed out, however, it did not appear that Nan was particularly concerned about Mary's behavior *until after* she learned—eight months later—that her former husband was a transsexual.

But for the majority of the court's justices, Suzanne's choices required the termination of her parental rights. The majority pointed out that Suzanne admitted on the stand that she wanted Mary to get to know her LGBT friends, a fact that it found disturbing. Furthermore, from the court's perspective, Suzanne chose to cease being Mary's father when she began her gender transition. And since she was not really a woman, she could not be her mother either. Being neither a father nor a mother meant that Suzanne, as a legal matter, could no longer be a parent. As the court explained, "it was strictly Tim Daly's choice to discard his fatherhood and assume the role of a female who could never be either mother or sister to his daughter."[2]

Cases like those of Suzanne Daly represent what one commentator has called the law's "unmaking" of transsexual parents.[3] As Suzanne transitioned from being a man to being a woman, she was unable to retain her parental rights and obligations. The law's response to Suzanne's gender transition was to strip her of her parental status. In effect, the law gave Suzanne a choice: if she wanted to remain being a legal parent, then she had to continue living as a man.

Suzanne's case was decided more than a quarter of a century ago. It might therefore be tempting to dismiss the legal outcome as little more than a reflection of its time. But as the next case illustrates, courts continue to "unmake" transsexual parents.

▲

Martha (formerly Michael) and Beth Boyd were married in Kentucky in 1974 and proceeded to have three children. Five years into their marriage, Martha revealed to Beth that she preferred wearing women's clothing and that she felt more comfortable thinking of herself as a woman. Although the marriage from that point on was rocky, it lasted for almost twenty more years. In 1998, the couple divorced and entered into a settlement agreement under which Beth got custody of the two children who were then still minors while Martha received visitation rights.

Eighteen months after the divorce, Martha had gender reassignment surgery, legally changed her name, and temporarily moved to Florida. When the children visited Martha there, they noticed, as a court would later put it, that she "exhibited various feminine features."[4] Shortly after the children returned to Kentucky, Beth began severely restricting Martha's ability to visit with them. In fact, the next time that Martha saw her youngest daughter Sarah, who at the time of the Florida trip was nine years old, was six years later when the adolescent testified at a hearing in favor of terminating Martha's parental rights.

Frustrated by Beth's unwillingness to allow her to visit with Sarah, Martha in 2001 filed a petition in Kentucky family court seeking to enforce her visitation rights under the original divorce decree. Beth, citing Martha's transsexuality, opposed the petition and instead asked the court to prohibit Martha from contacting Sarah, the only one of her children who was by then still under the age of eighteen. The court eventually granted Beth her wish, prohibiting Martha from contacting Sarah unless explicitly permitted to do so by a future court ruling.

As bad as this legal outcome was for Martha, matters soon got worse. In 2003, Beth and her new husband David petitioned the court to allow the latter to adopt Sarah without Martha's consent. If the court granted Beth and David's request, it would mean that Martha's parental rights would be terminated. Under Kentucky law, an adoption can be granted over a parent's objection only if (1) the child has been abandoned, neglected, or abused by the nonconsenting parent; (2) it would be in the child's best interest; and (3) the court makes one of ten specific findings, such as that the nonconsenting parent inflicted physical or emotional harm on the child.[5]

Several witnesses testified during a three-day hearing held in the spring of 2005 to consider the adoption petition, including an expert from each side. Martha's expert, a sexologist with a doctorate in human sexuality who had thirty-five years of experience working with transsexual clients, explained how she had supervised Martha's gender transition, which had gone smoothly and according to plan. In contrast, Beth and David's expert, a local psychiatrist with no experience treating transsexual individuals and who met with Martha only once, opined that Martha was "mentally ill." (It seems that the doctor had a rather broad definition of mental illness, given that he later told the court that anyone who was on antidepressant medications was also mentally ill.)[6]

Other witnesses included fifteen-year-old Sarah, who testified that she wanted David, her mother's new husband, to adopt her because she considered him to be her real father. "I want to be able to have a father in my life," she told the court, "a legal father. I don't have that with my biological father and I don't want it with" him.[7] Sarah also stated that Martha's sex change operation made her feel "abandoned," and that she cringed at the thought of having to tell her school friends that "I don't have a father [because] he's a woman."[8] For her part, Beth told the court that Sarah needed a "father figure," something that Martha was no longer able to be.[9]

When Martha took the stand, she explained how she had tried, in the years following the divorce, to visit with her children, only to be repeatedly rebuffed by Beth. She also reminded the judge that she had been, since 2001, under a court order prohibiting her from contacting Sarah. Martha made it clear in her testimony that far from abandoning her daughter, she had tried to remain a part of her life.

Several weeks later, the trial judge issued a ruling in which he concluded that Martha's gender transition was responsible for Sarah's bouts with depression and her difficulties in school. In particular, the court was troubled by the fact that Martha exhibited "physical changes in [her] appearance when the children visited in Florida, such as long finger nails, wearing tight shirts and short shorts (with shaved legs and arms) and breast augmentation, without any warning to prepare [Sarah] or the others for those changes." The judge also did not like the fact that Martha had sent "a letter to [Sarah's] sister with a photograph of [her] as a female and travel[ed] to Kentucky from Florida dressed as a woman."[10] As a result, the judge terminated Martha's parental rights and approved David's petition to adopt Sarah.

In defending the trial court's ruling on appeal, Beth and David's lawyer made three main arguments. First, he contended that Martha had "emotionally abandoned" her children when she "voluntarily chose to undergo a sex change operation and transform his identity from Michael to Martha."[11] Second, he charged that Martha, in seeking a gender change, acted selfishly by putting her interests ahead of her children. (The lawyer also complained that Martha "does not often attend church but [instead] spends time educating people about transsexualism.")[12] And third, the attorney claimed that Sarah needed a father and that that role could now be played only by David.

For her part, Martha's lawyer argued on appeal that even if it were true "that because Martha is no longer a man, she cannot be Sarah's *father*," that contention "fails to see that Martha may be a *parent* to Sarah, if given the chance and opportunity."[13] The attorney also pointed out that it was unfair to conclude that Sarah had abandoned her daughter when she was under a court order, sought by her former wife, that she not contact her children. In fact, an appellate court in Kentucky had earlier held that when a court denies a parent the right to visit with his or her children, that ruling cannot be used to support a later parental abandonment claim.[14] The lawyer added that there were reasons—other than Martha's transsexuality—that explained Sarah's depression and problems in school, including "the death of a close grandmother, [being subjected] to sexual abuse by a boy on her [school] bus, and boyfriend issues."[15]

None of these arguments made a difference. In 2007, the Kentucky Court of Appeals issued a unanimous opinion affirming the termination of Martha's parental rights. Although the court claimed it was not holding "that undergoing gender reassignment is, in itself, grounds" for terminating a parent's rights, it nonetheless concluded that Martha's gender transition caused Sarah emotional harm and constituted sufficient evidence to support the lower court's ruling that Martha had neglected her child.[16] Despite the court's protestations to the contrary, it seems clear that it did not believe it was possible for someone to be a fit parent after transitioning to a new sex.

By the time Martha lost before the appellate court, Sarah had already turned eighteen and the case was largely moot because, as an adult, she was now free to decide whether to have contact with Martha. (The case was not completely moot because issues of inheritance remained; after the court's ruling, Sarah became ineligible to inherit property from Martha if the latter were to die without leaving a valid will.) And even if Sarah someday decides to have a relationship with Martha, the latter still paid a heavy price for her decision to start living as a woman: she saw her daughter only once between the time the girl was nine years old and nine years later when the appellate court issued its ruling, and that was during the excruciatingly painful morning when her daughter took the stand to tell a judge that she no longer wanted Martha to be her parent.

▲

If one replaces gender identity for sexual orientation, the facts in Martha's case are essentially the same as those in Marianne MacQueen's case explored in chapter 1. In both instances, the former spouse of an LGBT parent remarried and the new spouse then sought to adopt the child over the objections of the LGBT parent. Also, in both instances, the trial court granted the adoption petition and ordered that the LGBT parent's rights be terminated because of her sexual orientation or gender identity.

There is, however, one crucial difference between the two cases: In Marianne's case, the Virginia appellate court overturned the trial court's judgment and restored her parental rights. In contrast, the Kentucky appellate court, twenty-six years later, ruled that Martha was no longer Sarah's legal parent.

The similarities between the two cases illustrate how lesbian and gay parents on the one hand and transsexual ones on the other face many of the same challenges, including allegations (raised in both Marianne's and Martha's cases) that LGBT parents act selfishly, putting their interests ahead of those of their children, when they insist in being open about their sexual orientation or gender identity.

But the different outcomes in the cases illustrate how transsexual parents face challenges that are in some ways even greater than those confronted by lesbian and gay parents. Once lesbian and gay parents attain parenthood status (which, as we saw in chapters 3, 4, and 5, is not always easy to do), they almost never lose it. In contrast, transsexual parents like Suzanne Daly and Martha Boyd are at risk of being permanently separated from their children after they begin the process of transitioning to a new gender.

The additional challenges faced by transsexual parents may be explained by Americans' seemingly greater tolerance for those who have a same-sex sexual orientation than for those who identify as transsexual. This "toleration gap" is reflected in the fact that many more states have laws prohibiting discrimination based on sexual orientation than gender identity.[17]

In addition, the number of lesbian and gay parents is larger than that of parents who are transsexual, making the former more visible than the latter. Indeed, over the last forty years, there have been more than four hundred reported court opinions involving lesbian and gay parents (and hundreds more that have gone unreported), while there have been fewer than twenty reported cases involving transsexual parents. This means that although judges have been seeing lesbian and gay parents in their courtrooms with some frequency, the same cannot be said of transsexual ones.

▲

Questions related to the intersection of parenting and gender commonly arise in legal cases involving transsexual parents, as they do in those involving lesbian and gay ones. For decades, lesbian and gay parents have had to contend with the argument that depriving a child of a mother (in the case of gay male parents) or of a father (in the case of lesbian parents) harms children. This argument is at its core grounded in the notion that there is something special, unique, and *complementary* about the supposed different nurturing styles of fathers and mothers. In response, lesbian and gay parenting advocates have argued, both inside and outside courtrooms, that whether and how parents love and care for their children is more important than their gender.

To some extent, however, courts grapple with the gender issue in the context of lesbian and gay parenting at a fairly abstract level. In lesbian and gay parenting cases, the question that frequently gets asked is whether mothers *in general* care for children in ways that are different, though not necessarily better, than fathers *in general* do.

But in a case involving a transsexual parent, the "gender in parenting" issue is significantly less abstract because there is an individual before the court *whose gender has already changed (or is in the process of changing).* Rather than grappling with generalities, courts in transsexual parenting cases must deal directly with the question of whether, for example, a particular parent who was formerly male can still be a parent after he becomes a woman. And, as we have seen, the courts in Suzanne Daly's and Martha Boyd's cases concluded that their gender changes meant that they could no longer continue being their children's legal parents.

Despite the courts' holdings and reasoning in those cases, it is not clear why the fact that a parent transitions from one gender to another should be relevant in determining whether he or she is entitled to remain a legal parent. To put the matter bluntly is to state the obvious: individuals do not parent with either their sexual organs or their secondary sexual characteristics. Indeed, neither Suzanne's nor Martha's attributes as parents changed simply because they took female hormones and had their sexual organs surgically altered.[18]

Although courts have not seen it this way, transsexual parents have the potential for undermining the traditional notion that gender is an essential component of a particular kind of parenting—that is, of *fatherhood* as understood as being significantly different from *motherhood* (and vice versa). At the end of the day, the case of the transsexual parent tells us, perhaps even more clearly than that of the lesbian or gay parent, that we need to pay considerably less attention than we currently do to parents' gender.

Admittedly, efforts to "degender" parenthood are quite controversial in some quarters. Many view the argument that gender should be irrelevant in matters related to parenthood as an attack on the traditional and familiar understandings of "motherhood" and "fatherhood." And to some degree these critics are right, at least to the extent that being a mother and being a man, for example, are thought to be mutually exclusive categories.

The time has come, however, to start thinking of "mother" and "father" as verbs rather than as nouns. In other words, we should focus on what it means *to* mother and *to* father a child, rather than on the sex of the parent who happens to be doing the mothering or fathering. If we do this, we will come to see that the only category that truly matters is that of "parent," and that the law should not rely on *any* sex-based assumptions about the capabilities of different individuals to promote and protect the well-being of their children.

Opponents of LGBT parenting frequently argue that children benefit in important ways from the unique contributions that mothers (as women) and fathers (as men) provide to their children. Although courts sometimes rule that such claims are part of "unprovable assumptions" that are supported by "intuition and experience," there is in fact little empirical support for them.[19] As stated in the introduction to a leading text on the role that fathers play in promoting the well-being of children, "fathers and mothers seem to influence their children in similar rather than dissimilar ways. . . . The differences between mothers and fathers appear to be much less important than the similarities. . . . Parental warmth, nurturance, and closeness are associated with positive child outcomes regardless of whether the parent involved is a mother or a father. *The important dimensions of parental influence are those that have to do with parental characteristics rather than gender-related characteristics.*"[20] Indeed, even Kyle Pruett, a parenting expert whose writings on the importance of fathers are sometimes cited by opponents of LGBT rights to support the claimed value of dual-gender parenting, has admitted that the most "enduring parental skills are probably, in the end, not dependent on gender."[21]

For more than three decades, the United States Supreme Court has been reminding us that it is constitutionally impermissible for the government to make assumptions about the abilities and aspirations of individuals based on their gender. In fact, as the demise of doctrines such as that of "tender years" (which held that young children were better off when cared for by their mothers rather than their fathers following a divorce) and the elimination of rules such as the requirement that former husbands but not former wives pay alimony,[22] there is little in family law *as applied to heterosexuals* that still calls for the differential treatment of men and women. As the Supreme Court has put it, the law no longer tolerates "overbroad generalizations about the different talents, capacities, or preferences of males and females."[23] And yet, when it comes to LGBT parents, many courts continue to give great legal significance to the supposed differences between mothers and fathers. It turns out, however, that assumptions about the supposed link between gender on the one hand and "talents, capacities, or preferences" on the other are as problematic when applied to LGBT parents as they are when applied to heterosexual ones. Unfortunately, until courts accept this proposition, transsexual parents in particular will remain at risk of having their parental rights terminated because of their decision to transition from one gender to another.

▲

Not all cases involving transsexual parents have raised the question of whether it is appropriate to terminate their parental rights altogether. Like lesbian and gay parents, transsexual ones sometimes find themselves in custody and visitation battles with their former spouses. As in the legal disputes involving lesbians and gay men profiled in chapters 1 and 2, the transsexual parenting cases involving custody and visitation raise the question of what is relevant in the judicial assessment of who is a good parent.

Interestingly, the first reported judicial opinion involving a transsexual parent—one from Colorado in 1973—upheld the right of a female-to-male transsexual to retain custody of his children. Mark (formerly Gay) Randall married Duane Christian in 1953 and the two divorced more than a decade later. The couple had four children, all girls. After the divorce, the girls lived with Mark, first in Arizona and then in Colorado. In 1972, Mark began dressing as a man and taking male hormones in preparation for undergoing sex reassignment surgery. Also in 1972, the state of Colorado, apparently not realizing that Mark was a biological woman, issued him and his new wife Ruth a marriage license.

When Duane—who had also remarried and who was living with his new wife in Nevada—learned that Mark was in the process of becoming a man, he quickly filed a petition with the Colorado district court seeking custody of his four daughters. At the hearing to consider Duane's petition, all four girls testified that they wanted to remain living with Mark and Ruth. The eldest daughter, who was then sixteen, told the judge that "about the transsexual thing, I believe in it very much and I think it's a very fantastic thing. And we were told about it six or seven years ago, and so it's no new thing to us. It may be new to Duane, [but] it's not that traumatic of a thing. . . . We have gone through the changes with Mark, and I consider Mark my father and Ruth my mother. But, naturally, we've always had respect for Duane and [his new wife] when we've gone out there."[24]

At the conclusion of the hearing, the trial judge granted Duane custody of the children based on the following findings of fact: "[1] That the defendant [Mark] is going through a transsexual change, and at this time he considers himself the father of the children, and not the mother of the children; [2] that the children also consider him the father and not the mother; [and 3] that this leaves the children with no natural mother."[25] The court also found that the two oldest daughters were mentally disturbed, apparently because they were supportive of Mark's gender transition.

Immediately after the hearing, Duane took the children to Nevada. Less than two months later, the four girls ran away and made their way back to

Colorado, where law enforcement officials found them and kept them in a county jail for three days until a new court hearing could be held. After that hearing, the court reaffirmed its initial ruling, noting that "if the Defendant [Mark] is still a female legally, then there is no 'man of the house' for the children; [and] if the Defendant is legally a man then . . . the Defendant has been living as a man and wife with Ruth without benefit of a ceremony. . . . This arrangement is not in the best interests of the children."[26]

Shortly after Duane took the children back to Nevada for a second time, he signed papers to have his eldest daughter sent to California to live in a foster home. The girl promptly ran away again, returning to Colorado to live with Mark and Ruth. In the meantime, Duane also placed his other three daughters, who had made it clear to him that they wanted to return to Colorado, in a foster care home while the case was on appeal.

In his brief to the Colorado Court of Appeals, Duane argued that Mark's "belief that she is now the father or father image of her four girls in her home" was evidence that he was mentally unstable, which Duane claimed justified the lower court's modification of custody.[27] In addition, the brief contended that if Mark was truly a man, he should be judged on his ability to be a "provider" for the family. Duane contended that Mark had failed in that role because a series of business failures had required him to declare bankruptcy. Duane added that he was a better provider for the children because he was a dentist with a successful practice.

For his part, Mark noted in his brief that Duane had failed to introduce any evidence that the four girls had been negatively affected by his gender transition. In doing so, the brief argued that it was improper to penalize someone simply for being a transsexual, because that would involve the imposition of legal disadvantages on individuals based on their status rather than their conduct. Although the brief acknowledged that Mark suffered from "gender disorientation," it suggested that whatever psychological complications might accompany that condition would be remedied by his upcoming gender reassignment surgery.

In chapters 1 and 2, we saw that only a few courts prior to the mid-1980s were willing to apply the nexus test—which demands evidence of actual or potential harm to children—in custody and visitation cases involving lesbian mothers or gay fathers. But that was precisely the test that the Colorado Court of Appeals applied when assessing the relevancy of Mark's transsexuality. In fact, the ruling in this case constituted the first time than an appellate court applied the nexus test in a case upholding the right of an LGBT parent to retain custody of children.

Specifically, the court observed that "the record contains no evidence that the environment of [Mark's] home . . . endangered the children's physical health or impaired their emotional development. On the contrary, the evidence shows that the children were happy, healthy, well-adjusted children who were doing well in school and who were active in community activities."[28] The court also found that Mark's gender transition "did not adversely affect [his] relationship with the children nor impair their emotional development." In deciding to overturn the lower court's decision, the judges were also influenced by the fact that the children had lived with Mark for several years after they learned about his transsexuality and that they clearly preferred to be in his home rather than in that of his former husband.

It is surprising that one of the strongest judicial condemnations of denying parental rights to individuals because they are lesbian, gay, bisexual, or transgender came as early as it did (in 1973) in a case involving a transsexual parent. But as the next case illustrates, not all such parents, in the decades that followed, have succeeded in persuading courts to look beyond gender identity in making custody decisions.

▲

Shortly after Robbie (formerly Robert) and Tracy Magnuson married in Spokane, Washington, in 1985, they moved to the Washington, D.C., area so that the former could attend law school and the latter medical school. After receiving their respective degrees and working on the East Coast, the couple returned to Spokane in 1995 with their four-year-old son, Benjamin. A second child, Maggie, was born a few years later.

A year before they moved back west, Robbie quit her job to care for Benjamin full-time. At the time, Tracy was completing her medical residency and working long hours. After returning to Spokane, Tracy got a job as a surgeon, and Robbie as an associate at a law firm. After Maggie was born, Robbie took a three-month leave of absence from work to care for her, something that no male associate had ever done in the firm's one hundred–year history.

Robbie later testified at trial that she had been struggling with gender identity issues all of her life. In 2003, she started seeing a psychologist, who diagnosed her as having gender identity disorder. Shortly thereafter, Robbie came out to Tracy as a transsexual. Tracy did not take the news well and insisted that Robbie get a second opinion. When the second opinion came back the same, she insisted on a third. She also asked that Robbie submit to an MRI exam because she suspected that her spouse's gender issues were being caused by a brain tumor. That test came back negative.

The couple divorced a few months later. Although they agreed that they would share legal custody, they each petitioned the court for primary physical custody of the children. During the custody trial, Tracy testified that she believed her husband was mentally ill rather than a transsexual. To dispute this claim, Robbie called Dr. Walter Bockting to testify. Bockting, a leading expert on transgender issues who taught at the University of Minnesota Medical School, explained that gender identity disorder was a diagnosis contained in the American Psychiatric Association's Diagnostic and Statistical Manual (DSM). He also noted that the designation was controversial, in the same way that the DSM's designation of homosexuality as a mental disorder had been controversial thirty years earlier.

The doctor added that there was a difference between a mental disorder (which included any diagnosis contained in the DSM) and a mental illness. Only the latter significantly affected the ability of individuals to function on a daily basis. The doctor finished his testimony by stating that there was no evidence that gender identity disorder negatively affected an individual's ability to function as a parent.

The court assigned a guardian at litem (GAL) to represent the children's interests. After speaking to several experts in the field, the GAL found that Robbie's transsexuality, and her planned gender reassignment surgery, was not causing the children emotional harm. The GAL also found that Robbie had been the children's primary caregiver and that she was the more nurturing and engaged of the two parents. Based on both of these findings, he recommended to the court that primary physical custody be given to Robbie. (Shortly after that recommendation, Tracy filed a complaint against him before the Washington State Bar Association and the GAL oversight committee claiming that he was unqualified, had a bias for "alternative lifestyles," and had failed to protect the children.[29] The complaint was eventually dismissed.)

The trial judge refused to follow the GAL's recommendation, concluding that awarding primary physical custody to Robbie would not be consistent with the children's best interests because of what the judge considered the uncertain impact of her transsexuality on the children. As the judge put it, Robbie's "surgery may be everything [she] has hoped for, or it may be disastrous. No one knows what is ahead, and the impact of gender reassignment surgery on the children is unknown."[30]

The court's conclusion was puzzling given that the only expert testimony presented at trial, which was corroborated by the GAL's findings, concluded that there was in fact no uncertainty. As the GAL explained, if there was any negative impact on the children from Robbie's gender transition, it was not because of the transition itself but because of Tracy's unwillingness to accept it.

On appeal, the main issue in Robbie's case was the extent to which custody cases involving gender identity in Washington State should be treated the same way as ones involving lesbians and gay men. As we saw in chapter 1, the Washington Supreme Court had made it clear almost thirty years earlier in Sandy Schuster and Madeleine Isaacson's case that a parent's sexual orientation was relevant only to the extent that it affected the children's well-being.[31] The court later reaffirmed that position in a case involving a gay father.[32]

The Washington Court of Appeals ostensibly followed the same approach in considering Robbie's appeal. Indeed, the court went out of its way to claim that it was not applying a per se standard based on Robbie's transsexuality but was instead focusing only on the children's needs.[33] However, the mere fact that a court says it is concerned about the children's well-being and not the parent's gender identity does not prevent it from being improperly swayed by a divorced parent's decision to transition from one gender to another. This is what happened in Robbie's case—despite the appellate court's protestations to the contrary, it ended up essentially applying a per se standard by approving the lower court's view that the mere decision to transition from one gender to another constituted evidence of parental instability.

The problem with this conclusion is that there was nothing in the record suggesting that Robbie—whom the GAL deemed to be the more nurturing and engaged of the two parents—would not be able to care for her children as a woman as she had as a man. In addition, there was no evidence in the record that the children had been in any way harmed by Robbie's transsexualism. In the end, Robbie lost her custody dispute because she was a transsexual, a defeat that is unfortunately reminiscent of the cases, explored earlier in this book, of lesbian and gay parents who have lost custody of their children because of their sexual orientation.

▲

The transsexual cases explored so far in this chapter have involved individuals who had children in heterosexual marriages that eventually dissolved. As with lesbian and gay parents who find themselves in similar circumstances, the issue in these cases is not whether, as an initial matter, the LGBT individuals are legal parents (they clearly are), but is instead whether they are *good* parents. But transsexuals, like lesbians and gay men, also sometimes find themselves in court trying to persuade judges that they should be deemed parents of children whom they helped raise despite not being biologically related to them.

This is what happened to Michael Kantaras. When Michael met Linda in Florida in 1988 and fell in love with her, Linda had been living with a boyfriend for four years. The boyfriend eventually moved out of state, but not before getting her pregnant. After Michael and Linda had dated for some time, they started discussing the possibility of getting married, with Michael offering to help care for the soon-to-be born child.

A few weeks later, Michael was approaching the supermarket where Linda worked when he saw her sitting outside on a bench experiencing contractions. Michael rushed her to the hospital where she gave birth—after eleven hours of labor—to a baby boy whom she named Matthew.

Early on in their relationship, Michael told Linda that he had traveled to Texas the year before to undergo several sex reassignment procedures, including a double mastectomy and a total hysterectomy. Prior to the operations, he had completed hormonal therapy and a fourteen-month program in which he lived openly as a man.

In 1989, Michael and Linda were married in a Florida courthouse with many family members—and six-week-old Matthew—in attendance. A few months later, Michael successfully petitioned a court to adopt Matthew with Linda's full support. In the adoption paperwork, Michael identified himself as Linda's husband.

Wanting to have more children, the couple began visiting a local fertility clinic. Michael's brother agreed to donate sperm, and after only the second attempt at insemination by one of the clinic's physicians, Linda became pregnant. Their second child, Irina, was born in 1992.

The couple had several happy years together, with Michael supporting the family through his job as a baker and Linda staying at home to take care of the kids. (Linda was on Michael's health and retirement plans at work, listed in both as his spouse, a fact that became relevant later when Linda attempted to deny the legal validity of their marriage.) And, with some financial help from their parents, they purchased a home together. But eventually the relationship soured. After Michael confessed to Linda that he had fallen in love with her best friend, the couple separated. In 1998, Michael brought a divorce petition and asked the court to award him physical custody of the children.

Linda replied by filing papers alleging that their marriage was void *ab initio* ("from the beginning") because Michael was a woman and their marriage therefore had been a same-sex one. Linda also claimed that Michael had never legally adopted Matthew because the adoption was based on a marriage that was invalid under Florida law. Furthermore, she contended that the adoption was invalid because it was prohibited by Florida's ban on gay adoption. Finally, Linda told the court that Michael was not Irina's father because he had not provided the sperm and he had not been legally married to her at the time of conception. According to Linda and her lawyers, when all these points were put together, the court had no choice but to conclude that Michael was not Matthew or Irina's legal parent and that he was therefore not entitled to either custody or visitation.

Although there were many issues raised during the Kantaras divorce and custody trial—which lasted three weeks and was televised nationally by Court TV—the most important one was whether Michael was, as a legal matter, a man or a woman.

▲

The first American appellate court that was confronted directly with the issue of how the law should determine the sex of an individual was a New Jersey one in 1976. That case began when a postoperative male-to-female transsexual filed a claim asking for support and maintenance from her husband. The latter responded in court by contending that his marriage to the plaintiff was legally void because the plaintiff was a man.

The New Jersey court refused to follow an earlier British court, which had held that sex "is irrevocably cast at the moment of birth."[34] Rather than looking only at the issue of biological sex, the New Jersey court noted the importance of a person's psychological sex. As the court saw it, when an individual's self-identification as a woman, for example, matches medically created anatomical or genital features that are female, then the law should consider that person to be a woman for purposes of marriage, even if she was born a male and had male chromosomes.

Although the New Jersey court could have ended its analysis there in ruling that the plaintiff was a woman at the time of the marriage, and that therefore the marriage was valid, it proceeded to explain the importance of sexual capacity in deciding whether an individual is, as a legal matter, a man or a woman. It was the plaintiff's ability to act sexually as a woman following her sex reassignment surgery that was dispositive for the court, because it showed "the coalescence" of anatomical features with gender self-identification.

Most American courts that have grappled with the question of how the law should determine an individual's sex have disagreed with the New Jersey ruling. In 1999, for example, when a Texas appellate court was confronted with the question of whether a postoperative male-to-female transsexual had legally married a man, it concluded that an individual's sex is established at birth, and, once so determined, it cannot later change, at least for purposes of marriage. In holding that the plaintiff could not bring a wrongful death suit after the death of the person whom she considered to be her husband, the court explained that the plaintiff "inhabits a male body [except for] what the physicians have supplied."[35] For the court, the "man-made" anatomy was irrelevant to the issue of the plaintiff's legal sex. "There are some things," the court explained, "we cannot will into being. They just are." The plaintiff, therefore, was legally a man and her marriage to another man was not valid under Texas law.

Three years later, the Kansas Supreme Court agreed with this reasoning when it held that a postoperative male-to-female transsexual could not inherit property from the person she claimed to be her husband after the latter died without leaving a will. While the New Jersey court twenty years earlier had placed much weight on the ability of a transsexual to have sexual intercourse, the Kansas court looked to the ability to procreate. "[A] male-to-female post-operative transsexual," the court stated, "does not fit the definition of a female. The male organs have been removed, but the ability to produce ova and bear offspring does not and never did exist. There is no womb, cervix, or ovaries, nor is there any change in his chromosomes."[36]

▲

Given these prior cases, much of the Kantarases' divorce and custody trial revolved around questions such as whether Michael considered himself to be a man, his precise anatomical features, the extent to which he could "perform" sexually as a man, and even whether he urinated standing up or sitting down. Linda, for example, made much of the fact that Michael still had a vagina and had not had a phalloplasty, a genital reconstruction surgery in which a penis is created with the individual's own tissue (usually taken from the leg or abdomen). For his part, Michael emphasized at trial that he had an enlarged clitoris that sexually served as a penis, that he had many typically male physical features, and that he had always considered himself a man.

Michael also noted that he was a transsexual and not a gay person. As he explained, he was a heterosexual man who had married a woman and therefore Florida's ban against same-sex marriage should not be used to invalidate his marriage. Similarly, since he was not gay, Florida's ban against gay adoption did not apply to his adoption of Matthew.

Several weeks after the trial's conclusion, circuit court judge Gerard O'Brien issued an 809-page opinion (easily the longest judicial opinion ever written in an LGBT parenting case) in which he ruled that Michael Kantaras was a man. O'Brien, who came out of retirement specifically to hear the Kantaras case, reached this conclusion based on the fact that Michael had always considered himself to be male, and had been so deemed by most people who knew him. The judge also pointed out that "Michael is visibly male. He has a deep masculine voice, a chin beard and moustache, a thinning hair line and some balding, wide shoulders, muscular arms and the apparent shifting of fat away from the hips toward the stomach. He has a pronounced 'maleness' that prompts one to automatically refer to Michael with the pronoun he or him."[37] At the same time, as a result of medical treatments, he "had no secondary female identifying characteristics and [no] reproductive female organs . . . such as ovaries, fallopian tubes, cervix, womb, and breasts."[38]

As Judge O'Brien saw it, what mattered for purposes of whether a valid marriage existed was the sex of the individual at the time the marriage license was issued rather than at the time the individual was born. By the time Michael married Linda, the judge concluded, he was legally a man and therefore the marriage was not a same-sex one.

It was also important to Judge O'Brien that the Kantaras case, unlike the transsexual marriage cases from other jurisdictions that preceded it, involved children. Indeed, the earlier cases had only been about the legal rights of the transsexual parties themselves. In contrast, this case was also about the rights (and well-being) of children. If Michael and Linda's marriage was void, that would leave the children without the right of support from Michael. Another reason why the judge concluded that the marriage was valid, therefore, was to protect the children from the loss of a legal parent.

Once Judge O'Brien recognized the validity of the marriage, it followed that Michael was the parent of both children. As Linda's husband, Michael had been eligible under the law to adopt Matthew. And as Linda's husband who consented to her insemination with the sperm of another man, he was, under Florida law, Irina's father.

Giving him a complete legal victory, Judge O'Brien then proceeded to grant Michael primary physical custody of the children. He did this for several reasons. First, he noted that Linda, during the course of the litigation, had unilaterally and abruptly revealed to the children that their father was a transsexual, causing them a great deal of emotional distress. Second, and unlike most of the other judges whose opinions we have considered so far in this chapter, the Florida trial judge refused to conclude that Michael's transsexuality rendered him unable to provide good care to his children. And third, the judge found that Michael had shown a greater commitment than Linda to promoting the children's academic interests.

After her loss at the trial level, Linda contacted Mathew Staver, the president and general counsel of Liberty Counsel, the same Christian legal organization that represented Lisa Miller in her protracted legal fight—profiled in

Transsexual parent Michael Kantaras testifying at his divorce and custody trial in 2002. Used with permission of the *St. Petersburg Times*.

chapter 3—to keep her former lesbian partner from visiting with their child. Staver quickly agreed to represent Linda—who had become a fundamental-ist Christian a couple of years before—on appeal because his organization was as opposed to transsexual rights as it was to gay rights.

It was the conservative lawyer's position that the law should not "permit a person to change their sex like one changes clothes. . . . A few hormones and plastic surgery do not change a person's sex, which is an immutable trait fixed at birth."[39] The lawyer added that "numerous mental disorders involve cognitive dissonance between mind and body (anorexia to name one), but the law cannot condone mutilating the body to match the mind."[40] As far as Staver was concerned, Michael was—and always would be—a woman. As a result, Judge O'Brien's ruling upholding Michael's marriage to Linda constituted an impermissible recognition of a same-sex marriage.

What anti-LGBT rights activists like Staver rarely acknowledge when discussing the intersection of same-sex marriage and transsexuality is that, regardless of how the law determines who is a man and who is a woman, transsexuality inevitably leads to the recognition of some types of same-sex marriages. In a jurisdiction like Texas, in which sex, for marriage purposes, is defined according to the biological sex at birth, a genetic male (for example) who has had sex reassignment surgery and who has many of the physical attributes of a woman will be permitted to marry a woman. The state's same-sex marriage ban will not apply to this marriage even if most people are likely to perceive both spouses as being female.

And in a jurisdiction like New Jersey, in which sex, for marriage purposes, is defined when the psychological sex matches the anatomical one, a postoperative male-to-female transsexual (for example) who identifies as a female will be permitted to marry a man. The state's ban against same-sex marriage will not apply even though the two spouses have male chromosomes. The issue raised in cases like that of Michael and Linda Kantaras, therefore, is not *whether* same-sex marriages will be recognized, but instead *which ones*.

Michael's lawyers made a similar point in a different way in their brief to the Florida appellate court following Judge O'Brien's ruling. Interestingly, they claimed that by recognizing the marriage between Michael—who considered himself, and was considered by others, to be a male heterosexual—and Linda as valid, the court would be promoting *heterosexual* marriage, which was precisely what the Florida legislature had wanted to accomplish when it enacted the state's Defense of Marriage Act. Quoting approvingly from Judge O'Brien's decision, the brief argued that "'the law should not hinder the 'heterosexualization' of transsexual people who undergo sex reassignment surgery and who wish to enter into heterosexual relationships. 'It is better that transsexuals be allowed to marry under certain legal conditions whereby they maintain what society wants, a heterosexual marriage of opposite sexes.'"[41]

It was ironic, to say the least, that an LGBT litigant used the state's prohibition against same-sex marriage to argue that the court should recognize *his* marriage. Despite the irony, the argument was available to Michael because of the trial court's conclusion that he was, legally speaking, a man.

The Florida Court of Appeals, however, agreed with Linda's position that sex is an immutable characteristic that is determined at birth. The court explained that whether advances in medical treatments—which make it possible to change male anatomical features into female ones (and vice versa)— affected the legal definition of what it means to be a man or a woman was a policy decision for the legislature. Since the Florida legislature had not spoken on that issue, the court concluded that Michael was a woman and that therefore his marriage to Linda had never been valid.[42]

Although Linda urged the appellate court to also reverse Judge O'Brien's custody ruling, the court refused to do so. Instead, it sent the case back to the lower court for a new custody determination given its conclusion that the couple had never been legally married.

As both sides geared up for another hearing before the trial judge, the TV talk show host Phil McGraw ("Dr. Phil") invited Michael and Linda onto his nationally syndicated program. In front of the cameras, Dr. Phil encouraged them to try to settle the case for the children's sake. This was followed by two all-day mediation sessions, after which the former couple agreed that they would share legal custody of the children, that Linda would have primary physical custody, and that Michael would enjoy extensive visitation rights.

▲

Even though most of the Kantaras litigation focused on the validity of the couple's marriage, whether Michael was legally a parent should not have depended on the answer to that question. Michael, after all, had helped to raise both children for many years with Linda's consent and encouragement. In addition, it was undisputed at trial that Matthew and Irina considered him their father. Under the equitable doctrine of de facto parenthood explored in chapter 3, therefore, Michael should have been deemed the children's father regardless of the validity of his marriage to Linda. Unfortunately, Florida is one of the states which does not recognize that doctrine.[43]

What Michael had cared about the most from the beginning of the litigation was that he be able to retain his parental rights and responsibilities; as a result of the settlement agreement he reached with Linda, he was able to accomplish that goal. But other transsexual parents, such as Sterling Simmons, have not been so fortunate.

Although Sterling was born a genetic female in 1959, by the age of seven he began to realize that he wanted to be a boy, a desire that confused him. In junior high school, he read an article profiling a transsexual person, and that helped him understand what he was going through. By his late teens, Sterling was taking hormones and developing male physical traits.

Sterling met Jennifer in 1984 and the two began dating. The couple married in Chicago the following year. In 1991, they engaged the services of a doctor to help Jennifer become pregnant through alternative insemination with sperm donated by an anonymous donor. Before the first insemination, Sterling signed an agreement acknowledging that any child born as a result of the procedure would be his and waiving any right to disclaim responsibility for the child. After six insemination attempts, Jennifer became pregnant, leading to the birth of a baby boy, whom the couple named Armando. Ten days after the child was born, Sterling underwent surgery to have his internal female reproductive organs removed. He did not, however, have his external female genitalia or his breasts altered.

Sterling, Jennifer, and Armando lived as a family until 1998, when Sterling filed petitions in court for divorce and for custody of his son. The hearing that followed was similar to the one that took place in the Michael and Linda Kantaras case, with Sterling presenting evidence that he was a man and Jennifer contending that he was a woman. The trial court eventually agreed with Jennifer. In so doing, the judge placed great weight both on the fact that Sterling had female chromosomes and on his decision not to undergo the surgical procedures that would have modified his external female genitalia.

Once the judge concluded that Sterling was legally a woman, it followed that his marriage was a same-sex one, which was invalid under Illinois law. But the judge did not stop there; instead, he went on to conclude *that because the marriage was void, Sterling was not Armando's parent.*

The Cook County public guardian, who represented Armando during the litigation, vigorously disputed this last conclusion. The public guardian argued on appeal that it made no sense to punish the twelve-year-old boy by denying him a second parent—the person whom he had considered to be his father all of his life—simply because his parents had entered into what the court retroactively deemed to be a same-sex marriage.

It was undisputed throughout the proceedings that Sterling and Armando had established a strong parent-child bond through the years. For example, a social worker employed by the court reported that although Armando "feels an attachment to both his parents[,] . . . his strongest attachment is to his father. . . . While Mr. Simmons is not the child's biological father, he is and has always been his father in every other meaningful sense of the word."[44] Furthermore, a psychiatrist who interviewed the two adults and the child, and who was called to testify by the public guardian, concluded that Sterling was a good father who had established a strong and lasting relationship with his son. The expert witness also told the court that Sterling's transsexuality had not negatively affected Armando's well-being.

In his brief to the Illinois Court of Appeals, the public guardian took issue with the lower court's holding that the invalidity of Sterling and Jennifer's marriage meant that the parental relationship between Sterling and Armando was not legally recognizable. The guardian noted that the biological children of unmarried individuals do not lose their parents simply because they are unmarried. In addition, under Illinois law, when a married woman gives birth to a child, her husband is presumed to be the child's father even if the marriage is later found to be invalid.[45] Armando was being told, however, that the legal validity of his relationship with his father depended on the legal validity of the marriage between his father and mother. The brief complained that the boy was "suffering from a punishment that is never inflicted on other children: his father was essentially taken away from him, based on his parents' mistake of entering into a same-sex marriage. There is no rational basis for depriving [this child] of parentage while other children enjoy it."[46]

Unfortunately for Armando, the Illinois Court of Appeals upheld the trial judge's ruling that Sterling was not his parent. The appellate court, like the judge below, concluded that Sterling was a woman because he "still possesses all of his female genitalia."[47] Placing great emphasis on surgical procedures that Sterling could have undergone but chose not to—including "a vaginectomy, reduction mammoplasty, metoidoiplasty, scrotoplasty, urethroplasty, and phalloplasty"—the court held that Sterling's anatomical characteristics determined his legal gender.

For the court, the fact that Sterling was legally a woman meant that none of the parenthood-recognition mechanisms available under Illinois law was applicable to him. Although an Illinois statute called for the recognition of a husband's parenthood when he consented in writing to the alternative insemination of his wife with another man's sperm, Sterling could not avail himself of that law because he was a woman and therefore could not be a *husband*. Similarly, the statutory presumption that a man is the father of children born to his wife during a marriage even if the marriage is subsequently held to be invalid did not help Sterling because (again) he was legally a woman and not a man.

In the end, the court could not have been more explicit in concluding that *it was Sterling's sex that determined whether he was Armando's parent*. But sex, like biology, should not be determinative of whether someone is a child's parent. The court was so focused on identifying Sterling's "true" legal sex that it completely ignored the actual, *parental* relationship that Sterling had had with the boy for more than a decade—what was best for Armando got lost in lengthy judicial discussions of the precise nature and attributes of Sterling's sexual organs. The result, as the public guardian put it, was that the boy "woke up one day and, after more than a decade, his father was no longer his father. There are not many more harsh and wrenching forms of injustice in this world."[48]

It bears noting that in Sterling's case, there was not a third party making a parentage claim. Unlike, for example, in Martha Boyd's case from Kentucky—in which her former wife's new husband filed a petition to adopt the child—there was no one else claiming that he would be a better parent than the transsexual litigant. The only issue for the Illinois court, therefore, was whether Armando had one or two parents. The court's ruling meant that the boy lost the rights of support and companionship from a parent without gaining those benefits from another party.

The Illinois court's ruling was misguided because it allowed the question of whether Sterling was a man or a woman to determine whether he was a parent. Indeed, the court's emphasis on the need to ascertain Sterling's "true" sex blinded it to the parental relationship that Sterling had established with his son for more than ten years. As in most of the other cases profiled in this chapter, the judges on the Illinois appellate court were unable to look beyond Sterling's transsexuality to see the human being (and the parent) who stood behind it. In the end, the real losers in cases like Sterling's are not the transsexual litigants, but are instead children like Armando who are deprived of parents through judicial rulings that improperly focus on an individual's sex to determine whether he or she is legally entitled to be (or remain) a parent.

The proper rule in these types of cases is as easy to discern as it is to apply: if an individual would be a parent as a female (for example), then the fact that she has changed her female identity to a male one should not lead a court to deprive him of the rights, or excuse him from the obligations, of legal parenthood. Or, to put it more succinctly, gender does not make a parent.

Conclusion

Although this book has profiled many different types of parenting cases, all of them involved individuals who decided—either before or after they became parents—to live openly as lesbians, gay men, bisexuals, or transsexuals. It is likely that the path to parenthood for most of these individuals would have been considerably easier if they had chosen to stay in the closet. But to remain in the closet is to hide an important part of who one is; to lead a closeted life is, to some extent, to live a lie. And it goes without saying that good and effective parenting cannot be based on dishonesty.

This book has explored the different ways that courts have grappled with the refusal of LGBT parents to lead closeted lives. We saw in chapters 1 and 2, for example, how many judges in the 1970s and 1980s denied custody and visitation rights to lesbians and gay men because of their decision to lead open lives, most frequently by sharing their homes with their partners. While some of these judges may have been willing to countenance unrestricted contact between lesbian and gay parents and their children following a heterosexual divorce had the parents in question remained in the closet, that was a price that none of the profiled parents was willing to pay. These parents, by refusing to stay in the closet, directly challenged long-held assumptions about the incompatibility of homosexuality and parenthood.

Most jurisdictions eventually turned to the nexus test—which demands specific evidence of actual or potential harm to children caused by a parent's same-sex sexual orientation and relationships—as the best way of addressing the question of what role parents' openness about their sexuality should play in custody and visitation cases. A court's adoption of the nexus test by no means guarantees that it will not be improperly swayed by a divorced parent's same-sex sexual orientation and relationships. But the fact that most jurisdictions today place the burden of proof on the heterosexual parent to show the existence of harm has been a positive development for lesbian and gay parents.

Chapter 5 illustrated how the willingness of lesbians and gay men to be open about their sexual orientation has also played an important role in their ability to serve as foster care and adoptive parents. Like many lesbian and gay parents who want to retain custody of or have visitation with their children following the dissolution of a different-sex marriage, many prospective lesbian and gay foster care and adoptive parents have refused to hide their sexual orientation. As a result, child welfare officials have had to grapple with the relevance, if any, of a prospective parent's same-sex sexuality and relationships in making foster care and adoptive placement decisions.

As chronicled in chapter 5, the initial reaction of many state officials was to place roadblocks in the way of prospective foster care and adoptive parents who were open about their same-sex sexual orientation. But largely as a result of litigation, many of those roadblocks have been gradually lifted. For example, while Massachusetts for several years during the 1980s made it practically impossible for openly gay people to serve as foster parents, and while Florida for more than three decades prohibited openly gay people from adopting children, neither policy remains in place today. Given that there are about half a million children in foster care in the United States and approximately one hundred thousand children waiting to be adopted, the lifting of these types of restrictions is a moral and policy imperative.[1]

It is interesting to note that of none of the legal provisions limiting the ability of lesbians and gay men to adopt still in place today applies to single individuals. Instead, the impediments are aimed at those in ongoing same-sex relationships. Mississippi law, for example, explicitly prohibits same-sex couples from adopting, while a Utah statute bans individuals in cohabiting relationships from doing the same.[2] The reasoning behind these laws seems to be not so much that lesbians and gay men should be prohibited from adopting, but that gay people *in open relationships* should not be allowed to do so.

Since it is unlikely that prospective lesbian and gay foster care and adoptive parents will retreat en masse back into the closet, the question of openness regarding sexual orientation is likely to continue to play an important role in both the setting of foster care/adoption policies and in future legal challenges to them. As with the issue of custody and visitation following the dissolution of different-sex marriages, the law's general trend in the foster care/adoption area has been to focus on the needs of individual children, and how those needs can be met by particular adults, rather than to rely on presumptions of harm based on the unwillingness of prospective parents to hide who they are and whom they love.

▲

Another crucial question in LGBT parenting cases has been the role that biology should play in determining who is a parent. The cases have repeatedly questioned the traditional, seemingly exclusive, correlation between biology and parentage status. Indeed, all the cases profiled in chapters 3 and 4 (as well as several explored in chapter 6) were, at their core, about whether the determination of who is a parent should be expanded beyond considerations of biology to include additional factors, such as the intent of the adults and their willingness to function as the children's parental caretakers.

To allocate parentage rights based exclusively on the existence of a biological connection would be relatively easy. All that would be required is for adults claiming parentage status to take blood tests to determine whether they have genetic links to the children. In contrast, determining whether two individuals intended, prior to conception, to raise the child together can be complicated, especially when the parties disagree between themselves on what their expectations were when they were considering the prospect of parenthood. Establishing at what point adults have sufficiently cared for children—and sufficiently established bonds of love and affection with them—to support the conclusion that the law should recognize and protect their relationships can also be a complex question with different possible answers.

Despite the clear challenges that inhere in making these types of fact-specific assessments, attempting to do so is preferable to the alternative, which would be for the law to refuse to look beyond biology when assigning parentage status. I have argued in this book that it is essential that courts look to issues of intent and to questions of functional parenthood, because only by doing so will they be able to account both for the actual relationships that children have with adult caretakers and for the wide diversity of familial structures that exist in the United States today. Although some conservative advocacy groups and others contend that biological parents have a categorical right to deny parentage rights to their former same-sex partners, such a view improperly ignores the relationships of love and care that adults routinely establish with children in the absence of biological links.

To allow the lack of a biological connection between an adult and a child to be dispositive in assigning parentage status is misguided not because it violates the rights of the adult, but because it harms the child. Although courts have traditionally placed great emphasis on the marital status, gender, and sexual orientation of individuals raising children together, those considerations are surely less important to the children themselves. Indeed, it seems factually indisputable that most, and perhaps even all, of the children in the cases profiled in chapters 3 and 6 established relationships with the adults to whom they were not biologically related that were indistinguishable from the relationships they enjoyed with their biological parents. To limit their ability to have contact with the former following the dissolution of the adults' relationships is as harmful as it is to deny children contact with one of their two biological parents after a heterosexual divorce.

One of the interesting consequences of adopting legal rules that look beyond biology to determine who should be deemed a parent is that it affects different LGBT parents differently. As we saw in chapters 3 and 4, there are often LGBT individuals on *both* sides of disputes involving the role that biology should play in assigning parental rights. Thus, for example, when a court recognizes the parentage status of an LGBT person who does not have a biological connection to a child, it often does so at the expense of the rights of another LGBT individual who is a biological parent. And when courts refuse to recognize as parents gay men who provide their sperm, or lesbian women who provide their eggs, so that (other) lesbian women can conceive, they end up denying the parenting claim of LGBT individuals who have biological links with the children.

Furthermore, to limit the rights of biological LGBT parents is not an insignificant issue from a gay rights perspective since, as we saw in the cases profiled in the introduction, those rights can be essential in preventing third parties, including grandparents, from interfering with the relationships between LGBT parents and their children. It cannot be said, therefore, that there is a clear pro–gay rights position to take in all LGBT parenthood status cases that revolve around the proper relationship between biology and parentage—at least not one that will benefit all LGBT parties equally.

But the lack of such a position should not worry us because LGBT parenting cases, unlike most other gay rights cases, are not ultimately about the rights of LGBT people, but are instead about the interests of children. At the end of the day, those interests must serve as the courts' polestars in this area of the law. And those interests require that the law be sufficiently flexible to account for considerations that go beyond biological links to include the intent of the adults and the lived experiences of the children.

▲

This book has dealt with hot-button issues of sex, sexual orientation, and transsexuality, which are particularly contentious when the well-being of children is at stake. These issues are likely to continue to generate controversy and disagreement in our society for years to come. But it is my hope, for two reasons, that the parents' stories told in this book will help to allay at least some of the concerns of those who question the motivations of LGBT individuals to become parents, as well as of those who worry about the implications for children of being raised by LGBT individuals.

First, it should be clear that the LGBT parents whose stories I have chronicled here were deeply and unshakably committed to their children. From their perspective, what was at stake in their lawsuits were not issues of politics or of civil rights; instead, the legal battles were about fighting efforts, either by the government or by former spouses or partners, to separate them from (or limit their access to) their children.

Second, in none of the cases profiled in this book were litigation opponents of LGBT parents able to show that their sexual orientation or gender identity harmed the children involved. Indeed, concerns about harm to children caused by the LGBT parents raised in the cases profiled in chapters 1, 2, and 6 amounted to little more than generalized allegations based on unwarranted presumptions and fears, rather than the showing of specific and causal connections between the sexual orientation and gender identity of particular parents and the well-being of their children.

It is true, of course, that the parents profiled here represent only a sliver of the thousands of LGBT individuals who have raised, or are currently raising, children. But there is no reason to believe that what is distinctive about them is the quality of the care or the amount of love that they provided their children. Instead, what is most distinctive about them is that they had the courage and determination to fight for their children in the courts. As a result of their efforts, the law of parenthood in the United States—while by no means perfect—has been transformed in ways that make it significantly more cognizant of the diversity and complexities of American families than it was just a generation ago.

Some of the parents whose stories we have shared won their court battles, while others lost. But they have collectively made it easier for the LGBT parents who have followed to pursue the dreams and joys of parenthood. And in that process, they have helped to make possible the raising of tens of thousands of children in loving homes. It is ultimately the success stories of the actual parenting—more than the litigation victories—that will lead the country to provide LGBT families with the legal recognition and social respect they deserve.

▲

The legal disputes explored in this book have involved efforts by one side to persuade courts to look at the actual relationships between adults and the children they care for, rather than to rely on presumptions about parental status and care that are based on sexual orientation and gender identity. Indeed, it is clear from the lawsuits chronicled here that what is left out of the legal analysis in parenting cases is as important as what is included. When courts are able to get past preconceived notions based on individuals' sexual orientation and gender identity, they are much more likely to focus on what should matter most, that is, whether parents are adequately—or prospective parents are capable of—caring for children by providing nurturing and supportive home environments.

Legal disputes involving LGBT parents make obvious the limitations that inhere in using criteria such as biology, marital status, sexual orientation, and gender identity as indicators of competent parenthood. These factors, by their very nature, operate at a high level of generality because they rely on presumptions of competency rather than on individualized assessments. As we have seen, courts sometimes assume that if an individual has a biological relationship with the child, or is in a marital relationship with someone of the opposite sex, or has a gender identity that is consistent with his or her biological sex, then that individual is likely to be a better parent than someone who meets none (or only some) of those criteria.

At the core of the legal struggles on behalf of LGBT parents has been a concerted effort to question the validity of using these proxies to determine parental competence. In the end, what should matter most in determining whether particular individuals are (or can be) good parents is not who they are but how they carry out their responsibilities of parenthood. If the character and the conduct of current or prospective parents show that they are able to love and care for children in ways that promote the latter's well-being, then it should not matter whether they are biologically related to the children, or whether they are men or women, or whether they are gay or straight. Going forward, what is required of judges and other decision makers who hold the future of children in their hands is, above all else, that they account for the actual relationships between adults and the children whom they care for rather than cling to rigid and outmoded conceptions of what every family (and every parent) should look like.

Notes

NOTES TO THE INTRODUCTION

1. B. Drummond Ayres, "Gay Woman Loses Custody of Her Son to Her Mother," *New York Times*, September 8, 1993, A7.

2. Transcript of Judge's Ruling, Bottoms v. Bottoms, Circuit Court of Henrico County, Virginia, No. 93JA0517, September 7, 1993, 195.

3. Deborah Kelly, "Lesbian Ruled Unfit to Raise 2 Year Old," *Richmond Times-Dispatch*, September 8, 1993, A1.

4. Deborah Kelly, "Lesbian Mother Tells Story," *Richmond Times-Dispatch*, September 10, 1993, B3.

5. Bottoms v. Bottoms, 1999 WL 1129720 (Va. Ct. App.). In 1996, ABC aired a made-for-TV movie based on Sharon Bottoms's case called *Two Mothers for Zachary*. Valerie Bertinelli starred as Sharon Bottoms and Vanessa Redgrave as her mother Kay.

6. Bottoms v. Bottoms, 457 S.E.2d 102, 108 (Va. 1995). The state supreme court reversed an intermediate appellate ruling that had concluded that Sharon should retain custody of her child. See Bottoms v. Bottoms, 444 S.E.2d 276 (Va. Ct. App. 1994).

7. Mason v. Moon, 385 S.E.2d 242 (Va. Ct. App. 1989).

8. Walker v. Fagg, 400 S.E.2d 208 (Va. Ct. App. 1991).

9. Deborah Kelly, "Mother Facing Setback in Quest to Regain Custody: Lesbian Relationship Was Factor in Case," *Richmond Times-Dispatch*, May 11, 1993, B3.

10. Brief of Appellee, Bottoms v. Bottoms, Virginia Supreme Court, No. 94-1166, December 28, 1994, 4–5.

11. Chaffin v. Frye, 45 Cal. App. 3d 39, 47–48 (Ct. App. 1975).

12. "A Display of Homophobia in Appeals Court," *Advocate*, March 12, 1975, 6; "Lesbian Appeals Custody Case for Lack of 'Reason,'" *Advocate*, September 11, 1974, 9. Several months after she lost before the California Court of Appeal, Lynda Chaffin, with the assistance of Cheryl Bratman, a lesbian and a third-year law student from Loyola Law School in Los Angeles, successfully brought a petition to modify the original order granting custody to her parents. During those proceedings, Lynda proved that her teenage daughters did not want to live with her parents—the children had run away from their grandparents' home several times. In addition, the judge who ordered that custody be modified noted that "Chaffin affirmatively submitted expert evidence which indicated that it was in the children's best interests to remain with their mother, and that it would be detrimental to the children to be taken away from her." *Mom's Apple Pie*, June 1975, 1. The court's opinion was Chaffin v. Frye, California Superior Court, Los Angeles County, No. 44465, May 19, 1975.

13. William A. Henry, "Gay Parents: Under Fire and on the Rise," *Time*, September 30, 1993, 66.

14. See, e.g., Editorial, "The Bottom Line for Sharon Bottoms," *St. Louis Post-Dispatch*, May 7, 1995, 2B; Editorial, "A Case of Justice Gone Badly Awry," *Chicago Tribune*, May 6, 1995, A20.

15. D.C. Code, § 16-914(a).

16. George Vecsey, "Approval Given for Homosexual to Adopt a Boy," *New York Times*, June 21, 1979, B1.

17. Cheri Pies, *Considering Parenthood* (San Francisco: Aunt Lute, 1985).

18. Lesléa Newman, *Heather Has Two Mommies* (Boston: Alyson, 1989).

19. Gina Kolata, "Lesbian Partners Find the Means to Be Parents," *New York Times*, January 30, 1989, A13; Jonathan Mandell, "The Lesbian Baby Boom," *Newsweek*, July 13, 1989, 8.

20. Michael Willhoite, *Daddy's Roommate* (Boston: Alyson, 1990).

21. April Martin, *The Lesbian and Gay Parenting Handbook* (New York: HarperCollins, 1993).

22. Susan Chira, "Gay Parents Become Increasingly Visible," *New York Times*, September 30, 1993, A1.

23. Ellen Lewin, *Lesbian Mothers: Accounts of Gender in American Culture* (Ithaca, N.Y.: Cornell University Press, 1993).

24. The only exception is Mary Jo Risher, a lesbian mother profiled in chapter 2 who, before she came out as a lesbian, adopted a child with her then husband.

25. I sometimes use the term "parentage" rather than "parenthood" to reflect the fact that some of the litigation explored in this book, in particular the cases discussed in chapters 3 and 4, involves the question of whether an LGBT individual should be recognized as a child's parent for certain purposes—such as seeking custody and visitation after the dissolution of a same-sex relationship—rather than for all purposes.

26. For a discussion of LGBT rights litigation led by movement lawyers, see Carlos A. Ball, *From the Closet to the Courtroom: Five LGBT Lawsuits That Have Changed Our Nation* (Boston: Beacon, 2010).

27. Many of the names of litigants in the cases explored in this book are real. I generally use pseudonyms only when discussing cases decided after 1985 in which the parties' actual names were not part of the litigation's public record and were not widely disseminated in the media.

28. In re Visitation of C. L. H., 908 N.E.2d 320, 328 (Ind. Ct. App. 2009).

NOTES TO CHAPTER 1

1. Donna Hitchens and Barbara Price, "Trial Strategy in Lesbian Mother Custody Cases: The Use of Expert Testimony," 9 *Golden Gate University Law Review* 451, 453 (1978/79) (emphasis added). The judge ended up awarding custody to the heterosexual father after advising the mother "to get therapy" and explaining that he could not "take the chance that something untoward would happen to [the child]" if she remained in her mother's care. Ibid., 454. The case in question was Nadler v. Nadler, California Superior Court, Sacramento County, No. 177331, November 15, 1967.

2. Gary Atkins, *Gay Seattle: Stories of Exile and Belonging* (Seattle: University of Washington Press, 2003), 152.

3. Ibid.

4. Gifford Guy Gibson, with Mary Jo Risher, *By Her Own Admission: A Lesbian Mother's Fight to Keep Her Son* (Garden City, N.Y.: Doubleday, 1977), 85.

5. Ibid., 151.

6. Ibid., 174.

7. Nan D. Hunter and Nancy D. Polikoff, "Custody Rights of Lesbian Mothers: Legal Theory and Litigation Strategy," 25 *Buffalo Law Review* 691, 727 (1976).

8. Ibid., 729.

9. Letter from Dr. Benjamin Spock to Dr. Bruce Voeller, June 19, 1973.

10. Gibson, *By Her Own Admission*, 167.

11. Lisa I. Schwartz, "Lesbian Mother Continues Custody Struggle," *Gay Community News*, March 20, 1976.

12. Gibson, *By Her Own Admission*, 165.

13. Ibid., 196.

14. Ibid., 200.

15. "Briefs," *Time*, January 12, 1976, 54.

16. "Custody Case Jury Begins Deliberation," *Fort Worth Star-Telegram*, December 23, 1975, A15; Don Mason, "Custody Undecided: Jury Deliberating Lesbian's Case," *Dallas Morning News*, December 23, 1975, 6A.

17. Jim Hardin, "Decision Expected in Custody Case," *Dallas Time Herald*, December 23, 1975.

18. Gibson, *By Her Own Admission*, 229.

19. Ibid., 236.

20. Lindsay Van Gelder, "Lesbian Custody: A Tragic Day in Court," *Ms.*, September 1976, 72, 73.

21. "Lesbian Plans Appeal," *Dallas Morning News*, January 8, 1977, 8A.

22. In 1978, ABC aired a sympathetic made-for-TV movie based on Mary Jo's custody fight, *A Question of Love*, starring Jane Alexander and Gena Rowlands. By that time, Mary Jo's relationship with Ann had ended due to the stress and strain caused by the trial and the loss of custody of her son.

23. "Colorful Lawyer Dies," *Spokane Daily Chronicle*, July 4, 1980, 6.

24. "Seattle: A Family First," *Seven Days*, September 14, 1974, 8.

25. Court's Oral Decision, Schuster v. Schuster and Isaacson v. Isaacson, Superior Court of the State of Washington, County of King, Nos. D-36867–68, September 3, 1974, 6.

26. Ibid., 8.

27. Findings of Fact and Conclusions of Law, Schuster v. Schuster and Isaacson v. Isaacson, Superior Court of the State of Washington, County of King, Nos. D-36867–68, November 7, 1974, 5.

28. Hunter and Polikoff, "Custody Rights of Lesbian Mothers," 695.

29. Nadler v. Superior Court, 255 Cal. App. 2d 523 (Ct. App. 1967).

30. In re Tammy, California Court of Appeal, First Appellate District, No. 32648, August 2, 1973, quoted in R. A. Basile, "Lesbian Mothers I," 2 *Women's Rights Law Reporter* 3, 21 (1974) (emphasis added).

31. In re Deanna P., Superior Court of California, Sonoma County, No. 10747-J, July 12, 1973, quoted in Basile, "Lesbian Mothers I," 22. This decision was affirmed on appeal. See

In re Deanna P., California Court of Appeal, First Appellate District, No. 34000, July 2, 1974.

32. Townend v. Townend, 1 *Family Law Reporter* 2830, 2831 (1975) (Ohio Ct. C.P., Portage County, March 14, 1975).

33. Order Continuing Temporary Wardship and Order of Custody, Koop v. Koop, Washington Superior Court, Pierce County, Nos. 28218–19, February 6, 1976, 5.

34. In re Jane B., 380 N.Y.S. 2d 848 (Sup. Ct. 1976).

35. Brief of Appellants, Schuster v. Schuster and Isaacson v. Isaacson, Washington Supreme Court, No. 3441-I, July 30, 1975, 18–19.

36. Nancy Driber and Marilyn Koop, a lesbian couple, filed separate divorce actions against their husbands in 1973, seeking custody of their respective three children after all eight began living together as a family. In an example of the arbitrariness of custody decisions, a judge granted custody to Driber, holding that her sexual orientation was "irrelevant," while a separate judge in the same county on the same day denied Koop custody of two of her children, calling her living arrangement "abnormal," "not stable," and highly detrimental to the children. Driber v. Driber, Washington Superior Court, Pierce County, No. 220748, September 17, 1973; Koop v. Koop, Washington Superior Court, Pierce County, No. 221097, September 17, 1973. It would take another five years for Koop to regain custody of her children, and then only because—wanting to live with their mother—they repeatedly ran away from their father's home. "Koop Wins," *Mom's Apple Pie*, May 1978, 9.

37. *Mom's Apple Pie*, November 1974, 1; *Mom's Apple Pie*, June 1975, 1.

38. A recent documentary tells the story of the LMNDF and its work on behalf of lesbian mothers during the 1970s. See *Mom's Apple Pie: The Heart of the Lesbian Mothers' Custody Movement* (2006).

39. Jen Collettaa, "Rosalie Davies, 70, Lesbian Activist," *Philadelphia Gay News*, July 2009, http://epgn.com/pages/full_story/push?article-Rosalie+Davies-+70-+lesbian+activist%20&id=3018545&instance=home_news.

40. "A Victory in Illinois," *Mom's Apple Pie*, May 1977, 1.

41. Schuster v. Schuster, 585 P.2d 130 (Wash. 1978).

42. Gaylord v. Tacoma School Dist. 10, 559 P.2d 1340 (Wash. 1977).

43. Appellant's Brief, Doe v. Doe, Virginia Supreme Court, No. 790824, December 28, 1979, 5–6.

44. Doe v. Doe, 284 S.E.2d 799, 802 (Va. 1981).

45. Appellant's Brief, Doe v. Doe, 8.

46. Final Order, in re Adoption of Jack Doe, Virginia Circuit Court of Franklin County, March 5, 1979, 2.

47. Compare Sylvander v. New England Home for Little Wonders, 584 F.2d 1103 (1st Cir. 1978) (not allowing use of writ in parental rights termination cases) with Davis v. Page, 640 F.2d 599 (5th Cir. 1981) (reaching the opposite conclusion).

48. The U.S. Court of Appeals for the Fourth Circuit eventually held that the writ of habeas corpus could not be issued in a parental termination case. Doe v. Doe, 660 F.2d 101 (4th Cir. 1981).

49. Interview with Marianne MacQueen in the documentary film *Labor More Than Once* (1983).

50. Doe v. Doe, 284 S.E.2d 799, 804–5 (Va. 1981).

51. See, e.g., S. N. E. v. R. L. B., 699 P.2d 875 (Alaska 1985); Bezio v. Patenaude, 410 N.E.2d 1207 (Mass. 1980).

52. For citations, see note 78.

53. See, e.g., Susan Golombok, Ann Spencer, and Michael Rutter, "Children in Lesbian and Single-Parent Households: Psychosexual and Psychiatric Appraisal," 24(4) *Journal of Child Psychology and Psychiatry* 551 (1983); Sharon L. Huggins, "A Comparative Study of Self-Esteem of Adolescent Children of Divorced Lesbian Mothers and Divorced Heterosexual Mothers," in *Homosexuality and the Family*, ed. Frederick W. Bozett (Binghamton, N.Y.: Haworth, 1989), 123; M. Kirkpatrick, C. Smith, and R. Roy, "Lesbian Mothers and Their Children: A Comparative Survey," 51(3) *American Journal of Orthopsychiatry* 545 (1981).

54. See, e.g., A. Brewaeys, I. Ponjaert, E. V. Van Hall, and S. Golombok, "Donor Insemination: Child Development and Family Functioning in Lesbian Mother Families," 12(6) *Human Reproduction* 1349 (1997); Raymond W. Chan, Barbara Raboy, and Charlotte J. Patterson, "Psychosocial Adjustment among Children Conceived via Donor Insemination by Lesbian and Heterosexual Mothers," 69(2) *Child Development* 443 (1998).

55. See, e.g., K. Vanfraussen, I. Ponjaert-Kristoffersen, and A. Brewaeys, "What Does It Mean for Youngsters to Grow up in a Lesbian Family Created by Means of Donor Insemination?," 20(4) *Journal of Reproductive and Infant Psychology* 237 (2002); Jennifer L. Wainwright and Charlotte J. Patterson, "Peer Relations among Adolescents with Female Same-Sex Parents," 44(1) *Developmental Psychology* 117 (2008); Jennifer L. Wainwright and Charlotte J. Patterson, "Delinquency, Victimization, and Substance Abuse among Adolescents with Female Same-Sex Parents," 20(3) *Journal of Family Psychology* 526 (2006).

56. See, e.g., Stephen Erich, Heather Kanenberg, Kim Case, Theresa Allen, and Takis Bogdanos, "An Empirical Analysis of Factors Affecting Adolescent Attachment in Adoptive Families with Homosexual and Straight Parents," 31(3) *Children and Youth Services Review* 398 (2009); Rachel H. Farr, Stephen L. Forsell, and Charlotte J. Patterson, "Parenting and Child Development in Adoptive Families: Does Parental Sexual Orientation Matter?," 14(3) *Applied Developmental Science* 164 (2010); Rachel H. Farr and Charlotte J. Patterson, "Transracial Adoption by Lesbian, Gay, and Heterosexual Couples: Who Completes Transracial Adoptions and with What Results?," 12(3/4) *Adoption Quarterly* 187 (2009); Patrick Leung, Stephen Erich, and Heather Kanenberg, "A Comparison of Family Functioning in Gay/Lesbian, Heterosexual and Special Needs Adoptions," 27(9) *Children and Youth Services Review* 1031 (2005); Scott Ryan, "Parent-Child Interaction Styles between Gay and Lesbian Parents and Their Adopted Children," 3(2/3) *Journal of GLBT Family Studies* 105 (2007).

57. See, e.g., Brewaeys et al., "Donor Insemination"; Tamar D. Gershon, Jeanne M. Tschann, and John Jemerin, "Stigmatization, Self-Esteem, and Coping among the Adolescent Children of Lesbian Mothers," 24(6) *Journal of Adolescent Health* 437 (1999).

58. See, e.g. , Brewaeys et al., "Donor Insemination."

59. See, e.g., ibid.; Megan Fulcher, Erin L. Sutfin, and Charlotte J. Patterson, "Individual Differences in Gender Development: Associations with Parental Sexual Orientation, Attitudes, and Division of Labor," 58(5/6) *Sex Roles* 330 (2008); Susan Golombok, Beth Perry, Amanda Burston, Clare Murray, Julie Mooney-Somers, Madeleine Stevens, and

Jean Golding, "Children with Lesbian Parents: A Community Study," 39(1) *Developmental Psychology* 20 (2003).

60. Richard Green, Jane Barclay Mandel, Mary E. Hotvedt, James Gray, and Laurel Smith, "Lesbian Mothers and Their Children: A Comparison with Solo Parent Heterosexual Mothers and Their Children," 15(2) *Archives of Sexual Behavior* 167 (1986).

61. See, e.g., Richard Green, "Sexual Identity of 37 Children Raised by Homosexual or Transsexual Parents," 135(6) *American Journal of Psychiatry* 692 (1978); J. Michael Bailey, David Bobrow, Marilyn Wolfe, and Sarah Mikach, "Sexual Orientation of Adult Sons of Gay Fathers," 31(1) *Developmental Psychology* 124 (1995); Ghazala Alzal Javaid, "The Children of Homosexual and Heterosexual Single Mothers," 23(4) *Child Psychiatry and Human Development* 235 (1993).

62. Susan Golombok and Shirlene Badger, "Children Raised in Mother-Headed Families from Infancy: A Follow-Up of Children of Lesbian and Single Heterosexual Mothers at Early Adulthood," 25(1) *Human Reproduction* 150 (2010).

63. Susan Golombok and Fiona Tasker, "Do Parents Influence the Sexual Orientation of Their Children? Findings from a Longitudinal Study of Lesbian Families," 32(1) *Developmental Psychology* 3 (1996).

64. Nanette K. Gartrell, Henny M. W. Bos, and Naomi G. Goldberg, "Adolescents of the U.S. National Longitudinal Lesbian Family Study: Sexual Orientation, Sexual Behavior, and Sexual Risk Exposure," 40 *Archives Sexual Behavior* (2011), http://www.springer-link.com/content/d967883qp3255733/fulltext.pdf.

65. Affidavit of Michael Lamb, Gill v. Office of Personnel Management, U.S. District Court for the District of Massachusetts, No. 1:09-CV-10309, November 11, 2009, 14.

66. See, e.g., Henry M. W. Bos, Frank van Balen, and Dymphna van den Boom, "Child Adjustment and Parenting in Planned Lesbian-Parent Families," 77(1) *American Journal of Orthopsychiatry* 38 (2007) (comparing one hundred planned lesbian families with one hundred heterosexual-parent families); Gershon, Tschann, and Jemerin, "Stigmatization, Self-Esteem, and Coping among the Adolescent Children of Lesbian Mothers" (studying seventy-six adolescents raised by lesbian mothers).

67. See, e.g., Golombok et al., "Children with Lesbian Parents"; Michael J. Rosenfeld, "Nontraditional Families and Childhood Progress through School," 47(3) *Demography* 755 (2010); Jennifer L. Wainwright, "Psychosocial Adjustment, School Outcomes, and Romantic Relationships of Adolescents with Same-Sex Parents," 75(6) *Child Development* 1886 (2004).

68. One longitudinal study is the USA National Lesbian Longitudinal Family Study. See Nanette Gartrell and Henny Bos, "U.S. National Longitudinal Lesbian Family Study: Psychological Adjustment of 17-Year-Old Adolescents," 126(1) *Pediatrics* 1 (2010). Another longitudinal study has followed children of lesbian mothers living in Avon, England. See Golombok and Badger, "Children Raised in Mother-Headed Families from Infancy."

69. American Psychological Association, *Lesbian and Gay Parenting: A Resource for Psychologists* (Washington, D.C.: APA, 1995), 8.

70. American Academy of Pediatrics, "Technical Report: Coparent or Second-Parent Adoption by Same-Sex Parents," 109(2) *Pediatrics* 341, 343 (2002).

71. Damron v. Damron, 670 N.W.2d 871, 873 (N.D. 2003).

72. Ibid., 876.

73. Ibid., 873.

74. Jacobson v. Jacobson, 314 N.W.2d 78, 80 (N.D. 1981). For other judicial opinions that considered a parent's homosexuality to be per se harmful to children, see Thigpen v. Carpenter, 730 S.W.2d 510 (Ark. Ct. App. 1987); S. E. G. v. R. A. G., 735 S.W.2d 164 (Mo. Ct. App. 1987).

75. Brief of Appellee, Damron v. Damron, Supreme Court of North Dakota, No. 2003-0135, August 20, 2003, 4.

76. Opening Brief of Appellant, Damron v. Damron, Supreme Court of North Dakota, No. 2003-0135, June 18, 2003, ¶ 47.

77. *Damron*, 670 N.W.2d at 875.

78. The court cited the following cases from other jurisdictions that similarly refused to hold that parents' same-sex sexual orientation and relationships could be used against them in custody and visitation cases in the absence of evidence of actual or potential harm: S. N. E. v. R. L. B., 699 P.2d 875 (Alaska 1985); Jacoby v. Jacoby, 763 So.2d 410 (Fla. Ct. App. 2000); In re Marriage of R. S., 677 N.E.2d 1297 (Ill. Ct. App. 1996); D. H. v. J. H., 418 N.E.2d 286 (Ind. Ct. App. 1981); Hassenstab v. Hassenstab, 570 N.W.2d 368 (Neb. Ct. App. 1997); Inscoe v. Inscoe, 700 N.E.2d 70 (Ohio Ct. App. 1997); Fox v. Fox, 904 P.2d 66 (Okla. 1995); Stroman v. Williams, 353 S.E.2d 704 (S.C. Ct. App. 1987); Van Driel v. Van Driel, 525 N.W.2d 37 (S.D. 1994); Matter of Marriage of Cabalquinto, 669 P.2d 886 (Wash. 1983). For similar rulings, see also In re Marriage of Birdsall, 197 Cal. App. 3d 1024 (Ct. App. 1988); McGriff v. McGriff, 99 P.3d 111 (Idaho 2004); Teegarden v. Teegarden, 642 N.E.2d 1007 (Ind. Ct. App. 1994); Paul C. v. Tracy C., 622 N.Y.S. 2d 159 (N.Y. App. Div. 1994).

79. Ex parte J. M. F., 730 So.2d 1190, 1194 (Ala. 1998).

80. Davidson v. Coit, 899 So.2d 904 (Miss. Ct. App. 2005).

81. Taylor v. Taylor, 110 S.W.2d 731 (Ark. 2003); Hollon v. Hollon, 784 So.2d 943 (Miss. 2001).

82. Downey v. Muffley, 767 N.E.2d 1014 (Ind. Ct. App. 2002).

NOTES TO CHAPTER 2

1. Bruce Voeller and James Walters, "Gay Fathers," 27(2) *Family Coordinator* 149, 155 (1978).

2. Marcia Chambers, "Ex–City Official Says He's Homosexual," *New York Times*, October 3, 1973, A1.

3. Richard Green and John Money, eds., *Transsexualism and Sex Reassignment* (Baltimore: John Hopkins University Press, 1969).

4. Richard Green, Jane Barclay Mandel, Mary E. Hotvedt, James Gray, and Laurel Smith, "Lesbian Mothers and Their Children: A Comparison with Solo Parent Heterosexual Mothers and Their Children," 15(2) *Archives of Sexual Behavior* 167 (1986); Richard Green, "Sexual Identity of 37 Children Raised by Homosexual or Transsexual Parents," 135(6) *American Journal of Psychiatry* 692 (1978).

5. Richard A. Gardner, *The Boys and Girls Book about Divorce* (New York: Science House, 1970).

6. Carol S. Bruch, "Parental Alienation Syndrome and Parental Alienation: Getting It Wrong in Child Custody Cases," 35(3) *Family Law Quarterly* 528 (2001); Stuart Lavietes, "Richard Gardner, 72, Dies; Cast Doubt on Abuse Claims," *New York Times*, June 9, 2003, B7.

7. In the Matter of J. S. & C., 324 A.2d 90, 96 (N.J. Super. Ct., 1974).

8. Ibid.

9. In the Matter of J. S. & C., 362 A.2d 54 (N.J. App. Div. 1976).

10. Brief of Appellant, J. L. P. (H.) v. D. J. P., Missouri Court of Appeals, No. 33116, June 2, 1982, 6.

11. Ibid., 2.

12. Brief of Respondent, J. L. P. (H.) v. D. J. P., Missouri Court of Appeals, No. 33116, June 15, 1982, 15.

13. Brief of Appellant, J. L. P. (H.) v. D. J. P., 33, quoting from ruling by Judge Gaitan.

14. Ibid., 37.

15. J. L. P. (H.) v. D. J. P., 643 S.W.2d 865, 869 (Mo. Ct. App. 1982).

16. See, e.g., N. K. M. v. L. E. M. 60 S.W.2d 179 (Mo. Ct. App. 1980); L. v. D., 630 S.W.2d 240 (Mo. Ct. App. 1982); S. E. G. v. R. A. G., 735 S.W.2d 164 (Mo. Ct. App. 1987).

17. Agreed Record, Conkel v. Conkel, Ohio Court of Common Pleas, Pickaway County, No. 81-CI-261, September 10, 1985, 1.

18. Judgment Entry, Conkel v. Conkel, Ohio Court of Common Pleas, Pickaway County, No. 81-CI-261, September 10, 1985, 2.

19. Brief of Appellant, Conkel v. Conkel, Ohio Court of Appeals, No. 85-CA-38, March 25, 1985, 4.

20. "AIDS Looms as an Issue in Visits by Fathers," *New York Times*, October 5, 1986, A17.

21. The trial court's ruling was overturned on appeal. See Stewart v. Stewart, 521 N.E.2d 956 (Ind. Ct. App. 1988).

22. Brief of Appellee, Conkel v. Conkel, Ohio Court of Appeals, No. 85-CA-38, November 18, 1985, 2.

23. Jacobson v. Jacobson, 314 N.W.2d 78, 81 (N.D. 1981).

24. Conkel v. Conkel, 509 N.E.2d 983, 987 (Ohio Ct. App. 1987).

25. Palmore v. Sidoti, 466 U.S. 429 (1984).

26. Roberts v. Roberts, 489 N.E.2d 1067, 1070 (Ohio Ct. App. 1985).

27. Roe v. Roe, 324 S.E.2d 691, 692 (Va. 1985).

28. Brief for Amici Curiae, American Civil Liberties Union of Northern Virginia, Roe v. Roe, Supreme Court of Virginia, No. 832044, November 5, 1984, 5.

29. Doe v. Doe, 284 S.E.2d 799 (Va. 1981).

30. Brown v. Brown, 237 S.E.2d 89 (Va. 1977).

31. Roe v. Roe, 324 S.E.2d 691, 694 (Va. 1985).

32. Mongerson v. Mongerson, 678 S.E.2d 891, 894 (Ga. 2009).

33. Associated Press, "Kids to Meet Gay Dad's Partner on Father's Day," June 20, 2009.

34. Brief of Amici Curiae, Lambda Legal Defense and Education Fund, Mongerson v. Mongerson, Supreme Court of Georgia, No. S09F0132, February 17, 2009, 6.

35. Brandenburg v. Brandenburg, 551 S.E.2d 721, 722 (Ga. 2001).

36. *Mongerson*, 678 S.E.2d at 895.

37. The question of who is eligible to be a parent, as we will see in chapter 5, has also been at the center of legal disputes between the government and (prospective) lesbian and gay parents in the context of foster care and adoption.

1. Martin Currie-Cohen, Lesleigh Luttrell, and Sander Shapiro, "Current Practice of Artificial Insemination by Donor in the United States," 300(11) *New England Journal of Medicine* 585 (1979).

2. Anne Taylor Fleming, "New Frontiers in Conception," *New York Times Magazine,* July 12, 1980, 14.

3. Jil Clark, "Sperm Bank Welcomes Unmarried Recipients," *Gay Community News,* October 30, 1982, 3.

4. Amy Agigian, *Baby Steps: How Lesbian Alternative Insemination Is Changing the World* (Middletown, Conn.: Wesleyan University Press, 2004), xvi.

5. U.S. Congress, Office of Technology Assessment, *Artificial Insemination: Practice in the United States: Summary of a 1987 Survey* (Washington, D.C.: U.S. Government Printing Office, 1988), 9.

6. Judie Telfer, "Artificial Insemination Solution for Lesbians Who Wanted Own Child," *Boston Evening Globe,* June 16, 1979, 31.

7. In fact, two years after the newspaper reports on the birth of their child, the lesbian couple from Oakland separated. In what may have been the first such ruling in the country, a California trial judge in 1984 held that the nonbiological mother had the right to visit with the child over the objections of the biological mother. See "Lesbians' Custody Fight on Coast Raises Novel Issues in Family Law," *New York Times,* September 9, 1984, A14. The court issued its written ruling the following year. See Loftin v. Flournoy, California Superior Court, Alameda County, No. 569630-7, January 2, 1985.

8. It is not clear from the public record what role, if any, Virginia continued to play in the life of the couple's second child.

9. Elliot Grossman, "City Boy at Center of Lawsuit That Aims to Change State Law," *Poughkeepsie Journal,* July 24, 1988, 1A.

10. Ibid.

11. Ibid.

12. 1973 Uniform Parentage Act, § 5(a).

13. See, e.g., Connecticut General Statutes, § 45a-772; Oregon Revised Statutes, § 677.360.

14. New York Domestic Relations Law, § 73(1). There were two main differences between the New York statute and the UPA. First, the former, but not the latter, required that the consent of both the husband and the wife be in writing. Second, while the UPA required that the insemination be conducted "under the *supervision* of a licensed physician," the New York statute required that it be "*performed* by persons duly authorized to practice medicine" (emphasis added).

15. New York Domestic Relations Law, § 70(a).

16. Grossman, "City Boy at Center of Lawsuit," 2A.

17. Oral Argument, Alison D. v. Virginia M., New York Court of Appeals, March 20, 1991.

18. Ronald FF. v. Cindy GG., 511 N.E.2d 75 (N.Y. 1987).

19. Carter v. Broderick, 644 P.2d 850 (Alaska 1982); Spells v. Spells, 378 A.2d 879 (Pa. Super. Ct. 1977); In re Custody of D. M. M., 404 N.W.2d 530 (Wisc. 1987).

20. Tubwon v. Weisberg, 394 N.W.2d 601 (Minn. Ct. App. 1986); In re Adoption of Young, 364 A.2d 1307 (Pa. 1976); In re Paternity of D. L. H., 419 N.W.2d 283 (Wisc. 1987).

21. Alison D. v. Virginia M., 552 N.Y.S. 2d 321 (N.Y. App. Div. 1990).

22. Braschi v. Stahl Associates, 543 N.E.2d 49 (N.Y. 1989). I explore the *Braschi* case in some detail in my book *From the Closet to the Courtroom: Five LGBT Lawsuits That Have Changed Our Nation* (Boston: Beacon, 2010), 21–65.

23. Oral Argument, Alison D. v. Virginia M., New York Court of Appeals, March 20, 1991.

24. Alison D. v. Virginia M., 572 N.E.2d 27, 28 (N.Y. 1991).

25. Kevin Sack, "Lesbian Loses a Ruling on Parent's Rights," *New York Times*, May 3, 1991, B1.

26. In re Interest of Z. J. H., 471 N.W.2d 202 (Wisc. 1991).

27. Deposition of Elsbeth Knott, In re Custody of H. S. H.-K., Circuit Court of Wisconsin, Dane County, No. 93-FA-1668, September 27, 1993, 22.

28. Decision and Order, In re Custody of H. S. H.-K., Circuit Court of Wisconsin, Dane County, Wisconsin, No. 93-FA-1668, October 28, 1993, 7–8.

29. In re Custody of H. S. K.-H, 533 N.W.2d 419, 428 (Wisc. 1995).

30. In re Angel Lace M., 516 N.W.2d 678 (Wisc. 1994).

31. Guardian at Litem's Brief, In re Custody of H. S. H.-K, Wisconsin Court of Appeals, No. 93-2911, February 16, 1994, 11.

32. See, e.g., V. C. v. M. J. B., 748 A.2d 539 (N.J. 2000).

33. The District of Columbia and New Mexico are rare in that they have statutes that allow the *unmarried* partners of inseminated women to become parents by consenting to the insemination. See D.C. Code, § 16-909(e)(1) and N.M. Laws, 215 § 7-703. The same is true in Oregon for lesbian partners. This is due to a judicial ruling rather than legislative action. In 2009, an Oregon appellate court held that same-sex couples are constitutionally entitled to the same protections afforded to married couples by the state's insemination statute. See Shineovich v. Kemp, 214 P.3d 29 (Or. Ct. App. 2009). This ruling allows a lesbian woman who consents to her partner's insemination to be deemed the child's mother.

34. King v. S. B., 837 N.E.2d 965 (Ind. 2005); C. E. W. v. D. E. W., 845 A.2d 1146 (Me. 2004); E. N. O. v. L. M. M., 711 N.E.2d 886 (Mass. 1999); Mason v. Dwinnell, 660 S.E.2d 58 (N.C. Ct. App. 2008); T. B. v. L. R. M., 753 A.2d 873 (Pa. Super. Ct. 2000), aff'd, 786 A.2d 913 (Pa. 2001); In re Parentage of L.B., 122 P.3d 161 (Wash. 2005).

35. See Delaware Code Title 13, § 8-201(a)(4), (b)(6), and (c); D.C. Code, § 16-831.01 et seq.

36. Smith v. Gordon, 968 A.2d 1 (Del. 2009). The Delaware statute is also interesting because it grants de facto parents the status of full legal parents. In Delaware, in other words, biological, adoptive, and de facto parents are all equal under the law. In contrast, while the District of Columbia statute awards de facto parents equal custody and visitation rights, and imposes equal child care obligations, it does not confer on them the status of full legal parents with all of the other corresponding rights and obligations.

37. *Principles of the Law of Family Dissolution: Analysis and Recommendations* (Philadelphia: American Law Institute, 2002), § 2.03(1)(b)(iii).

38. Ibid., § 2.03(1)(b)(iv).

39. Matter of Visitation with C. B. L., 723 N.E.2d 316 (Ill. Ct. App. 1999); Wakeman v. Dixon, 921 So.2d 669 (Fla. Ct. App. 2006); B. F. v. T. D., 194 S.W.3d 310 (Ky. 2006); Janice

M. v. Margaret K., 948 A.2d 73 (Md. 2008); White v. White, 293 S.W.3d 1 (Mo. Ct. App. 2009); Jones v. Barlow, 154 P.3d 808 (Utah 2007).

40. Debra H. v. Janice R., 930 N.E.2d 184 (N.Y. 2010).

41. "Groups Issue Standards for Custody Disputes in Same-Sex Relationships," Lambda press release, May 3, 1999, http://www.lambdalegal.org/news/pr/ny_19990503_groups-issue-standards-custody-dispute-same-sex-relationships.html.

42. Gay & Lesbian Advocates & Defenders, "Protecting Families: Standards for Child Custody in Same-Sex Relationships," 10 *UCLA Women's Law Journal* 151 (1999).

43. Ibid., 154–55.

44. In re Adoption of B. L. V. B., 628 A.2d 1271 (Vt. 1993). The lesbian attorney later wrote about the experience of seeking to adopt her partner's children. See Deborah Lashman, "Second Parent Adoption: A Personal Perspective," 2 *Duke Journal of Gender Law & Policy* 227 (1995).

45. Adam Liptak, "Parental Rights Upheld for Lesbian Ex-Partner," *New York Times*, August 5, 2006, A11.

46. April Witt, "About Isabella," *Washington Post Magazine*, February 4, 2007, 14.

47. Lisa Miller, "Prayer Letter," *Only One Mommy*, May 12, 2007, http://imgodschild. wordpress.com/2007/05/12/prayer-letter-3/.

48. Mathew D. Staver, *Same-Sex Marriage: Putting Every Household at Risk* (Nashville: Broadman & Holman, 2004), 47.

49. Brief of the Appellee, Miller-Jenkins v. Miller-Jenkins, Supreme Court of Vermont, Nos. 2004-443, 2005-030, June 7, 2005, 2.

50. Prior to the enactment of the PKPA, it was not clear whether the constitutional doctrine of full faith and credit—which requires states to recognize the judicial judgments issued by other states' courts—applied to custody and visitation rulings, because those rulings are never truly final given that they can be modified if the circumstances of the children or the parents change. The PKPA clarified that custody and visitation judgments were indeed subject to the doctrine of full faith and credit.

51. For example, a Virginia appellate court in 2008 refused to recognize the doctrine of de facto parenthood in a visitation case brought by a former lesbian partner of a biological mother. See Stadter v. Spirko, 661 S.E.2d 494 (Va. Ct. App. 2008).

52. Defense of Marriage Act, 1996, § 2.

53. Miller-Jenkins v. Miller-Jenkins, 912 A.2d 951, 967 (Vt. 2006).

54. As of 2011, Connecticut, Iowa, Massachusetts, New Hampshire, New York, Vermont, and the District of Columbia recognize same-sex marriages. In addition, civil unions or domestic partnerships are recognized in California, Hawaii, Illinois, Maine, Nevada, New Jersey, Oregon, Rhode Island, Vermont, Washington, and Wisconsin.

55. Miller-Jenkins v. Miller-Jenkins, 637 S.E.2d 330 (Va. Ct. App. 2006).

56. The Vermont Supreme Court eventually upheld the lower court's order transferring custody from Lisa to Janet. See Miller-Jenkins v. Miller-Jenkins, 12 A.3d 768 (Vt. 2010).

57. Erik Eckholm, "Pastor Is Accused of Helping to Kidnap Girl at Center of Lesbian Custody Fight," *New York Times*, April 24, 2011, A16.

58. See Kyle Mantyla, "Lisa Miller's Supporters Praise Her Heroic 'Civil Disobedience,' Compare Her to Harriet Tubman," *Right Wing Watch*, March 8, 2010, http://www. rightwingwatch.org/content/lisa-millers-supporters-praise-her-heroic-civil-disobedience-compare-her-harriet-tubman.

. 59. Eckholm, "Pastor Is Accused of Helping to Kidnap Girl at Center of Lesbian Custody Fight."

60. ABC News, *Nightline*, January 28, 2010, http://abcnews.go.com/Nightline/lesbian-custody-battle-vermont/story?id=9686772.

61. Ali Lorraine, "Mrs. Kramer vs. Mrs. Kramer," *Newsweek*, December 15, 2008, 33.

62. As already noted, Sandy was eventually named as Harrison's permanent legal guardian, but that was because Elsbeth was experiencing psychological challenges at the time.

63. V. C. v. M. J. B., 748 A.2d 539, 554 (N.J. 2000) (emphasis added).

64. Opinion, Jones v. Jones, Court of Common Pleas of Bucks County, Pennsylvania, No. A06-00-64229-C-19, December 14, 2001, 4.

65. Opinion, Jones v. Jones, Court of Common Pleas of Bucks County, Pennsylvania, No. A06-00-64229-C-19, March 9, 2005, 4.

66. Charles v. Stehlik, 744 A.2d 1255, 1259 (Pa. 2000).

67. Jones v. Jones, 884 A.2d 915 (Pa. Super. Ct. 2005).

NOTES TO CHAPTER 4

1. Ry Russo-Young, "Thank God My Moms Are Lesbians," *The Daily Beast*, June 21, 2010, http://www.thedailybeast.com/blogs-and-stories/2010-06-21/growing-up-with-lesbian-moms-by-ry-russo-young/full/.

2. Donna J. Hitchens, *Lesbians Choosing Motherhood: Legal Implications of Donor Insemination* (San Francisco: Lesbian Rights Project, 1984), 4. In one of the earliest disputes between a known sperm donor and a mother, a New Jersey trial court in 1977 granted visitation rights to the former over the objections of the latter. After claiming to take "no position as to the propriety of the use of artificial insemination between unmarried persons," the court held that it would be in the child's best interests to grant visitation to "a man [who] wants to take upon himself the responsibility of being a father to a child which he is responsible for helping to conceive." "Sperm Donor Granted Visitation," *Mom's Apple Pie*, September 1977, 5.

3. 1973 Uniform Parentage Act, § 5(b).

4. Thomas S. v. Robin Y., 618 N.Y.S. 2d 356 (N.Y. App. Div. 1994).

5. Cheri Pies, *Considering Parenthood* (San Francisco: Aunt Lute, 1985), 211.

6. In re Jacob, 660 N.E.2d 397 (N.Y. 1995).

7. Thomas S. v. Robin Y., New York Family Court, New York County, No. P3884/91, exhibit 16, 2.

8. Thomas S. v. Robin Y., 599 N.Y.S. 2d 377, 380 (N.Y. Family Ct. 1993).

9. Ibid., 382.

10. Arthur Leonard, "Judge Denies Parental Standing to Gay Sperm Donor," *Lesbian/Gay Law Notes*, May 1993, 33–34.

11. "Letters to the Lesbian/Gay Law Notes," *Lesbian/Gay Law Notes*, June 1993, 1.

12. This position was defended in a 1996 law review article about the Tom Steel case. See Fred A. Bernstein, "This Child Does Have Two Mothers . . . And a Sperm Donor with Visitation," 22 *NYU Review of Law and Social Change* 1 (1996).

13. This lawsuit was the first time that the National Center for Lesbian Rights took a position in a case involving lesbian or gay litigants on both sides. See "Our Day in

Court—Against Each Other: Intra-Community Disputes Threaten All of Our Rights," *NCLR Newsletter*, Winter 1991/92, 1. Two San Francisco–area gay parenting groups, the Lesbian and Gay Parenting Group and the Gay Fathers Group, initially filed an amicus brief on behalf of Tom Steel. The organizations later withdrew their briefs.

14. In 1990, Polikoff published what quickly became the leading academic article on lesbian parenthood and the law. See Nancy D. Polikoff, "This Child Does Have Two Mothers: Redefining Parenthood to Meet the Needs of Children in Lesbian-Mother and Other Nontraditional Families," 78 *Georgetown Law Journal* 459 (1990).

15. Nancy D. Polikoff, "Lesbian Mothers, Lesbian Families: Legal Obstacles, Legal Challenges," 14 *NYU Review of Law and Social Change* 907, 910 (1986).

16. *Thomas S.*, 618 N.Y.S. 2d at 359.

17. David W. Dunlap, "Sperm Donor Is Awarded Standing as Girl's Father," *New York Times*, November 19, 1994, A27.

18. Susan Dominus, "Growing Up with Mom and Mom," *New York Times Magazine*, October 24, 2004, 69.

19. Abby Rubenfeld and Dennis DeLeon, "Letter to the Editor," *Lesbian/Gay Law Notes*, April 1995, 64.

20. Nancy D. Polikoff, "What's Biology Got to Do with It? The Specter of Norms in Gay/Lesbian Parenting Disputes," *Gay Community News*, Spring 1995, 4, 14.

21. See, e.g.,, Dunlap, "Sperm Donor Is Awarded Standing as Girl's Father"; "Gay Man Can Visit Child He Fathered for Lesbian," *Orlando Sentinel*, November 20, 1994, 26.

22. Bernstein, "This Child Does Have Two Mothers . . . And a Sperm Donor with Visitation," 47.

23. Jhordan C. v. Mary K., 179 Cal. App. 3d 386 (Ct. App. 1986); In re Interest of R. C., 775 P.2d 27 (Colo. 1989); McIntyre v. Crouch, 780 P.2d 239 (Or. Ct. App. 1989).

24. April Martin, *The Lesbian and Gay Parenting Handbook* (New York: HarperCollins, 1993), 86.

25. Some sperm banks have more recently adopted policies that allow the child, usually when he or she reaches the age of eighteen, to learn the identity of the anonymous donor, as long as the donor, at the time of donation, consented to have his identity revealed. These sperm banks inform prospective mothers whether donors have agreed to have their identity revealed in the future, so that they can take this information into account when choosing a donor.

26. Jacob v. Schultz-Jacob, 923 A.2d 473 (Pa. Super. Ct. 2007).

27. Trial Transcript, Jacob v. Schultz-Jacob, Court of Common Pleas, York County, Pennsylvania, No. 2006-FC-0363, August 2, 2006, 186.

28. 1973 Uniform Parentage Act, § 5(b).

29. 2002 Uniform Parentage Act, § 703. This version of the UPA no longer requires that the sperm be provided to a licensed physician in order for the sperm donor's parental rights to be terminated.

30. See, e.g., Del. Code title 13, § § 8-702–4; Kan. Stat., § 38-1114(f); N.H. Rev. Stat. Ann., § § 168B:11–12; N.J. Stat. Ann., § 9:1744; N.M. Stat. Ann., § 40116; N.D. Cent. Code, § § 14-2060–62; Tex. Fam. Code, § § 160.702, 160.7031; Wyo. Stat. Ann., § § 142902–4.

31. John Bowe, "Gay Donor or Gay Dad?," *New York Times Magazine*, November 19, 2006, 66.

32. Matter of Baby M., 537 A.2d 1227 (N.J. 1988).

33. See, e.g., Ginia Bellafante, "Surrogate Mothers' New Niche: Bearing Babies for Gay Couples," *New York Times*, May 27, 2005, A1; Judy Keen, "Surrogates Relish Unique Role: And Science Has a Place in the Family, Too," *USA Today*, January 23, 2007, D1.

34. Elizabeth S. Scott, "Surrogacy and the Politics of Commodification," 72(3) *Law and Contemporary Problems* 109, 121 (2009).

35. 750 Illinois Compiled Statutes, § 47/1–75.

36. C. on Behalf of T. v. G. & E., Supreme Court of New York, New York County, *New York Law Journal*, January 12, 2001, 29.

37. Decker v. Decker, 2001 WL 1167475 (Ohio Ct. App. 2001).

38. A. G. R. v. D. R. H. & S. H., Superior Court of New Jersey, Hudson County, No. FD-09-001838-07, December 23, 2009.

39. In re Paternity and Custody of Baby Boy A., 2007 WL 4304448 (Minn. Ct. App.).

40. K. M. v. E. G., 13 Cal. Rptr. 3d 136 (Ct. App. 2004).

41. Johnson v. Calvert, 851 P.2d 776 (Cal. 1993).

42. K. M. v. E. G., 117 P.3d 673, 679 (Cal. 2005).

43. Respondent's Answer Brief on the Merits, K. M. v. E. G., Supreme Court of California, No. S125643, December 29, 2004, 19.

NOTES TO CHAPTER 5

1. Kenneth J. Cooper, "Some Oppose Foster Placement with Gay Couple," *Boston Globe*, May 8, 1985, 21.

2. Dudley Clendinen, "Homosexual Foster Parents Debated," *New York Times*, May 19, 1985, A24.

3. Brad Pokorny, "The Foster Care Controversy Resurfaces: Boys Allegedly Abused in New Home," *Boston Globe*, January 19, 1986, 33.

4. Lucinda Franks, "Homosexuals as Foster Parents: Is Program an Advance or Peril?," *New York Times*, May 7, 1974, 47.

5. "Judge Places Gay Teenage Boy in Lesbian Foster Parents' Home," *Advocate*, May 22, 1974, 8.

6. "New Rules Proposed: Seek to Block Gay Foster Homes," *Advocate*, May 22, 1974, 8.

7. Randy Shilts, "Foster Homes for Gay Children—Justice or Prejudice," *Advocate*, December 17, 1975, 11.

8. Ibid. The judge's order was reported in In re Davis, 1 *Family Law Reporter* 2845 (Wash. Super. Ct., 1975).

9. Kay Longcope, "Gay Couple Express Anger, Grief and Hope," *Boston Globe*, May 16, 1985, 1.

10. Line Item Amendment No. 4800-001 to Administrative Budget, Massachusetts House of Representatives, H.R. 6000, 174th Legislature, 1st Session (1985).

11. Philip W. Johnston, Official Statement from the Executive Office of Human Services of the Commonwealth of Massachusetts, May 24, 1985, quoted in "Policy Statement on Foster Care," *Boston Globe*, May 25, 1985, 24.

12. Dudley Clendinen, "Curbs Imposed on Homosexuals as Foster Parents," *New York Times*, May 25, 1985, A24.

13. Editorial, "A Model Foster Care Policy," *Boston Globe*, May 28, 1985, A14.

14. Ellen Goodman, "Who Lost in Foster-Care Case?," *Boston Globe*, May 30, 1985, A23.

15. Babets v. Secretary of the Executive Office of Human Services, 526 N.E.2d 1261 (Mass. 1988).

16. Renee Loth, "State's Gay Foster Care Policy Politically Based, Memos Show," *Boston Globe*, August 19, 1988, 22.

17. John Milne, "Starting Today, N.H. Bars Gay Foster Parents," *Boston Globe*, July 24, 1987, 13.

18. Anita Bryant, *The Anita Bryant Story: The Survival of Our Nation's Families and the Threat of Militant Homosexuality* (Old Tappan, N.J.: Revell, 1977), 146.

19. Tom Matthews, "Battle over Gay Rights," *Newsweek*, June 6, 1977, 22.

20. Lofton v. Secretary of the Department of Children and Family Services, 377 F.3d 1275, 1303 (11th Cir. 2004) (Barkett, J., dissenting from denial of en banc review).

21. The New Hampshire legislature repealed its gay adoption ban in 1999.

22. The regulation added that "a decision to accept or reject when homosexuality is at issue shall be made on the basis of individual factors as explored and found in the adoption study process as it relates to the best interests of adoptive children." 18 N.Y.C.R.R., § 421.16(h)(2).

23. "Families by Adoption: A Gay Reality," *Advocate*, August 28, 1974, 1.

24. Denise Sudell, "Gay Couple Adopts Child: Believed a First," *Philadelphia Gay News*, March 1979, 2.

25. George Vecsey, "Approval Given for Homosexual to Adopt a Boy," *New York Times*, June 21, 1979, B1.

26. Doug MacEachern, "A Homosexual Fights for a Chance at Parenthood," *Phoenix Magazine*, July 1980, 82.

27. In re Pima County Juvenile Action, 727 P.2d 830, 835 (Az. Ct. App. 1986).

28. Transcript, In re Adoption of Charles B., Licking County (Ohio) Juvenile Court, No. 87-A-78, April 14, 1988, 43.

29. Ibid., 135.

30. Ibid., 139.

31. Ibid., 119.

32. In re Adoption of Charles B., 1988 WL 119937 (Ohio Ct. App.).

33. Portage County Welfare Department v. Summers, 311 N.E.2d 6 (Ohio 1974); In re Adoption of Baker, 185 N.E.2d 51 (Ohio 1962).

34. Brief of Respondent, In re Matter of Adoption of Charles B., Supreme Court of Ohio, No. 88-2163, May 17, 1989, 5–6.

35. In re Adoption of Charles B., 552 N.E.2d 884 (Ohio 1990).

36. J. Limbacher, "Giving a Gay Couple a Boy," *News-Herald* (Willoughby, Ohio), July 4, 1990.

37. For a detailed account of the gay couple's journey to parenthood, see Jon and Michael Galluccio, *An American Family* (New York: St. Martin's Press, 2001).

38. In re Adoption of a Child by J. M. G., 632 A.2d 550 (N.J. Super. Ct. 1993); In re Adoption of Two Children by H. N. R., 666 A.2d 535 (N.J. Super. Ct. 1995).

39. Ronald Smothers, "Court Lets Two Gay Men Jointly Adopt Child," *New York Times*, October 23, 1997, B5.

40. Kelly Heyboer, "State Clears Adoption by Gay Couples," *Star-Ledger* (Newark), December 18, 1997, 1. Ten years after Michael and Jon's legal victory, the Maine Supreme Court held that the state adoption statute, which explicitly permitted married couples to

file joint adoption petitions, did not implicitly prohibit an unmarried same-sex couple from seeking to adopt their foster children. See In re Adoption of M. A., 930 A.2d 1088 (Me. 2007). Other appellate courts have reached similar conclusions in interpreting their state's adoption statutes. See In re Adoption of Carolyn B., 774 N.Y.S. 2d 227 (N.Y. App. Div. 2004); In re Infant Girl W., 845 N.E.2d 229 (Ind. Ct. App. 2006).

41. The first judicial approval of a second-parent adoption took place in Alaska in 1985 in a case litigated by Allison Mendel. See In re Adoption of A. O. L., Alaska Superior Court, First Judicial District of Juneau, No. 1JU-85-25, August 7, 1985. (As a result of this ruling, the child was left with three legal parents: two mothers, who had the primary responsibility for raising the child, and the biological father, who retained the right to have some contact with her. This outcome was highly unusual for its time.) The Alaska case was followed by several others in which trial judges in California, Oregon, and Washington State recognized second-parent adoptions in families headed by lesbian couples.

42. Report and Recommendation, District of Columbia Department of Human Services, Ex Parte in the Matter of the Petitions of Laura Solomon and Victoria Lane for Adoption, March 8, 1991, 5.

43. Memorandum Opinion, In re Adoption of Minor T., Superior Court of the District of Columbia, No. A-269-90, August 30, 1991, 3. This ruling was reported in 17 *Family Law Reporter* 1523 (1991).

44. D.C. Code, § 16-312(a).

45. Memorandum of Points and Authorities in Support of Petitions for Adoption, Superior Court of the District of Columbia, No. A-269-90, May 17, 1991, 35.

46. Memorandum Opinion, In re Adoption of Minor T., 4.

47. Deb Price, "Girl Would Be Orphan If They'd Lost," *Minneapolis Star Tribune*, January 5, 1994, E4.

48. Memorandum Opinion and Order, In the Matter of Adoption by Bruce M. and Mark D., Superior Court of the District of Columbia, No. A-62-93, April 20, 1994, 12, quoting from Matter of Adams, 473 N.W.2d 712, 715–16 (Mich. App. 1991).

49. In re M. M. D. and B. H. M., 662 A.2d 837 (D.C. Ct. App. 1995).

50. In re Adoption of Tammy, 619 N.E.2d 315 (Mass. 1993); In re Adoption of B. L. V. B. & E. L. V. B., 628 A.2d 1271 (Vt. 1993).

51. In re Angel Lace M., 516 N.W.2d 678 (Wisc. 1994).

52. See, e.g.,, Sharon S. v. Superior Court, 73 P.2d 554 (Cal. 2003); In re Adoption of M. M. G. C., 785 N.E.2d 267 (Ind. Ct. App. 2003); In re Jacob, 660 N.E.2d 397 (N.Y. 1995); In re Adoption of R. B. F. & R. C. F., 803 A.2d 1195 (Pa. 2002).

53. Connecticut General Statutes, § 45a-724(3), abrogating In re Adoption of Baby Z., 724 A.2d 1035 (Conn. 1999); Colorado Revised Statutes, § 19-5-203(1)(d.5)(1), abrogating Adoption of T. K. J., 931 P.2d 488 (Colo. Ct. App. 1996).

54. In re Adoption of Luke, 640 N.W.2d 374 (Neb. 2002); In re Adoption of Doe, 719 N.E.2d 1071 (Ohio Ct. App. 1998); In re Angel Lace M., 516 N.W.2d 678 (Wis. 1994).

55. Mississippi Code, § 93-17-3(5).

56. Utah Code, § 78-30-1-3(b).

57. In addition to caring for Frank, Ginger, Tracy, and Bert for many years, Steven and Roger also cared for four additional HIV-positive children. The latter placements, however, were for shorter periods of time.

58. See, e.g., Florida Department of Health & Rehabilitation Services v. Cox, 656 So.2d 902 (Fla. 1995).

59. Memorandum from Naomi Goldberg and M. V. Lee Badgett to Florida State Representative Mary Brandenburg titled "Cost of Florida's Ban on Gay Adoption by GLB Individuals and Same-Sex Couples," March 12, 2009, http://www.law.ucla.edu/williamsinstitute/pdf/Florida_Adoption.pdf.

60. In re Matter of Adoption of X. X. G. and N. R. G., 45 So.3d 79, 95 (Fl. Ct. App. 2010).

61. Lofton v. Kearney, 157 F.Supp.2d 1372 (S.D. Fla. 2001).

62. Abby Goodnough, "Woman Accused of Killing a Missing Child in Florida," *New York Times*, March 17, 2005, A24; Dana Canedy, "Case of Lost Miami Girl Puts Focus on an Agency," *New York Times*, May 3, 2002, A19; Megan O'Matz, "Two More Child Deaths Revealed Since Five Were Reported Dec. 29," *Fort Lauderdale Sun-Sentinel*, January, 26, 2003, A14.

63. David Damron, "DCF's Workers Fail to Visit 1,841 Children in June," *Orlando Sentinel*, July 6, 2002, B1; Megan O'Matz, "DCF Is Still Losing Track of Children, Data Show," *Fort Lauderdale Sun-Sentinel*, July, 24, 2003, B4.

64. Rene Stutzman, "Foster-Care Abuse Rises Sharply," *Orlando Sentinel*, June 22, 2002, B1.

65. Megan O'Matz, "Report: DCF Misses Re-Abuse Goals," *Fort Lauderdale Sun-Sentinel*, January 28, 2004, B5.

66. Brief of Appellant, Lofton v. Secretary of the Department of Children and Family Services, U.S. Court of Appeals for the Eleventh Circuit, No. 01-16723-DD, February 14, 2005, 8–9.

67. Curtis Krueger, "Gay Dads Get Daughters Plus Praise from Judge," *St. Petersburg Times*, September 9, 2004, A1 (emphasis added).

68. Ibid.

69. Julian Sanchez, "All Happy Families: The Looming Battle over Gay Parenting," *Reason*, August 1, 2005, 30.

70. Lofton v. Secretary of the Department of Children and Family Services, 358 F.3d 804, 822 (11th Cir. 2004).

71. Lofton v. Secretary of the Department of Children and Family Services, 377 F.3d 1275, 1299 (11th Cir. 2004) (Barkett, J., dissenting from denial of en banc review).

72. In re Adoption of Doe, 2008 WL 5006172 (Fla. Dist. Ct), 2.

73. *Adoption of X. X. G.*, 45 So.3d at 82.

74. John Schwartz, "Scandal Stirs Legal Questions in Anti-Gay Cases," *New York Times*, May 19, 2010, A15.

75. Ibid.

76. *Adoption of X. X. G.*, 45 So.3d at 87.

77. Department of Human Services v. Howard, 238 S.W.3d 1 (Ark. 2006).

78. Department of Human Services v. Cole, 2011 WL 1319217 (Ark. 2011).

79. Gary J. Gates, M. V. Lee Badgett, Jennifer Ehrle Macomber, and Kate Chambers, *Adoption and Foster Care by Gay and Lesbian Parents in the United States* (Williams Institute and Urban Institute, 2007), http://www.law.ucla.edu/williamsinstitute/publications/FinalAdoptionReport.pdf. "About 19 percent of same-sex couples raising children reported having an adopted child in the house in 2009, up from just 8 percent in 2000." Sabrina Tavernise, "Adoptions Rise by Same-Sex Couples, Despite Legal Barriers," *New York Times*, June 14, 2011, A11.

1. Brief of Appellee, Daly v. Daly, Supreme Court of Nevada, No. 15423, August 10, 1984, 12.

2. Daly v. Daly, 715 P.2d 56, 60 (Nev. 1986).

3. Taylor Flynn, "The Ties That (Don't) Bind: Transgender Family Law and the Unmaking of Families," in *Transgender Rights*, ed. Paisley Currah, Richard M. Juang, and Shannon Price Minter (Minneapolis: University of Minnesota Press, 2006), 32, 42.

4. M. B. v. D. W., 236 S.W.3d 31, 33 (Ky. Ct. App. 2007).

5. Kentucky Revised Statutes, § 625.090(2).

6. Brief for Appellant, M. B. v. D. W., Kentucky Court of Appeals, No. 2006-CA-002285, January 29, 2007, 6.

7. *M.B.*, 236 S.W.3d at 37.

8. Ibid., 35.

9. Brief for Appellant, M.B. v. D.W., 11.

10. *M. B.*, 236 S.W.3d at 35.

11. Brief for Appellees, M. B. v. D. W., Kentucky Court of Appeals, No. 2006-CA-002285, March 1, 2007, 11.

12. Ibid., 8.

13. Brief for Appellant, M.B. v. D.W., 14.

14. Wright v. Howard, 711 S.W.2d 492 (Ky. Ct. App. 1986).

15. Brief for Appellant, M. B. v. D. W., 19.

16. *M. B.*, 236 S.W.3d at 38.

17. As of 2011, twenty-one states have statutes prohibiting employment discrimination based on sexual orientation, but only twelve have laws that provide the same protection based on gender identity.

18. It is important to note that not every transsexual person chooses to undergo medical treatment that leads to anatomical changes.

19. The first quoted phrase is from Lofton v. Secretary of Department of Children and Family Services, 358 F.3d 804, 819 (11th Cir. 2004). The second phrase is from Hernandez v. Robles, 855 N.E.2d 1, 7 (N.Y. 2006).

20. Michael E. Lamb and Catherine S. Tamis-LeMonda, "The Role of the Father: An Introduction," in *The Role of the Father in Child Development*, ed. Michael E. Lamb, 4th ed. (Hoboken: Wiley, 2004), 1, 10 (emphasis added).

21. Kyle Pruett, *Fatherneed: Why Father Care Is as Essential as Mother Care for Your Child* (New York: Free Press, 2000), 18.

22. Orr v. Orr, 440 U.S. 268 (1979).

23. United States v. Virginia, 518 U.S. 515, 533 (1996).

24. Brief of Defendant-Appellant, Christian v. Randall, Colorado Court of Appeals, No. 73-100, June 8, 1973, 5–6.

25. Ibid., 7.

26. Ibid., 8.

27. Brief of Plaintiff-Appellee, Christian v. Randall, Colorado Court of Appeals, No. 73-100, August 13, 1973, 16.

28. Christian v. Randall, 516 P.2d 131, 133 (Colo. Ct. App. 1973).

29. Appellant's Brief, Magnuson v. Magnuson, Supreme Court of Washington, No. 78841-3, October 19, 2006, 21.

30. Magnuson v. Magnuson, 170 P.3d 65, 66 (Wash. Ct. App. 2007).

31. Schuster v. Schuster, 585 P.2d 130 (Wash. 1978).

32. Cabalquinto v. Cabalquinto, 669 P.2d 886 (Wash. 1983).

33. *Magnuson*, 170 P.3d at 67.

34. M. T. v. J. T., 355 A.2d 204 (N.J. App. Div. 1976); Corbett v. Corbett, 2 All ER 33 (1970).

35. Littleton v. Prange, 9 S.W.3d 223, 231 (Tex. Ct. App. 1999).

36. In re Estate of Gardiner, 42 P.3d 120, 136 (Kan. 2002).

37. Opinion, Kantaras v. Kantaras, Florida Circuit Court, Pasco County, No. 98-5375CA, February 2003, 761.

38. Ibid., 796.

39. See "Florida Court Holds There Is No Right to Transsexual Marriage," *Liberty Alert*, July 23, 2004, http://www.lc.org/libertyalert/2004/la072304b.htm.

40. Brief of Appellant, Kantaras v. Kantaras, Florida Court of Appeal (2nd District), No. 03-1377, August 29, 2003, 9. The brief added that "finding [Michael Kantaras], who was born female, to be male because she had several surgeries and popped some testosterone is clearly erroneous. Does a female bodybuilder who had a hysterectomy due to cancer and who supplements her muscle growth with testosterone thereby become male?" (11).

41. Brief of Appellee, Kantaras v. Kantaras, Florida Court of Appeal (2nd District), No. 03-1377, October 15, 2003, 39–40, quoting Kantaras v. Kantaras, Florida Circuit Court, Pasco County, No. 98-5375CA, February 2003, 741.

42. Kantaras v. Kantaras, 884 So.2d 155 (Fla. Ct. App. 2004).

43. Wakeman v. Dixon, 921 So.2d 669 (Fla. Ct. App. 2006) (en banc).

44. Brief of the Public Guardian, Simmons v. Simmons, Illinois Court of Appeals, Nos. 1-03-2284, 1-03-2348, 6.

45. 750 Illinois Compiled Statutes, § 45/5(1).

46. Brief of the Public Guardian, Simmons v. Simmons, 37.

47. In re Marriage of Simmons, 825 N.E.2d 303, 309 (Ill. Ct. App. 2005).

48. Brief of the Public Guardian, Simmons v. Simmons, 34. It also did not help Sterling's case that Illinois does not recognize the doctrine of functional or de facto parenthood. See Matter of visitation with C. B. L., 723 N.E.2d 316 (Ill. Ct. App. 1999).

NOTES TO THE CONCLUSION

1. For national statistics on foster care and adoptions, see U.S. Department of Health and Human Services, *Trends in Foster Care and Adoptions, FY 2002–2009*, http://www.acf.hhs.gov/programs/cb/stats_research/afcars/trends.htm.

2. Mississippi Code, § 93-17-3(5); Utah Code, § 78-30-1-3(b).

Index

About the Author

CARLOS A. BALL is Professor of Law and Judge Frederick Lacey Scholar at the Rutgers University School of Law (Newark). He is the author of several books on LGBT rights issues, including *From the Closet to the Courtroom* and *The Morality of Gay Rights*. He lives with his family in Brooklyn, New York.